Living Racism

Living Racism

Through the Barrel of the Book

Edited by Theresa Rajack-Talley and
Derrick R. Brooms

LEXINGTON BOOKS
Lanham • Boulder • New York • London

Published by Lexington Books
An imprint of The Rowman & Littlefield Publishing Group, Inc.
4501 Forbes Boulevard, Suite 200, Lanham, Maryland 20706
www.rowman.com

Unit A, Whitacre Mews, 26-34 Stannary Street, London SE11 4AB

Chapter 1 was previously published as "The 'Race' Concept and Racial Structure." In *Racial Structure and Radical Politics in the African Diaspora. Journal of Africana Studies*, Vol.3: 61–79, (2009).

British Library Cataloguing in Publication Information Available

Library of Congress Cataloging-in-Publication Data Available

ISBN 978-1-4985-4431-3 (cloth : alk. paper)
ISBN 978-1-4985-4433-7 (pbk. : alk. paper)
ISBN 978-1-4985-4432-0 (electronic)

∞™ The paper used in this publication meets the minimum requirements of American National Standard for Information Sciences Permanence of Paper for Printed Library Materials, ANSI/NISO Z39.48-1992.

Printed in the United States of America

This book is dedicated to Dr. Clarence R. Talley, his father Carl R. Talley, and to all Black men who continue to mentor their children and channel them into enlightened education.

Contents

Acknowledgments

Theresa Rajack-Talley

There is never enough space to thank everyone who in different ways supported this project. There are, however, those whose direct input made this book a reality. First, I would like to thank my co-editor and colleague, Derrick R. Brooms; without his collaboration and valuable input, completing this project would have been much more difficult. Moreover, his support and friendship carried us through long hours of labor, face-to-face discussions, texts, and emails. I would also like to thank each of the young men, most former students of Clarence, who willingly and enthusiastically shared their experiences and/or co-authored chapters in the book. I name these in alphabetic order: Camara Douglas, Cameron Khalfani Herman, Lamar Johnson, Eric A. Jordan, Thomas J. Mowen, Oliver Rollins and Willie J. Wright. I would also like to thank some of my colleagues who read and gave positive feedback on drafts of chapters, in particular Joy Carew and Margaret D'Silva. Special thanks to one of my few mentors, Dr. James Conyers, who, when I had doubts about the project, always encouraged me to write the book because he thought it would make a valuable contribution to the discourse.

I must thank my graduate students who patiently listened and at times allowed me the space to write. Lastly, I would like to thank Clarence's sister, Ustaine Talley, who provided me with the information for the preface, and the other Talley family members, Richard and Karen, who supported the project for so many years. I am very fortunate that I have the un-relentless support and love of my own family, my mom (Ayesha), Uncle Truman, my siblings (Claire, Helen, Charmaine and Patrick) and their spouses. Although much of this book is focused on black scholarship and student mentorship, it is also about brotherhood. As such, I would like to acknowledge the supportive and oftentimes entertaining role that Clarence's male friends played in his life: Ted, Jerry, Robert (Hindu), Melville (Blues), Taylor-Lee, Terry and Jan. From all of us, we thank you Clarence for your love, dedication and intellectual contributions to understanding and helping change social inequality for all peoples.

Derrick R. Brooms

The opportunity to work on and contribute to this project is indeed a blessing. As such, I give great thanks to Theresa Rajack-Talley for her vision and leadership on this project. I am thankful for our many conversations and discussions and for our collaborations—here and elsewhere. I was able to witness firsthand the importance and meaning of this project through your efforts, attention to detail, and dedication to the quality of all of our work. Your commitment is inspiring and helps to elevate us all. I give thanks to each of the contributors to this volume; your work here and the work you will do in the future is incredibly important. I give thanks to all of the students that I have opportunities to work and connect with, through a number of different ventures, and especially as you pursue your goals. Additionally, I give thanks to Dr. Edgar Epps for your encouragement of my intellectual curiosities and Andre Phillips for engaging me in a number of critical conversations and offering your office as a space for me to "be" during my college years; also, many thanks to Dr. Ayana Karanja for sharpening my critical eye and enhancing my academic goals during my graduate school years—your example helped enhance how I envisioned my own roles. Also, I give thanks to family, friends and my many communities. And, finally, I give thanks to Rufus Brooms, Jr.; you are and forever will be my model of all I want to be. All of these efforts, spaces, and people helped to strengthen my resolve to be in and of service to others. Let our collective efforts continue to move us forward.

Preface

This book is based on the efforts and scholarship of many but was conceived around the ideas and mentorship of one man. It is an example of how one person can make a difference in resisting racism and changing racial thinking. Clarence R. Talley was a sociologist who crossed over on January 28, 2011, before completing this manuscript. As his wife, I collected his drafts and outlines and completed the co-authored chapters in the book. His students, whom he mentored and supervised, called themselves his "warriors" on social media and many went on to graduate with their doctorates. A handful of these young scholars, all African Americans but one, agreed to write chapters in this book as a display of black male mentorship and scholarship. The co-editor and author of some of the book chapters, Derrick R. Brooms, was hired to replace Clarence in the Department of Sociology at the University of Louisville. Little did we know that Derrick would not only teach some of the seminal courses on "Race in the U.S." that Clarence developed, but that he would continue with a level of mentorship and intellectual devotion to students, particularly black males, that is so important.

The preface for a book is usually one of the easiest parts to write. In this case, the content and the emotions are difficult and painful. As the horrors of racial history unfolded, I had to accede that these encounters were the experiences of my beloved husband and all African Americans and their families. Moreover, Clarence not only spent his entire life living racism but as a scholar he studied and understood the context for the negative racial thinking and the consequences. As a socially conscious individual he also resisted racism and social inequality of all hues. Early in his life Clarence negotiated his identity and chose to embrace his black maleness. From that time onwards, Clarence devoted the rest of his life to becoming a change agent. After several turns in this his life's journey, Clarence eventually selected education as his weapon of choice. This is not surprising given the lessons that were passed on from his mentor and father, Carl R. Talley.

Carl Talley was not easy on his three sons. As the youngest son of Carl Talley, Sr., Clarence got the best lessons and stories, and he got the hardest lessons and stories from his father. Carl Talley knew what challenges his sons would face as black men in America and he did his best to make sure that his sons were tough enough and smart enough to make a good life for themselves, and to grow healthy families in a sometime hostile environment. Carl grew up on the former Kaw Indian reservation land settled by his grandfather, Robert Payne, in 1891. He and his sister Alice Jane grew up in an all-black farm colony with other black settlers from Tennessee and Kentucky in the Kansas Flint Hills region. The farm community was connected to the Dunlap Village in Morris and Lyon Counties and was chartered by land developer Benjamin "Pap" Singleton from Nashville, Tennessee, as the Singleton Colony in 1879. A school and a church were built near the farm community. Carl's father, Isaiah, was called to a Baptist ministry in St. Joseph, Missouri, in 1917 and the family left the colony in Morris County, Kansas.

When Carl grew up he moved to the South, attended Tuskegee University, and taught at an all-black elementary school. He then moved to Arkansas where he was consistently threatened by the white community because of his defiance and commitment to educating black children and including a science curriculum. Carl's strong devotion to education as a way to combat the effect of racism eventually led to him to leave Little Rock in the middle of the night because it was no longer safe for himself and his family. After several years of moving from one town to the next, Carl and his family settled on a historically owned family farm in Dunlap, Kansas. Life on the farm settled into routine work for Carl, growing crops and building a home, both took a lot of ingenuity. One of the first pieces of furniture Carl built in the family home was a bookcase. Carl also installed a furnace, fireplace and bathroom, none of which he had done before. He wired the house for electricity and applied to the Rural Electrification Act for service. When he was denied, Carl went to the library in Council Grove, Kansas, and studied electricity. He began locating and buying glass storage batteries, a generator motor (actually a model A Ford motor) and other parts. He built a generator house and began assembling his generator plant. He figured out how to make his system automatic—when the stored electricity fell below a certain level, the generator motor would automatically come on. When the system was complete, Carl threw the switch and he had electricity. No more studying by lamplight! When asked how he knew he would succeed, he replied with one of the many maxims that he taught his children, "The information is there. Use your mind."

Carl Talley believed in playing a major role in his children's education. He would always inquire, "What did you learn in school today?" When he received a reply, he would often ask, "Is that true? Is that correct? How do you know that is correct?" These frustrating questions urged his children to seek other sources to corroborate or refute any information they were given. This approach to education was passed from Clarence's father to Clarence, and from Clarence to his students. Clarence's students noted that as a teacher he allowed no uncritical assertions to go unnoticed; his singular goal mentoring scholars was for them to arrive at deeper levels of thought and become critical thinkers. Clarence, like his father, had a disdain for injustice, cruelty, and unfairness. As his father did, Clarence transmitted this to those whom he was close to, including his students. Not to enrage, but to encourage one to be systematic and rigorous in questioning the knowledge that surrounds us. For them both, there was too much work to be done to be mired in rage. This book is a product of this on-going mentorship, education and social activism.

Introduction

This Is Not the America We Know!

Theresa Rajack-Talley and Derrick R. Brooms

It is hard to imagine that in August 2017, as the introduction to this book is being written, that white, arms-bearing nationalists, Ku Klux Klan members and neo-Nazis are creating havoc on the streets of Charlottesville, Virginia, over the removal of the Confederate statue of Robert E. Lee from Emancipation Park. Several people were injured and one white female, Heather Heyer, was killed by a twenty-year-old neo-Nazi supporter who was born in Florence, Kentucky. Both Heather and her young killer are far removed from the eras of slavery and Jim Crow, nevertheless, the racial thinking of these times is what brought them together in Charlottesville at a "Unite the Right Rally" organized by the alt-right movement.

It is no secret that there are hundreds of hate groups in this country—their members living largely in the shadows. However, as a fairly large number of white supremacist protesters descended upon Charlottesville on Saturday, August 12, many felt that this was a belated coming-out party for an emboldened white nationalist movement in the United States. Torch-wielding white nationalists marched on the grounds of the University of Virginia, on the eve of the planned rally. They shouted "White lives matter!" and alternated chants of "You will not replace us," "Jews will not replace us," and "One people, one nation, end immigration!" One white supremacist shouted, "You sound like a n—" at counterprotesters. In an interview on MSNBC (8/12/2017), Reverend Traci Blackmon suggested that the rhetoric and structure of Donald Trump's presidency has given permission to white nationalists to unleash their deep hatred. These and other current events indicate that the United States is not yet a post-racial society. Instead, the white sheets have come off as white nationalists from different groups remain united around a

1

white supremacy ideology and now feel empowered to openly seek their agenda for a "White America."

Responses from public figures and everyday Americans are mixed, reflecting a diversity of racial ideologies within and across racial and ethnic groups. In today's rallies and social movements it is interesting to see a lot more white Americans demonstrating against overt racism, and in some instances leading, the anti-racist and anti-hatred counterprotests. Banners with "Black Lives Matter" and "White Lives Matter" are accompanied by sometimes heated debates on what do we mean when we say "Make America Great Again." Equally perplexing for us scholars is when folks are appalled at the clashes of overt racism and remark that, "This is not the America I know." As we unpack these slogans and innocent comments, it is clear that most Americans do not know their history—at least their racial history. In this book we try to uncover "the America lived" through racial lenses. We show that the varying positions of current White America, that include extremist, populist, conservative, liberal and progressive views are not so different from the historically diverse racial ideologies of the America we know and describe in this book.

Since the Civil Rights Movement most Americans, Black and white, hoped for a post-racial society where social stratification was not based on race and racism. Decades later the Black Power Movement reminded us that this was still more of a dream than a reality. Hope again was raised when Barack Obama became America's first Black president and optimistic citizens, political pundits, and some race scholars considered that finally the United States had become a post-racial, color-blind society. The *World Today* reported that a poll taken a few days after Obama won the election in November 2008 showed that 70 percent of Americans thought race relations would improve under his presidency. Eight years later a *New York Times/ CBS* poll taken in July 2016 showed that 69 percent of Americans felt that race relations between whites and Blacks were bad. These shifting poll results reflect the dilemma, confusion and complexity of race relations in the United States, as well as the frustrations because racial thinking and racism will not go away.

During the post-Obama era, it was felt by many that overt racial prejudice was mainly practiced by a few, small, historically white supremacist groups like those that showed up in Charlottesville. Indeed, covert racism, which is the more common form of racism, is believed to be practiced by some prejudiced individuals. Today, most white Americans do not consider themselves racist. Nevertheless, we are *all* socialized into racial thinking. For the vast majority of non-Black Americans (and some Blacks) social class, urban culture, family values and/or individual characteristics are contemporary reasons why African Americans and other minority groups are "failing" and why their racial etiquette is "deviant" to the American norm. But the enormity of the economic and social disparities by racial and ethnic groupings cannot be ignored. For example, the U.S. Bureau of Labor Statistics (BLS) reported that in 2016 unemployment for Blacks was roughly twice (8.4 percent) that for whites (4.3 percent). Based on Consumer Expenditure (CE) data, combined from 2010 to 2012, the average pretax income for the total U.S. population was $63,935, annually; however, Black households within the same reference period reported average pretax income of $45,287. Moreover, the distribution of Black household pretax income was skewed whereby most households sampled were on the lower end of the income continuum, falling between $12,500 and $37,499.

In addition, the U.S. World News Report (2016) showed that health disparities between Blacks and whites run deep. Blacks have higher rates of diabetes, hypertension and heart disease than other groups. And, African American adults with cancer are much less likely to survive prostate, breast and lung cancer than white adults. Alarmingly, Black children have a 500 percent higher death rate from asthma compared to white children. Yet Blacks of all ages are twice as likely to not have health insurance coverage. Economic and social disparities between whites and Blacks (and other minority groups) are hidden in statistical reports. They are less noticeable because we live in geographically divided communities by race and class. This makes it easier to rationalize disparity using stereotypes and propaganda of living in a post-racial society, that slavery and its repercussions are history and that structural racism is a distant past. Such thinking assumes that the playing field is now level and racial disparities are individualized and can be explained away as deviant socio-cultural behavior, social inabilities, or are pathological because of certain genetic persuasion. Many Americans and citizens around the world get their information about the "Other," specifically African Americans and minority populations living in the U.S., from the television screen, videos and social media. Consequently, negative stereotypes form the basis for their perceptions and racial viewpoints.

What is less hidden and forces us to question the reality of a 'post-racial' state are incidents like the Unite the Right rally in Charlottesville, as well as the string of mass protests and riots triggered by the killing of Black men and women by white police officers and others. These mass uprisings, often led by Black women, have been interpreted as "Black rage" or "Black defiance of the white man's laws." Conversely, others see it as resistance to the criminalization of the Black body. Regardless, the disparity by race in the criminal justice system warrants urgent attention. According to the Federal Bureau of Prisons (2016), Blacks comprise 37.7 percent of all incarcerated inmates and are only approximately 13 percent of the American population. Blacks are also three times more likely to be killed by police. In the last three years (2014–2016), thirteen glaringly worrisome cases have fueled outrage, heightened racial tensions and instigated protests around the nation. It is not enough to reference the cases but to write their names below is to rehumanize the Black body.

> Keith Lamont Scott, Terence Crutcher, Philando Castile, Alton B. Sterling, Christian Taylor, Samuel DuBose, Sandra Bland, Freddie Gray, Walter L. Scott, Tamir Rice, Laquan McDonald, Michael Brown, and Eric Garner.

The outcry linked to these thirteen cases and others, triggered those within and external to the justice system to closely investigate and take measures to reduce the level of violence on the Black body. As a result, for the same period in 2017 the total number of unarmed Black men and women killed is less. However, Black males continue to represent a disproportionately large share of unarmed people killed. Those who have lost their lives as of June 29, 2017, include: J. R. Williams, Darrion Barnhill, Nana Adomako, Chad Robertson, Raynard Burton, Alteria Woods, Jordan Edwards, and Aaron Bailey. The Black men and women killed range in ages and locations across the United States. In some of the cases, the police offered explanations for their actions, mainly that they feared for their lives. Video showings have oftentimes challenged this excuse, and as Tulsa police chief Chuck Jordan explains, "His agency reviewed its use-of-force policy after the surge in shootings in 2016 but that there was not much the department could change. We're a reflection of the society we live in" (the *Times* July 1, 2017). The police chief is accurate in his observation, however, it is not only the criminal justice system but all U.S. institutions that reflect the racist thinking of American society, with unfortunate outcomes.

African Americans have made tremendous advancement since the Civil Rights Movement on all fronts. However, progress and change have been accompanied by continued attempts of racial subordination, oppression and criminalization. Moreover, the extent of racial disparities cannot be the result of the actions of prejudiced individuals, they can, however, be explained by persistent racial structures, racial ideology, practices, traditions and customs. The killings of predominantly Black men (and women) and the justifications given about their deaths reveal the pervasive nature of racial thinking and point directly to the impact of years of unremitting racial stereotyping. Moreover, the current racial beliefs, stereotyping and justifications are not very dissimilar to the past.

Further, the presidential campaign, the attempted policies and the organizational structure of Donald Trump's presidency openly challenge whether the U.S is now a post-racial society. The desire and fear associated with maintaining white privilege and control were bluntly expressed in the public arenas and political forums of the presidential election, including the right to violence. Many believe that Donald Trump won the White House, in part, by pushing messages and policies that white nationalists liked. For this reason, he was hesitant to condemn the white nationalists, neo-Nazis and Ku Klux Klan groups for their actions in Charlottesville because doing so would anger his political base. But the number of full-fledged neo-Nazis, for example, or KKK members is small, so then what is the thinking of the wider population of Trump supporters?

This book attempts to explain the contradictions as well as the divergence in ideology and positions of members of the same group. It does this by exploring the nature of race and racism through three important epochs in the development of American society. The earlier chapters analyze why and how racial structures, ideology, beliefs and practices emerge, change and continue long after the Emancipation Proclamation of 1863. The latter chapters illustrate the impact of continued racism by examining the rationalization of racial disparities in the criminal justice system, education, the media, urban housing and governance, and on Black farmers and landowners. Collectively, the chapters offer structural and ideological arguments on change and continuity of racial domination, of white supremacy, and of Black oppression and resistance. The knowledge, evidence, perspectives and discussions shared in this book suggest that this work is not only important, but timely. It is something that all Americans should read if we are to move forward as a nation. This is the America we know.

THE BOOK

This book explores how racism is lived. It delves into why and how racial beliefs and practices persevere over time through the interactions of Black and white Americans. It adopts a socio-historical approach to highlight the complexities, nuances, atrocities and survival of people through slavery and the plantation society, the Jim Crow era, and the post–Civil Rights epoch. By introducing the concept of human agency the discussions allow for diversity and similarity in perspectives within group. Further, it explores how white privilege and white supremacy are rationalized by the Black image in the white mind (portrayed in the illustration on the book's cover) and played out through racial etiquette and racial practices. Parallel to this, is Black resistance to the Black image in the white mind and to racial oppression. Sociologist and race scholar, Clarence R. Talley, whose ideas on which this book is founded, points out that historically under slavery, and still today in contemporary America, seeking an education is a vibrant and rewarding form of Black resistance. He also believed that mentorship was key to successful learning, a theme explored in chapter four on the role of Black male mentorship. It is within this understanding that the persistent nature and outcomes of racism are analyzed and critiqued through the scholarship and voices of predominantly Black males. Hence, the title "Living Racism: Through the Barrel of a Book."

Organization of Chapters

The research for the book takes the position that to understand racism in the United States requires that the literature on race incorporate the conceptual development of race as both structure and ideology. From this perspective, race is an autonomous social force interrelated but separate from the concepts of class, ethnicity, nation, and gender. The first three chapters provide a unique theoretical perspective that explores the "race" concept as structure, ideology and etiquette, the interactions of the three elements, and the role they play in creating and reproducing racism. Collectively they provide the theoretical framework for the context and discussions in the other chapters of the book where outcomes of racism are highlighted. The evidence and discussions of the latter chapters (5–9) illustrate how the theoretical arguments are manifested in the living experiences of Blacks and other minority groups. They show how with change, structural racism is retooled to continue in all the major institutions of American society.

Chapter 1, "The 'Race' Concept and Racial Structure," offers important and unique theoretical perspectives that explain the race concept, racial structure and the link to racial theories. To avoid misunderstandings, the intermixture of racial structure with ideas and practices within a society is what is referred to as racialization. Racialization, although linked with elements of class and gender stratification, exists as a separate system of racial stratification. In a racialized society, the legitimation of racial stratification occurs through the promulgation of overt and covert ideologies of racial difference and privilege. Talley argues that current racial theories on racial formation and the racialized social systems do not adequately address how and why racial structures emerge in society and thus cannot address the nature of racial structures. Talley concludes that the plantation economy and society model is helpful in providing a theoretically consistent explanation of how and why racial structures and racism emerge and persist in the contemporary United States. Moreover, the model suggests that white privilege is an inherent aspect of the development of racial structures.

In chapter 2, "Racial Ideology, Beliefs and Practices," Talley and Rajack-Talley maintain that existing race-based theories provide useful understandings of how race as a concept is central to the organizing of American society. They point out, however, that these racial theories are unclear on whether white privilege is inherent in racial structures or is an outcome of white racial ideology that produces racial structures. Neither can they adequately explain why race as structure and race as ideology, can vary in form and extremes. The perspective offered in this chapter is therefore different to other race-based theories in that it adds explanations, with evidence, in what way race as structure and ideology varies in forms and extremes. It does this by incorporating human agency to show how within one racial group, in this case whites, there can be divergent racial ideologies, within and across time. This includes extremist, populist, conservative and liberal white perspectives, among others. Talley and Rajack-Talley show how these different ideologies can vary in any one individual over time, as well as how they persist across historical moments including in the contemporary post–Civil Rights period. Again employing human agency in the analysis, the chapter concludes that integral to white domination is Black resistance.

Chapter 3 on "Racial Etiquette and Racial Stereotypes" explains how racial ideologies are expressed through racial etiquette and racial stereotypes, and how they create and perpetuate a racialized American society. Talley and Rajack-Talley use racial etiquette to describe how social relations between persons, bounded by hierarchical racial classifications, are displayed in the private and public spheres. Racial etiquette is observed through racial beliefs, practices, traditions and customs of individuals and groups. They examine and discuss the rules of engagement of racial etiquette through the same historical periods as in the chapters before on racial structure and racial ideology. Talley and Rajack-Talley also discuss the role that racial stereotypes play; how they change with socio-economic and political shifts, and at the same time continue to support the notion of white superiority and Black inferiority. The link between racial etiquette, racial stereotyping, and racial ideology is made clear.

Chapter 4 is titled "Black Male Mentorship" and focuses on key understandings for mentoring. Derrick R. Brooms splits the chapter into two main parts. First, the chapter uses a strengths-based approach to provide an overview of the inherent possibilities of mentoring Black males. The impact of mentoring relationships is a significant finding across a range of studies on student success and personal development. Mentoring here is used to frame and discuss how building relationships with Black males can enhance personal development, self-efficacy, and capital (i.e., aspirational capital, navigational capital, and linguistic capital). Additionally, relationships developed through mentoring can help build community and extend social networks. The second part of the chapter highlights the role of Black male mentorship, how it works, citing the narratives of the authors, and the desired outcomes—one of which is this book. Brooms posits that exploring mentorship, both formal and informal, and the mentoring experiences of Black males helps reveal unique opportunities to build on the "cultural wealth(s)" of Black males. Mentoring relationships, especially among Black males, can provide heightened attention and caring to Black males to help ensure and support their success.

Chapter 5 on "Risky Bodies: Race and the Science of Crime and Violence" is a study of crime at the biological level and its long and contentious history with the question of race. In this chapter, Oliver Rollins makes the argument that biological knowledge (assumptions) of violence help to both reinforce the *myth* of race as a unique biological variable and justify the creation of new bio-political forms of racial control and governance—such as eugenics. According to Rollins, many bio-criminologists today have taken meticulous steps to avoid the issue of race; even going as far as to declare that today's bio-criminology is "race-neutral." He argues that we cannot simply separate scientific ways of investigating violence from our social representations and cultural interpretations of such behavior. Today's bio-criminology may be more wary of the misuses of race, but are there *new* ways that race can get re-envisioned, reduced, or naturalized through the construction and proposed management of risky and at-risk bodies? Moreover, what role does or can contemporary bio-criminology play in reconstituting, sustaining, or challenging the myth of the "dangerous Black male"? Rollins contends that we must engage more with contemporary racial theory to understand the potential function and effects of today's bio-criminology. Thus, the chapter draws attention to the manner in which the everyday conceptualizations and practices of living with and negotiating systemic racism are captured, ignored, or shaped by bio-criminological knowledge and technology. The chapter simultaneously helps to clarify the ways in which everyday engagements, practices, and ideologies of race influence the production and potential uses of biological and techno-scientific knowledge of crime and violence.

Chapter 6 is titled "Racialized School Discipline and the School-to-Prison Pipeline." Here, Thomas J. Mowen argues that although public schools in the United States have never been safer or more secure, schools continue to adopt increasingly castigatory forms of discipline, punishment, and security. Racial inequality in school discipline has existed since the founding of the public school system and historical issues are relatively well known among the public (e.g., separate but equal). However, racial inequality continues to exist in contemporary school discipline and punishment. This chapter explores this racial disproportionality in school punishment as well as the school-to-prison pipeline (STPP). It does this by first examining some of the theoretical explanations for racial inequality in school discipline. Secondly, the chapter investigates why both school punishment and the STPP mirror broader racialized trends in punishment in the United States. Additionally, the chapter addresses some of the consequences of the punitive school discipline and the STPP including both individual- and structural-level outcomes, as well the negative consequences of racialized school discipline within the hallways of schools in the United States.

In chapter 7, "Black and Blue: Analyzing and Queering Black Masculinities in *Moonlight*," Eric A. Jordan and Derrick R. Brooms examine representations of Black maleness in film. The chapter investigates how the film *Moonlight* "queers" black masculinities and how that queering of Black males shows more nuanced representations of Black masculinities. In particular, the chapter focuses on three key points: (a) performance of Black masculinities; (b) the impact of environment on expressing and performing masculinities; and (c) the limitations of heteronormative masculinity. In films, Black males often are represented one-dimensionally in ways that maintain the myth that Black men are to be aggressive, criminal, and detached—which primarily is informed and projected through the white gaze. Critical analysis of *Moonlight* demonstrates a potential shift in the presentation of the Black male in film, and offers an image of Black men who discover, explore, and embrace their feelings and sense of self in ways Black males have not been able to do in previous films. *Moonlight* offers an opportunity to discern and investigate heteronormative masculinity and its impact on Black males, and a look into how Black males can unlearn myths of hegemonic (or traditional) masculinity. The chapter addresses the need for providing more complex representations of Black maleness, which ultimately can offer greater understanding and insight into Black men's interiorities.

Chapter 8 is titled "New Rules to the Game: Neoliberal Governance and Housing in Atlanta, Georgia." In this chapter, Cameron Khalfani Herman and Theresa Rajack-Talley explore how economic and political shifts continue to marginalize individuals based on race and social class. The chapter begins with a discussion of the neoliberal restructuring of economies in the 1970s that has reshaped governance strategies at the global, national, and sub-national levels of society. Since that period, many U.S. cities have taken on entrepreneurial strategies to maintain local development in the face of declining federal fiscal support. As a result, cities have grown increasingly less responsive to the needs of economically marginalized citizens. Focusing on the demolition of public housing and the local implications of the housing market collapse in 2008 as specific examples of neoliberalization, Herman and Rajack-Talley examine coalition governance's treatment of housing issues in Atlanta between 1992 and 2012. The analysis of Atlanta's governing structure during this twenty-year period found that the city displayed a strong commitment to business-first governance reflecting the entrepreneurial thrust of neoliberalism. Additionally, the dwindling relationship between Atlanta's public housing residents, largely African American, and the city's political leadership affirms Adolph Reed's assessment of the Black Urban Regime's commitment to its business and middle-class constituency. The chapter concludes that Atlanta's citizens' collective action to protect residents from foreclosed home seizures provides a glimpse into extra-political resistance to neoliberalism.

Chapter 9 focuses on one of the least researched topic on race in the United States. Moreover, the tale of Black farmers is diminished in African American history. In this chapter on "Black Farmers' General and Gendered Strikes against the USDA," Willie Jamaal Wright analyzes the role of Black agrarians in resisting systemic racism within the United States Department of Agriculture (USDA). The chapter first highlights the historical importance of farming and landownership to African Americans. Congruent with the analytical framework of the book, the chapter provides some details on attempts to dispossess Black farmers and Black farmers' resistance to exploitation. Wright cites the class-action lawsuit, *Pigford et al. v. Glickman* (Pigford I), levied by Black farmers against the USDA in 1997 as an example of Black resistance and what the late sociologist W. E. B. Du Bois called a *general strike*. Du Bois coined the term *general strike* to describe the self-emancipatory praxis of formerly enslaved Black men and women during the Civil War. Wright also discusses gendered resistance, citing the case of agricultural advocate Shirley Sherrod, who was forced to negotiate and resist a particular patriarchal brand of white supremacy within the USDA. Wright concludes that Pigford I and Sherrod's solitary stance represents a general and gendered strike against the USDA, both furthering Black agrarians' contemporary struggles for land, livelihood, and justice.

In the concluding chapter, Brooms and Rajack-Talley present a brief summary of the discussions of all the chapters. They suggest that to properly understand racism and the negative outcomes, one must first study race as a separate construct and its intersectionality with gender, social class, sexuality and other social factors. Moreover, the nature of race is linked to both structure and ideology and their dialectical relationship that gives rise to white privilege and white supremacy. Brooms and Rajack-Talley conclude that human agency is integral to understanding the diversity in white racial thinking as well as to Black resistance to perceptions of Black inferiority and racial domination and oppression.

Chapter One

The "Race" Concept and Racial Structure

Clarence R. Talley

The study of the social phenomena of race in the social sciences has become increasingly dominated by the idea that race is socially constructed.[1] This consensus, however, serves only as the point of departure for academic debates about the conceptual nature of race. The meaning of the term race or "race" illustrates the divergent approaches and conceptualizations involved in the debate. In fact, the discourse on race may serve to obscure rather than clarify issues because of difficulties reconciling the different conceptual constructions to signify the race concept. A central tenet of the literature is the assumption that racism results from the social construction of groups of people as races. The social construction of race approach conceptualizes both structural and ideological components as the common elements used to define and account for the emergence, persistence, and continuing effects of racism. However, one problem that emerges from this literature is a tendency to conflate the structural and ideological processes so that racism creates racial positions subsequently manifested through racism. The circularity in this reasoning is what prompts Robert Miles to argue that race and racism although interrelated and interpenetrated must be analyzed separately.[2]

An important group of perspectives emerging over the last several decades could be termed "race-based" theories because of their focus on race as the central organizing feature of specific societies (Bell 1992; Knowles and Prewitt 1969; Blauner 1972, 2001; Bonilla-Silva 1996, 2001, 2017; Carmichael and Hamilton 1967; Feagin and Vera 1995, 2000; Omi and Winant 1986, 1994, 2015).[3] The "race-based" approaches conceptualize race as an autonomous social force with both structural and ideological elements that are integral to the operation of society. The centrality of race in these approaches is an attempt to avoid the reductionism of conceptualizing racial boundaries and racism as ephemeral and the outcome of other social hierarchies of class, ethnicity, gender, and nation. This literature has furthered debate about the concept of race by showing that racial phenomena operate at both institutional and individual levels and that different forms of racism may emerge across time in any one society as well as across societies with different histories.

The emergence of the "race-based" approaches while enlightening has not solved many of the conceptual problems that have always existed within the discourse on race. The conceptual issues stem, in part, because much of this research has searched for models that would explain racism, racial inequality, and/or racialized social structures and thus have neglected the conceptual development of race. The focus on racism rather than race has placed ideology at the center of the analyses. As a result, these models suffer from circular logic because explanations of racism do not rely on structural determinants but upon previous and contemporary ideological forces. The circularity of logic is due to conceptualizing racial ideologies as the determining factor in the emergence of race and racism. The effect of which is to explain the emergence and persistence of a social phenomenon through its own existence.

The problems stemming from the focus on racism as primarily an ideological phenomenon are seen in the confusing and non-comparable use of concepts and terminology to signify racial processes. For instance, some research views the concept of white privilege as an element of racial structure inherent in the system of ranking and evaluation in society (Blauner 1972, 2001; Bonilla-Silva 1996, 2001, 2017; Carmichael and Hamilton 1967). Alternatively, other researchers view white privilege as the outcome of contested material and ideological interests (Bell 1992; Omi and Winant 1986, 1994, 2015; Knowles and Prewitt 1969; Wellman 1993). The confusion over whether white privilege is an inherent aspect of racial structure or is an outcome of racial contestation has not been resolved. Thus, the literature cannot explain why a structuring of white privilege should emerge in society and why racism and racist practices persist with such tenacity in contemporary society.

The current debates over the conceptual status of race does not adequately address questions about the historically specific context for the emergence of racial structures, questions about whether racial processes emerge from primarily structural or ideological sources, and whether races exist in society as structural or ideological social phenomena. These questions have significant implications for the study of race and racism as well as the relationship of these social phenomena within the organization of the society. The idea that racism emerges as the result of the need for facilitating, legitimating, or explaining racial subordination has resulted in a general tendency to undertheorize the nature of racial structures. This position influences the social and academic debate over the relative significance of race and class, the desirability, attainability, and meaning of a color-blind society, assessments of progress in race relations, and debates about personal responsibility and the culture of poverty. All of which are important elements in explaining why "races" diverge in measures of social well-being. Centering study on racial structures can contribute to understanding the social context for framing these issues as public policy debates.

The argument of the current chapter is that the plantation economy and society model contributes to the development of race as a concept by providing a theoretically consistent explanation of why and how racial structures emerge within American society. From this perspective, past and current forms of racism persist because of the continued existence of racial structures. The plantation economy and society model incorporates insights from the "race-based" approaches to provide consistent explanations about why racial structures emerge in some societies and not others, as well as explanations for the nature of racial structures. The model focuses attention on the autonomous development of racial structures as well as the interconnectedness of racial structures with class structures. The chapter will first discuss some of the conceptual problems of the development of the race concept within the "race-based" perspectives and then offer a framework for viewing racialization within the plantation economy and society model.

RACE-BASED THEORIES AND RACIAL STRUCTURE

Much of the discourse about race consists of debates about explanations of the causes and consequences associated with race and racism as well as the nature of these concepts. Fundamental to this discourse is the need for broad agreement of acceptable frameworks, concepts, and terminology necessary to develop a theory of race and society. This chapter treats race and racism as distinct types of social phenomena that are interconnected but should be separate areas of study. The literature focusing race as a concept commonly understands the racialization process as the hierarchical ranking of the population into distinct segments and placement of social actors into these racial categories.

In general, theories that examine race and racism place different emphasis on racial structure and racial ideology. They also have diverse interpretations about the relationship between racial structures and racial ideology. To make clear the distinctions the next chapter of the book interrogates race-based theories and their perspectives on the emergence, manifestations, and continuance of racial ideology. This chapter focuses on the emergence and nature of racial structures where the literature tends to treat racial structures as the outcome of the process of racialization (Omi and Winant 1986, 1994, 2015), or as racialized outcomes of other social structures in society (Bonilla-Silva 1996, 2001, 2017). However, this minimizes racial structures as an autonomous aspect of the social structure of society. In order to conceptualize racial structures as an integral part of the social system requires understanding the logic for the emergence of racialization as well as the nature of racial structures emerging from this process.[4]

The Emergence and Nature of Racial Structures

The theory of racial formation of Omi and Winant (1986, 1994, 2015) and the racialized social system approach of Bonilla-Silva (1996, 2001, 2017) offer discussion of racial structure but largely take the structural elements of the race concept as given. The relative neglect of a focus on racial structure prevents these models from developing systematic explanations of how and why racial structures emerge in the United States. The two positions offer different explanations for the emergence of racial structures as well as differing conceptualizations about the nature of racial structures. For instance, Omi and Winant (1986) minimize the emergence and role of racial structures by conceptualizing racialization as a historically specific ideological process whereby the emergence of racial ideology affects the content of racial categories and the construction of racial identities. According to the authors, racialization is a process that signifies, "the extension of racial meaning to a previously racially unclassified relationship, social practice or group" (64).

The notion of racial structure in racial formation theory is complex and is not ultimately helpful in disentangling competing notions about the nature of racial structure. In the original formulation of a theory of racial formation, Omi and Winant (1986) argue that the racialization process produces racial classifications structured by differential levels of power and privilege. In a later work, however, Omi and Winant (1994, 2015) present a rather more detailed discussion of racial structure but one that focuses on racial outcomes as racial structure. The authors argue that racial formation processes have both structural and representational aspects and clearly state their conceptualization of the social role of racial structures "to interpret the meaning of race is to frame it social structurally" (Omi and Winant 1994, 56). According to this view, racial structures are conceptualized as structures of domination that operate through the political areas as demonstrated in this statement of the authors "[h]ere, the focus is on the racial dimensions of social structure—in this case of state activity and policy" (Omi and Winant 1994, 57).

The racial formation perspective views the role of racial structure in the social system to be one of re-enforcing the ideological elements of racial ideologies and racial identities through the political arena (Omi and Winant 1986, 1994, 2015). In this view, racial structure has no direct relationship with other structural aspects of society and its effects occur indirectly through the ideological realm. This is to say that racial structure does not directly affect the meaning of race or the racial distribution of resources. Racial structures result from racial projects. According to Omi and Winant (1994) "a racial project is simultaneously an interpretation, representation, or explanation of racial dynamics, and an effort to reorganize and redistribute resources along particular racial lines" (56). Thus, racial projects link the elements of structure and representation and give meaning to race at the institutional macro-level and micro-level of social relations.

This approach leaves several unanswered questions about racial structure. How does racial structure, as the system of racial classification, directly relate to other structural aspects of society? Are racial structures simply the aggregate outcome of the racial distribution of goods and services? How is the process of racial classification linked to the processes of social evaluation and ranking? Also problematic is the question of whether white privilege is an aspect of the system of racial classification or is white privilege an ideology arising from racial classifications?

A more recent theoretical approach that explains the social construction of race in society adopts a racialized social systems framework in an attempt to remedy prior theoretical shortcomings in conceptualizing racism. From this perspective, racial structure is inherent in the hierarchical ranking of the racial classification system and the resultant system of racial ideologies, race relations, and racial practices (Bonilla-Silva 1996, 2001, 2017). In racialized social systems, other social hierarchies are the source of hierarchical racial structures and racial structures are an explicit and autonomous aspect of the social structure. Racial structures emerge from other social structures and directly affect other social structures as well as the content and form of racial ideologies. The racialized social systems approach explicitly recognizes racial structure as the emergence of racial hierarchies that are themselves the outcome of processes of ranking and evaluation. In racialized social systems, the racial structure of white advantage and Black disadvantage emerges from the white supremacist racial order of European imperialist expansion. Racial hierarchies, in turn, produce specific social relations and social practices of domination and subordination between the races.

From the racialized social system perspective, racial classifications constitute only one aspect of the racial structure of society (Bonilla-Silva 1996, 2001, 2017). A second aspect of racial structure is reflected in autonomous racial ideologies that include systems of race relations, social practices, and racial etiquette that serve the interests and privilege of the dominant race and limits the life chances of members of subordinate races (Bonilla-Silva 1996, 2001, 2017). These ideological elements of racial structure emerge from the hierarchical system of racial classification and affect the operation of the labor market, practices of segregation, and practices of racial etiquette. From this perspective, the racial structure of society is "[the] totality of the racial-ized social relations and practices constitutes the racial structure of society" (Bonilla-Silva 2001, 37).

The theory of racialized social systems tries to avoid problems of circu-larity by explicitly discussing the emergence of racial structures but succeeds only in introducing racial structure as an explanation for the emergence of an autonomous racial ideology (Bonilla-Silva 1996, 2001, 2017). Once operat-ing as an autonomous feature of society, racial ideologies are the primary causal factor producing subsequent ideological practices and social relations. Thus, racial ideology reproduces itself in different forms of racism. The circularity in this formulation is perhaps a more general problem of theoriz-ing racial classifications, race relations, and racial practices among the ele-ments of the racial structure of racism. The homogenization of all conceptual elements of race into the concept of racial structure deflects attention away from the nature of racial structures and the direct relationship of racial struc-tures to the organization of society.

Institutional Racism, Internal Colonialism, and Critical Race Theories

The theories of racial formation and racialized social systems draw on previ-ous "race-based" approaches in the conceptualization of racial structure and racial ideology. In fact, fundamentally similar ways of viewing racial struc-ture and racial ideology are present in the literature on institutional racism, internal colonialism, and critical race theory. These approaches, with few exceptions, have tended to view racial ideology as the important causal agent in racial processes and racial structures as institutionalized white privilege and white racial domination.

According to the institutional racism perspective, the race concept has both structural and ideological elements but focuses primarily on racial ideol-ogy as cause and racial structure as outcome. Racial structures derive from an ideologically driven process resulting in racial subordination at the macro-level of institutional racism and the micro-level of personal racism. More-over, the structure of white privilege leads to the development of a racial ideology of white supremacy that serves both to unify whites and hold Blacks in subservient positions in the society. Thus, Black racial oppression and discrimination occur as the result of institutionalization of racism within the structure and organizations of society (Carmichael and Hamilton 1967; Knowles and Prewitt 1969; Wellman 1993). According to Wellman (1993), institutionalized racism is simply the societal organization of white privilege. This concern with racial ideology as a causal factor and racial structures as outcome also appears in research that examines the origins of institutional racism. Knowles and Prewitt (1969) argue that institutional racism is integral to the organization of American society beginning with the institution of slavery. For these authors, institutional racism has its origins in the ideology and institutional arrangements of British colonialism. The ideologies of "manifest destiny" and the "white man's burden" signify white supremacy and are the basis of subsequent racial ideologies and institutional arrangements.

Other writers supply logic for the institutionalization of racism in American society by drawing analogies to colonialism. For example, Stokely Carmichael (Kwame Ture) and Charles V. Hamilton in their book, *Black Power: The Politics of Liberation in America*, argue that the internal colonialism of the Black population occurs as the purposeful relegation of the Black population to inferior political and economic status both during and subsequent to slavery. From this perspective, white privilege emerges in American society because of the relations of colonialism and exploitation. Institutional racism is the form of domination under internal colonialism because it acts to deny rights to the Black population in spite of full citizenship status and standards of formal legal equality. More specifically, institutional racism is a covert form of racism that originates in the operation of established and respected forces in the society and relies on active and pervasive anti-Black attitudes and practices. The generally pluralistic character of American politics tends toward racial polarization when race emerges as a public issue and challenges white advantage. The polarization is the unity and solidarity of whites against Black encroachment upon vested rights and privileges. This notion suggests that racial structures emerge in American society because of the need to protect white privilege.

The institutional racism and colonialism perspectives view racial structure as the outcome of ideologically driven processes of racial subordination. However, Blauner (2001) argues that racial structures in American society emerged from the inherent structures of exploitation and control under colonialism. Colonialism produced races and ethnic groups of people of color throughout the third world in much the same way as it produced racial structures in the United States. Thus, the racial structure of the United States reflects the superiority of whites and the subordination of African Americans (Blauner 1972, 2001).[5] In this view, the hierarchical system of racial classification that emerged in the United States is inseparable from the white superiority inherent in the structure of colonialism. Thus, Blauner (2001) accounts for the emergence of racial structure in the United States but is unable to explain why racial structure varies from one colonial system to another and can vary over time within any one society.

Critical race theorists, a group of lawyers who engage in critical legal studies, also focus on the institutionalization of racial classifications and racial privilege and disadvantage within the political and legal structures of society (Bell 1992; Delgado and Stefancic 2000, 2001, 2012). Derrick Bell writing from a critical race theory perspective argues that specific ideologies of colonialism produce specific racial structures. These racial structures intersect with social class formations and the broader system of power in the United States (Bell 1992). This approach suggests that a particular "world view" contributes to the structural subordination of Blacks and the privileging of whites. The argument relies on two levels of analysis that are important: the macro-level racism of political institutions and the micro-level racism present among the dominant white population. The images of Blacks as the "other" and as "beyond the pale of the American Dream," are core ideas of the two racisms. Alternatively, whites, even those with no power, subscribe to a "privileged racial identity" that leads to a process of "racial bonding." The racism resulting from this "world view" is the basis for the justification of slavery, as well as ignoring the effects of slavery and the continuing institutional and individual discrimination against African Americans. Thus, racism, by which Bell means racial ideology, maintains and supports the white power structures and can be overt as was practiced prior to the civil rights movement or subtle and covert as is practiced in contemporary society.

THE PLANTATION ECONOMY AND SOCIETY

The plantation economy and society model draws on the experiences of colonialism to understand patterns of economic underdevelopment, processes of class formation, and racialization in Latin America, the Caribbean, and the southern United States. The process of racialization suggested by the model links the emergence and maintenance of racial structures in the United States to similar structures created by colonialism and imperialism throughout the third world. The plantation system, not the institution of slavery, is the context for racialization because slavery represents only one labor regime consistent with the needs and requirements of the planter elite for labor exploitation and control. The basic structural elements of the plantation economy and society, including racial structures, arise from the prevailing patterns of labor exploitation and control. These structures of control, in particular racial structures, persist past the initial period of slavery. Other coercive labor regimes such as indentureship and sharecropping may emerge within the constraints of the plantation structures of exploitation and control.

The application of the plantation economy and society model to the racialization process in the United States shares areas of communality as well as divergence with the theories of racial formation and racialized social systems. For instance, Omi and Winants' racialization process is an important key to understanding the period through which rigid definitions of racial classifications and meanings associated with racial categories were developed. An equally important area of commonality is the emphasis of Bonilla-Silva (1996, 2001, 2017) on the racial classification process as one of the inherent ranking and evaluation systems based upon white domination. The criteria for ranking and evaluation used in the system of racial classification are, in essence, privileging whites and disadvantaging Blacks. This hierarchical racial structure produces racial ideologies, racial inequalities, as well as racial contestations.

The plantation economy and society model departs from Omi and Winant as well as Bonilla-Silva in its explanations of the emergence and nature of racial structures. The break with Omi and Winant arises from their central assumption that the racialization process is ideological in nature and that racial ideologies are the central social forces initiating the racialization process. The primary difference between the plantation economy and society model and Bonilla-Silva is that the former focuses on racial structures while the latter focuses on racism. Bonilla-Silva reduces the study of race to the study of racism and argues that racial structures encompass racial hierarchies, racial ideologies, racial practices, and race relations.

Economic and Social Dynamics of Plantation Labor

The plantation economy and society model argues that racialization developed in the New World colonies of the Americas because of the nature of their economic insertion into the world system. The colonies of the Americas developed as one of three major types of colonies: colonies of settlement, conquest, and exploitation. Colonies of exploitation are the ones that emerge as plantation economies and societies because they evolve from a system of labor and resource exploitation characterized by production for trade (Best 1968). The plantations, as units of production within plantation economy and society, must form linkages with joint trading companies located in the metropolis. These investors would provide plantation units with economic enterprise, organization, and initial capital.

The conditions under which plantation units could gain access to sources of capital located in the metropolis were restrictive and provided constraints to social, economic, and political developments in the plantation economy and society (Beckford 1972; Best 1968; Mandle 1978, 1992; Thompson 1975). For instance, some of the requirements for plantation production units to do business with the joint trading companies forced the plantation units to limit production in the plantation economy to terminal activity and to surrender discretion over the regulation of monetary and fiscal relationships. This included control over the origin, destination, and carriage of trade, and disposition of plantation production.

The plantation economy and society approach extends the social context of the racialization process from a preoccupation with the system of slavery as primary cause to encompass the entire system of social relations (Thompson 1975). Thus, the planter class stood at the center of a process of social differentiation that resulted in the formation of social classes, racial structures, and racial ideology (Billings 1979; Cox 1948; Thompson 1975). The process of social differentiation stems from the need for authority and control over the resources of land and labor within the plantation economy and society. The authority and control of the planter class required a set of ideas and beliefs common to all members of the society and became possible for the relatively small planter class, in part, by emphasizing racial differences between Black and white workers rather than class differences among whites (Thompson 1975).

Social Control and Racial Structures

The perspective that relates the racial structure of the United States to racial hierarchies in the world economy is not new and appears in much of the literature on racialization.[6] However, the key insight provided by the plantation economy and society approach is the identification of specific types of colonies and colonial conditions that produced racial structures. For example, the major initial constraint of a plantation economy and society is the scarcity of labor needed for plantation export production. The problem of labor scarcity occurs because of the transfer of migrant labor to colonies of settlement rather than to colonies of exploitation. Therefore, plantation economies and societies are unique because they exist in a situation of open resources where land is widely available and the supply of labor is scarce and inadequate for plantation export production. The individual plantations solve the problem of labor and labor control by imposing a labor regime that creates the environment of a total economic institution (Best 1968; Thompson 1975). From this perspective, plantations evolved as economic units producing agricultural commodities for export with a unique labor system of organization and supervision where a small group of highly skilled managers controls a large, unskilled workforce.

On the other hand, plantation systems consist of individual plantations that collectively encompass the totality of institutional arrangements surrounding the production and marketing of plantation crops (Best 1968; Mandle 1978, 1992; Thompson 1975; Wagley 1957). The plantation system of production dominates the plantation economy and society and provides the basis for the plantation structures of control as a means of labor control. The plantation structures of control form the institutional basis for the plantation economy and society and allow the planter class to maintain relative control over social, economic, and political institutions (Beckford 1972; Best 1968; Mandle 1978; Thompson 1975; Wayne 1983). Thompson (1975) argues that the plantation system is a system of agricultural production for export that has historically acquired land through acts of conquest, migration, and/or importation of labor. The planter class provides an ordering or regimentation by race and class to the extent that they exercise certain judicial functions within plantation economy and society.

The relationship of labor and race in the plantation economy and society in the United States is unique because substantial numbers of whites did not benefit from the system of plantation production. The literature argues that racial structures were important because they provided social stability by helping to eliminate job competition between white and Black labor and because the control over the labor of the slaves and control of the slave population was a central problem for the plantation economy and society (Beckford 1972; Harris 1964; Thompson 1975).[7] The legal and extra-legal forms of social control that comprised the plantation structures of control were the basis for the development of racial structures. The plantation structures of control developed as racial structures with an inherent system of ranking and evaluation, explicit hierarchical racial status, and racialized expected roles and behavior.

The control over slaves occurred through the direct use of force as well as the use of various benefits and privileges extended to productive or obedient slaves. In fact, some researchers believe that the system of plantation production with slave labor could not have existed with only the use of force and that a system of privilege among slaves was a logical means of control over a diverse labor force and population (Genovese 1967; Gutman 1976; Patterson 1979). There is substantial evidence, however, to support the view that most slaves did not see Southern slavery as a benevolent, paternalistic way of life. For instance, open resistance to work or expressing a deferential attitude toward planter authority resulted in harsh punishment (Franklin 1947; Gutman 1976; Patterson 1979; Wilson 1975). It is clear that paternalistic attitudes of the planter class did not supplant the more or less unrestricted use of force to punish violations of behavioral norms.

There is, of course, no one accurate description of the division of labor that characterized the slave labor force on individual plantations because the work routines and activities of the slaves varied by the size of the plantation operation and the type of crops produced. However, some estimate that eighty percent of the slave population worked as field hands (Fogel and Engerman 1974). If this estimate is accepted, it means that about one fifth of the slaves were skilled laborers and thus the differentiated slave labor force required complex combinations of methods of supervision and control. Larger plantation operations recognized good management of the slave labor force was central to the development of a highly disciplined, highly specialized, and well-coordinated labor force. The industrial disciplining was necessary in establishing a steady and intense rhythm of work and accounts for the superior efficiency of large-scale plantation operations. The rigid organization of plantation slave labor was as in a factory with each laborer assigned a specific task or organized into work gangs or teams in which interdependence of labor was crucial. In this regard, Fogel and Engerman (1974) argue that large slave plantations were about thirty-four percent more efficient than free Southern farms because of the efficiency of the plantation, as well as the efficiency of slave labor. Of course, this type of work organization was possible because of the harsh methods of control over slave labor; methods of labor control that were not possible with nominally free white labor.

The racial structures that emerged in the plantation economy and society to control the labor of the slaves and to consolidate white rule did not dissipate with the end of slavery. Research has noted that change in the structure of the labor regime is possible without effecting the dominance and control of the planter class within the plantation economy and society. For example, the persistence of plantation structures of control is consistent with other coercive labor regimes such as indentureship and sharecropping (Beckford 1972; Best 1968; Mandle 1978, 1992). The latter forms of labor control as well as the slavery fit the demands of the planter class for control over the social, political, and economic aspects of the plantation economy. Weiner (1976) argues that, as a class, the planter elite survived the Civil War and Reconstruction. In fact, rather than decimating the power of this class, the planter elite went through a process of centralization and concentration with the strongest concerns remaining in operation.

The use of racialization to control the labor supply and labor force means that racial separation and subordination tends to remain a characteristic of plantation economies even after emancipation of the slaves (Beckford 1972; Best 1968; Wagley 1957). In fact, Best (1968) argues that emancipation of the slaves did little to alter the general institutionalized structures of the plantation economy. The plantation structures operate to control labor under established methods of production and persist through periods of decline and eventual collapse of the plantation system. Social change in the plantation structures of control, especially economic adjustments, do occur, but they usually come about through the institutionalized framework of the plantation economy determinate upon the nature of resource (land and labor) allocation. From this perspective, changes in methods of social control occur because of social and economic change and not as a reflection of fundamental change in ideology or racial structures (Billings 1979; Mandle 1978, 1992; Weiner 1976).

Social Control and Social Class

Control over the condition of servitude of the slaves was a problem that required the assistance of the other class segments of plantation society. In addition to the everyday resistance to work regimes, slaves engaged in other forms of resistance such as insurrection and escape. Slaves also resisted the system of slavery by engaging in forbidden family, cultural, and religious practices as well as resistance by obtaining education. In order to facilitate the consolidation of control, the planter class exerted legal dominance over Southern legislatures and in many cases influenced state policies to support the plantation economy and society. For example, legally established slave patrols helped to keep slaves within the boundaries of the plantation and off the plantation served to restrict illegitimate slave gatherings (Bartley 1983; Billings 1979). The slave codes that emerged from Southern legislatures from the middle of the 1600s through the emancipation of the slaves served to institutionalize the status, rights, and appropriate behavior of the Black slaves, free Blacks, and the white populations along racial lines (Franklin 1947). Franklin describes the climate of colonial Virginia in the period of enactment of the first slave codes as "an armed camp in which masters figuratively kept their guns cocked and trained on the slaves in order to keep them docile and tractable and in which the assembly, the courts, and the custodians of the law worked for the maintenance of peace and order among the Black workers" (Franklin 1947, 73). These measures to control the lives and labor of the slaves ultimately meant that race and whiteness became crucial indicators of freedom. In fact, W. E. B. Du Bois (1935) focused attention on the interconnectedness of race and class formation. This author argued that racial ideology and racist practices did not originate with white workers but that white workers adopted and acted upon pre-existing racial ideology and racist social practices. More important, white workers came to identify themselves and their interests with whiteness even when tangible results were negligible, and thus to accept their class position. The structure of controls over the slaves and the associated class structure emerging from slavery resulted in the creation of racial ideology and racist practices that affected both Black and white workers. Thus, white privilege and Black disadvantage are integral elements of racial structures in the plantation economy and society.

The Southern plantation economy and society was simultaneously a class society and a slave society built upon a complex set of race and class relationships. Plantation economy and society could not sustain itself, including maintain control over slave labor, without the allegiance and assistance of white non-slave owners. The race and class relationships of dominance allowed the planter class to maintain control over the plantation economy and society. Acquiring what amounted to racial allegiance, however, was problematic because of the exploitative class relationships that brought the yeoman farmers, industrialists, and merchants into political, economic, and social hierarchical relationships with the planter class. The exploitative class relationships, however, did not destroy the unity that existed among the white population of the plantation economy and society. The unity of the white population, based on the exploitation of slave labor, was central to the existence of the plantation economy and society. The exercise of more or less complete control over the lives and labor of the slaves came at the expense of minimizing class differences within the white population and accentuating racial differences.

In spite of the role and participation of the white lower classes within the plantation society, they faced class exploitation and/or exclusion by the wealthy planters who tolerated but scorned them. Many landless whites moved away from the Cotton Belt to settle in the Piedmont or Appalachian regions in hopes of becoming independent small farmers and herdsmen (Billings 1979; Franklin 1947; Hahn 1983; Wright 1978). In the Cotton Belt South, planters exploited the small farmers in several ways and took advantage of falling cotton prices to force many independent small (yeoman) farmers to become sharecropper and tenant producers. More generally, the planter class used the weak economic situation of the independent yeoman farmers to further the patron-client relationship of economic dependency of the small farmers on planters. For example, few yeoman farmers could afford cotton gins and other machinery and as a result turned to the planters as brokers that would gin and market their crop for a fee. In addition, market fluctuations in prices would often result in widespread poverty and food shortages that forced small farmers to turn to the planters for essential supplies.

The dominance of the planter class extended to the middle classes of plantation society to include industrialists and merchants. Literature on Southern economic development has indicated that an industrial middle class existed but did not develop because the planter class was effective in controlling the magnitude and form of industrialization. The industrialists who operated in the South had to accept the prevailing social system and the restrictions the planter class imposed on the expansion of their wealth and power as a class (Cobb 1984; Wright 1978). Genovese (1967) suggests that the industrialists found themselves in a paradox. On the one hand, manufacturing during the antebellum period played a supportive albeit subordinate role to agricultural production and concentrated mainly on the processing of agricultural goods (flour, corn, tobacco, cotton, etc.). The relationship of the industrialists to the planter class, however, had an exploitative character because, in many cases, the industrialists relied on the planter class as their main source of investment, their main customers, and often as their only client or market.

The merchant class of the slave regime, because their fortunes were linked to those of the planters, supported the plantation system of production against their long-term economic interests. Most merchants found either their business dependent on the patronage of the slaveholder, in which case they assumed a servile attitude toward the planters, or they became planters themselves (Genovese 1967). As part of the commercial class, merchants had little desire or opportunity to invest capital in industrial expansion. Their main interest was to expand their role as intermediary between the planters and outside merchants rather than try to reshape the economic order of the plantation society. This patron-client relationship, strengthened by the tendency of the planters to prefer imported goods for personal consumption, led planters to use merchants located in metropolitan centers to provide supplies and products of mass consumption for the plantation (Wayne 1983). The use of alternative sources of supplies, outside of the local merchants' network, limited the economic horizons and status of the local merchant class.

CONCLUSION

This chapter proceeded from the assumption that a paradigm shift is underway in studies of race and racism. This shift is indicated by the volume of research and writing emerging from theories that view the concept of race as central to the organization of certain societies. The very richness of the literature produces both areas of theoretical commonality as well as divergence and debate. The literature, however, does not provide a theoretically consistent understanding of the process of racialization. This is true, in part, because the literature fails to incorporate racial structures as an integral and direct aspect in the process of racialization. One of the main contestations arising from this body of literature is whether white privilege is inherent in racial structures or is an outcome of racial ideology that produces racial structures. The lack of clarity about the nature of racial structures introduces problems in the way that the concept of race connects with other social forces in the larger society.

The argument presented in this chapter is that the plantation economy and society model provides a framework for synthesizing divergent perspectives on conceptual questions about the nature and emergence of racial structure. Further, the plantation economy and society model can explain the emergence of racial structures and the persistence of racism over time within any one society and across societies. Thus, the model has application to the persistence of racial structures and racism as separate but interconnected concepts within the contemporary United States. Race is understood and treated in much the same way as class, ethnicity, and gender boundaries. Within this context, the interrelationships between racial structure and class formations are fundamental to the racialization process.

The synthesis of the various conceptual debates within the plantation economy and society model provides avenues for future studies of the race concept. Such studies could focus on processes of racialization, the persistence of various forms of racism, the relationship between racial structure and racial ideology, and the relationship of the race concept to other social forces. Crucial to this endeavor is to recognize the nature and role of both racial structures and racial ideologies.

NOTES

1. This chapter is a slightly edited and updated reprint titled "The 'Race' Concept and Racial Structure." In *Racial Structure and Radical Politics in the African Diaspora. Journal of Africana Studies*, Vol. 3: 61–79 (2009).

2. See Robert Miles (1993) for arguments that deconstruction of the "race" concept allows for the separate study of the effects of racialization and expressions of racism within a capitalist world system.

3. This is not to ignore the pioneering work of Du Bois, Drake, Clayton, etc., without whose work and insights none of this work would have been possible.

4. Past conceptualization of social structure acknowledged it to encompass, at least minimally, status viewed as a position within a set of positions and roles as the expected behavior of particular status positions. See Bourdieu (1984) for more relational and human agency aspects of social structure and McNall (1988) for a definition of class based upon the relational aspects and human agency.

5. Robert Blauner (2001) continues to argue that racial oppression plays a central and autonomous role in American Society although he no longer adopts the internal colonialism model that characterized his important work, *Racial Oppression in America.* Blauner acknowledges that accepted models of imperialism and colonialism would have to be adapted in several ways to explain the experiences of the African American community and that the use of the colonial model within the national framework can distort the context of advanced industrial capitalism. More specifically, the internal colonialism model cannot address the interconnectedness of race with the dynamics and structure of political and economic contexts that has produced groups, group politics, and social movements quite different from that of European colonialism.

6. Some good discussion of the importance for racialization of the economic and social context of Europe are Miles (1982, 1989); Balibar and Wallerstein (1991); and Wolpe (1975). Jan Carew (1988) takes a different position and argues that social and religious dynamics of the period preceding Spanish colonialism fostered initial racialization of the Americas.

7. In some views of race and class interconnections, racism emerges from the class structure (Cox 1948; Genovese 1967). Other views question the proposition of whether racism is an autonomous process that interpenetrates the class formation process (Du Bois 1935; Franklin 1991; Jones 1992; Roediger 1991).

REFERENCES

Balibar, Etienne and Immanuel Wallerstein. (1991). *Race, Nation, Class Ambiguous Identities.* London/New York: Verso.

Bartley, Numan, V. (1983). *The Creation of Modern Georgia.* Athens: University of Georgia Press.

Beckford, George. 1972. *Persistent Poverty: Underdevelopment in Plantation Economies of the Third World.* New York: Oxford University Press.

Bell, Derrick. 1992. *Faces at the Bottom of the Well: The Permanence of Racism.* New York: Basic Books.

Best, Lloyd. 1968. "Outlines of a Model of Pure Plantation Economy." *Social and Economic Studies* (September): 283–326.

Billings, Dwight B., Jr. 1979. *Planters and the Making of a "New South": Class, Politics and Development in North Carolina, 1865–1900.* Chapel Hill: University of North Carolina Press.

Blauner, Bob. 2001. *Still the Big News: Racial Oppression in America*. Philadelphia: Temple University Press.

Blauner. Robert. 1972. *Racial Oppression in America*. New York: Harper and Row.

Bonilla-Silva, Eduardo. 1996. "Rethinking Racism: Toward a Structural Interpretation." *American Sociological Review* 62:465–80.

———. 2001. *White Supremacy and Racism in the Post-Civil Rights Era*. Boulder: Lynne Rienner.

———. 2017. *Racism without Racists: Color-Blind Racism and the Persistence of Racial Inequality in America*. Lanham, MD: Rowman & Littlefield.

Carmichael, Stokely and Charles V. Hamilton. 1967. *Black Power: The politics of Liberation in America*. New York: Random House.

Carew, Jan. (1988). *Fulcrums of Change: Origins of Racism in the Americas and other Essays*. Trenton, New Jersey: Africa World Press, Inc.

Cobb, James C. 1984. *Industrialization and Southern Society, 1877–1984*. Lexington: The University Press of Kentucky.

Cox, Oliver Cromwell. 1948. *Caste, Class and Race: A Study in Social Dynamics*. New York: Doubleday and Company.

Delgado, Richard and Jean Stefancic. 2000. *Critical Race Theory: The Cutting Edge*. Philadelphia: Temple University Press.

———. 2001, 2012. *Critical Race Theory: An Introduction*. New York: New York University Press.

Du Bois, W. E. B. 1935. *Black Reconstruction in America, 1860–1880*. New York: Atheneum.

Feagin, Joe and Hernan Vera. 1995, 2000. *White Racism: The Basics*. New York: Routledge.

Fogel, Robert W. and Stanley L. Engerman. 1974. *Time on the Cross: The Economics of American Negro Slavery*. Boston: Little, Brown.

Franklin, John Hope. 1947. *From Slavery to Freedom: A History of African Americans*. New York: Alfred A. Knopf.

Franklin, Raymond. 1991. *Shadows of Race and Class*. Minneapolis: University of Minnesota Press.

Genovese, Eugene D. 1967. *The Political Economy of Slavery: Studies in the Economy and Society of the Slave South*. New York: Vintage Books.

Gutman, Herbert G. 1976. *The Black Family in Slavery and Freedom, 1750–1925*. New York: Pantheon Books.

Harris, Marvin. 1964. *Patterns of Race in the Americas*. New York: Norton.

Hahn, Steven. 1983. *The Roots of Southern Populism: Yeoman Farmers and the Transformation of the Georgia Upcountry, 1850–1890*. New York: Oxford University Press.

Jones, Jacqueline. 1992. *The Dispossessed: America's Underclasses from the Civil War to the Present*. New York: Basic Books.

Knowles, Louis L. and Kenneth Prewitt. 1969. *Institutional Racism in America*. New Jersey: Prentice- Hall.

Kuhn, Thomas. 1970. *The Structure of Scientific Revolutions*, 2nd ed. Chicago: University of Chicago Press.

Mandle, Jay R. 1992. *Not Slave, Not Free: The African American Economic Experience since the Civil War*. Durham, NC: Duke University Press.

———. 1978. *The Roots of Black Poverty: The Southern Plantation Economy After the Civil War*. Durham, NC: Duke University Press.

McNall, Scott G. (1988). *The Road to Rebellion: Class Formation and Populism, 1865-1900*. Chicago: University of Chicago Press.

Miles, Robert. (1989). *Racism*. (Reprint). New York, NY: Routledge.

———. (1993). *Racism After Race Relations*. New York, NY: Routledge.

Omi, Michael and Howard Winant. 1986, 1994, 2015. *Racial Formation in the United States: From the 1960s to the 1980s*. New York: Routledge.

Patterson, Orlando. 1979. "On Slavery and Slave Formations." *New Left Review* 117: 31–67.

Roediger, David. (1991). *The Wages of Whiteness: Race and the Making of of the American Working Class*. London: Verso.

Thompson, Edgar. 1975. *Plantation Societies, Race Relations and the South: The Regimentation* of *Populations.* Durham, NC: Duke University Press.

Wagley, Charles. 1957. "Plantation America: A Cultural Sphere." In *Caribbean Studies: A Symposium*, edited by Vera Rubin, 3–13. Seattle: University of Washington Press.

Wayne, Michael. 1983. *The Reshaping of Plantation Society: The Natchez District, 1860–1880.* Baton Rouge: Louisiana State University Press.

Weiner, Jonathan M. 1976. "Planter Persistence and Social Change: Alabama, 1850–1870." *Journal of Interdisciplinary History* 7: 235–260.

Wellman, David T. 1993. *Portraits of White Racism.* Oxford: Cambridge University Press.

Wilson, William J. 1975. *Power, Racism, and Privilege: Race Relations in Theoretical and Sociohistorical Perspectives.* New York: Macmillan.

Wolpe, Harold. 1975. "The Theory of Internal Colonialism: The South African Case," in I. Oxhaal et al.,*Beyond the Sociology of Development.* London: Routledge & Kegan Paul, 1975.

Wright, Gavin. 1978. *The Political Economy of the Cotton South: Households, Markets, and Wealth in the Nineteenth Century.* New York: Norton.

Chapter Two

Racial Ideology, Beliefs, and Practices

Clarence R. Talley and Theresa Rajack-Talley

The previous chapter presented a syncing argument and framework for understanding the emergence of racial structures and the persistence of racism. In this chapter, we focus on the role of racial ideology in maintaining racial beliefs of white supremacy and practices of white privilege. This is important today because public recognition of issues relating to racial ideologies in contemporary society usually occurs with little common understanding about the exact beliefs and practices associated with those ideologies. Therefore, people often have problems understanding the contradictions between the ideals through which they envision their lives, and the realities of the lives they actually live. It is possible to see this more clearly in moments in the largely still unacknowledged, racial history of the nation. Such moments include the accommodation to racial slavery, legal segregation, the process of desegregation, the Civil Rights Movement, and the post–Civil Rights Era where the first Black man was elected, twice, as the president of the United States.

However, striking evidence that this country's racial history is not resolved continues to surface with increasingly high rates of imprisonment and the killing of Black males commonly justified because of a "fear of the Black male." Additionally, the fact that in a supposedly "post-racial" society there is cause to advocate that "Black Lives Matter" can be confusing. Moreover, should Americans be surprised by the racial, sexist, and other homophobic overtones and anger that ensued during the 45th American presidential elections and spurred numerous street protests afterwards? Or that a candidate, who was popular with various white supremacist groups, was elected as president under the banner of "Make America Great Again?" These moments certainly stretch the logic of a system of racialization and the racism that maintains and rationalizes the system.

29

This chapter is based on the understanding that the United States of America is a racialized society in which persistent racial ideologies legitimize continued racial stratification of disadvantage and privilege based on race. First, we explain the nature of ideology and some of the main theoretical perspectives on racial ideology and their limitations. Second, we examine racial beliefs at three important moments in the United States. Starting with slavery and the plantation society, we illustrate how, even in contemporary times, a racialized society continues to produce and maintain racial beliefs and racial ideology that are based on and create discord. Throughout this chapter, we highlight how racial ideology is a coercive social force imposed upon the population. These discussions are important, as they shape the construction of whether we view racial ideology, at one extreme, as a social illusion or, at the other extreme, as the lived reality of the population.

THE NATURE OF IDEOLOGY

The treatment of ideology in the social science literature suggests that ideology is a multi-dimensional concept. At a general level of definition, racial ideology can refer to social ideals, practices, symbols, and beliefs acted on by rulers and citizens. Despite this basic definition, the literature is not clear about what we know of the nature of ideology. Are racial ideologies totalizing ideas within a population? Are racial ideologies products of the dominant group imposed upon subordinate racial groupings? To what extent are racial beliefs expressed as conceptual thoughts associated with actual behavior manifested in racial practices, traditions, and customs? Moreover, can we examine and analyze racial ideology because of its complexity and nuanced characteristics?

The Problem of Ideology

Antonio Gramsci presents a promising approach to the study of racial ideology in his writing about hegemony. Gramsci's perspective allows us to conceptualize ideology as an organic expression of people's lives. According to Gramsci (1971), ideology emerges within a specific group and grows out of their lived experiences. However, in every society there is a dominant ideology, which incorporates some aspects of the various subordinate ideologies into a central value system. He further explains that the central value system is organized around an "articulating principle" to which all constitutive elements can subscribe and this system, then, becomes a method of hegemonic control. Gramsci contends that hegemony occurs when a fundamental class exercises political, intellectual, and moral leadership within a hegemonic system united by a common worldview. The common worldview is not imposed from the top but is the organic expression of different forces in the system and includes ideological elements from varying sources. The nature of ideology is, therefore, elaborate and spreads across civil society through social institutions (such as schools, churches, and media), the cultural structure (such as architecture), and even in the cultural landscape (such as the naming of streets). For Gramsci, ideology provides the basis for ruling and, in its material existence, produces subjects of the social system.

While Gramsci postulates an approach to the study of ideology, the German sociologist, Karl Mannheim, provides a method for studying ideology. Mannheim (1955) suggests that in order to understand the sociology of knowledge, one has to study mental products as the underlying complex of real social forces. Key among these social forces is the struggle among the various social strata that define the nature of ideology. Mannheim argues that the struggle between various social strata results in ideological discourse. Equally important, the nature of the ideological discourse can be uncovered and understood. According to Mannheim, there are four steps necessary to identify and understand the nature of ideological discourse. First, identify a particular style of thought and trace the style of thought to a particular social stratum. This helps uncover the particular context out of which that style of thought evolved. Second, identify efforts of particular individuals, and their particular worldview, whose commitment to this view makes it "world-striving"—that is, more or less encompassing of the views of all social strata. This is called the spiritual strata. Third, identify the material aspects and objectives of the members recognized as part of this spiritual strata. Last, use specific historical events, temporally and historically, to link the spiritual with specific social strata through examining the political, intellectual, and aspirational contents of that strata.

Ideology through Time and Space

Gramsci's (1971) approach and Mannheim's (1955) method of studying ideology suggest that racial ideologies can be studied from known historical events, but we must interpret these events as being integral parts of the story of racialization and not simply events of nation building. Moreover, in a racialized society, the history of that society will be a racialized history and the social contexts of racial interactions are most clear at those historical moments when challenges to status quo beliefs make the various and opposing positions evident. It is the social context of the interaction between racial groups or strata in a social milieu of domination, subordination, and human agency that reveals racial ideologies. However, a dilemma arises in the United States context as racial ideologies persist even after peoples' lived experiences and social contexts changed in the three key moments of U.S. history—the period of plantation production with slave labor, the period of enactment of Jim Crow legislation, and in the post–Civil Rights period. Interestingly, the idea that racial ideologies persist came into question with the election of Barack Obama as president of the United States. Dawson and Bobo (2009) write about the myth that with the election of Obama America was becoming a "post-racial" society. They found many news commentators, both conservative and liberal, clamoring this idea.

This existence of racial ideologies is central to the work of Barbara Jean Fields (1966, 1985) who examines slavery and freedom in Maryland during the nineteenth century. Fields argues that racial ideologies are rooted in the lived experience and that all ideologies are real. Further, racial ideologies are the embodiment in thought of real social relations. Fields (1985) argues that racial ideologies are linked to specific social structures and conditions and, as these change, social relations and the social experience of people will vary. Within this understanding, the same racial ideologies cannot persist over time; instead, they must be created anew to reflect changing social conditions. Fields explains that there can be some confusion because some racial beliefs and attitudes persist. She gives the example of the antebellum planter who believed in his own superiority over his slaves whom he thought could not survive outside the tutelage of slavery. While the reality stemming from Emancipation should have changed his ideology (freed slaves did survive figuratively and literally), and the slave-master social relations were different, the antebellum planter continued to speak of, and believe in, white racial superiority. This, Fields suggests, can lead many historians (and others) to the spurious inference that the racial ideology of institutionalized slavery had not changed.

Fields makes a compelling argument that while there may be examples of substantial continuity in racial attitudes, this does not demonstrate continuity of the same racial ideology. She also claims that there is no single ideology used by everyone to understand the social world. What sometimes appears to be a single ideology cannot hold the same meaning for everyone. For example, if ideology both shapes and is shaped by experience, then human agency dictates that this same ideology will most likely convey different meanings to people with diverse social experiences. According to Fields (1985), "to suppose otherwise is to take another false step onto the terrain of racialist ideology" (156).

On the other hand, Oliver Cromwell Cox, a sociologist and theorist on the caste-class model of race relations, recognizes race as a product of social relations within history and the political economy, but does not place much credence on the relationship of ideology to the lived experience of people. Instead, he prefers to address issues of socialization and the internalization of racial thinking. Cox (1948, 1976, 2000) argues that the development of racial prejudice initially served the interests of the Southern plantation economic elites and that Blacks suffered less racial prejudice in the North because of the advancement of capitalism and industrialization. He suggests that the race problem and race prejudice in the U.S. are the result of a socio-attitudinal matrix that supports the efforts of a white ruling class to keep exploiting people of color and their resources. Within this theoretical framework, he links racial exploitation to class exploitation, but Cox believes that race prejudice can never be removed completely under capitalism, although the form of exploitation may change.

Cox explains that racial prejudice persists, even after it no longer serves the same economic purpose, because of the socialization of a small percentage of people into racial thinking. This type of socialization occurs as individuals from an early age either consciously or subconsciously internalize the messages of racial thinking contained in the media, schools, and among peer groups, as well as in most arenas of society. The socialization and internalization of racial thinking are quite effective because most people move within well-defined social groups that shelter them from experiencing other people's livelihoods or ways of living.

Similarly, Pierre Bourdieu (1990) argues that past structures and experiences can give substance to contemporary thought and practices. Bourdieu argues that within the subconscious is the "Habitus," a product of history that produces individual and collective practices—as more history—in accordance with schemes generated by history. Habitus is not simply a result of free will, nor is it determined by structures. Instead, it is created by a kind of interplay between the two over time. Consequently, dispositions are shaped by past events and structures and they, in turn, shape current practices and structures. More importantly, Habitus conditions our very perceptions of our practices and structures. According to Bourdieu, Habitus "ensures the active presence of past experiences, which are deposited in each new organism in the form of schemes, practices, thought, and action" (54). Thus, Habitus guarantees the constancy of social action over time through a means above and beyond formal rules and explicit norms. The linking of structure, Habitus, and social practices allow us to conceive of the persistence of racial ideologies even though the social context changes constantly.

The foregoing discussion of ideology and racial ideology provides clues about the multi-faceted nature of racial ideology. Some aspects of racial ideology may result from the lived experiences of people; other aspects can result from historical structures and experiences; and still other aspects may result from the socialization and internalization of racial thinking embedded in society. The combination of all three explanations assists in clarifying the nature of racial ideology and the persistence of diverse views on white superiority and white supremacy in contemporary citizens long after slavery, Jim Crow, and the Civil Rights Era.

Characteristics of racial ideology include racial beliefs, racial stereotypes, racial customs and traditions, and racial practices. The manner in which racial ideologies are used results in racism. Tzvetan Todorov (2000) reminds us that while racism has meanings other than hatred for other races, racism is a behavior that results from race hatred. Todorov argues that racialism is a doctrine or ideology born in western Europe and found worldwide. Moreover, racialism is built on a coherent set of five propositions: (i) the existence of the races, (ii) the continuity between physical type and character, (iii) the action of the group on the individual, (iv) a unique hierarchy of values, and (v) knowledge-based politics (64–67). The latter, knowledge-based politics, is the result of acceptance of the first four propositions as being 'self-evident' and the desire to conform to these facts through the subordination or elimination of inferior races. Racialism joins racism when the theory is put into practice.

While research on racism and the outcomes of racism continues to grow, we need to examine concrete ways that racial thinking derives from the more formalized racial ideology. Further, within this research, it is important to note the differences that exist among various factions of the white and of the Black community. The diverse ideologies, as well as the relative dominance of any one idea at a particular moment in history, reveal the role of human agency and the negotiated nature of racial ideology. In the U.S. context, racial theories all tend to focus, to varying degrees, on white privilege, white superiority, and/or white domination. However, racial ideologies differ in their perspectives on how to view white privilege and white supremacy, and on the relationship between white supremacy, racial structures, and racial ideologies.

RACE-BASED THEORIES AND RACIAL IDEOLOGY

Do racial ideologies produce racial structures and white privilege? Alternatively, do racial structures produce racial ideologies of white superiority? Understanding the dialectic relationship between structure and ideology remains ambiguous. In the previous chapter, we briefly discussed some of the differences among racial theories and their perspectives on racial structures. Here, we examine how the same race-based theories vary along areas of emphasis on racial ideology. Some center their attention on racial formations (Omi and Winant 1986, 2015; Winant 2004), others on racism and the social relations of racial power (Bonilla-Silva 2001, 2006, 2017), some on institutional racism (Blauner 1972, 2001; Carmichael and Hamilton 1967), and more recently on critical race theories (Bell, 1987, 1992).

From the perspective of racial formation theory, racial ideologies emerge in society from pre-existing conceptual elements. That is, they are historically produced from competing political movements in conflict over the social meaning of the ideas of race (Omi and Winant 1986, 2015; Winant 2004). Moreover, racial formation is a social process through which racial classifications and racial meanings result from the interplay of specific economic, political, and social forces that are themselves shaped by racial meanings. The racial identities forged from racial meanings form the basis for collective action by the racial group. The two major architects of racial formation theory, Michael Omi and Howard Winant, believe that racial meanings pervade U.S. society and shape individual racial identities as well as structure collective political action. For Omi and Winant (2015), racialization is "the extension of racial meaning to a previously racially unclassified relationship, social practice, or group" (111). According to these racial formation scholars, the racialization process started during the period of slavery out of efforts of colonizers to justify the exploitation of Black slave labor. The political movements signified by the institutionalized and systemic nature of racial ideology are important on-going influences on the contours of racial boundaries and associated racial meanings.

The discussion of racial ideology by Omi and Winant (1986, 2015) is an important step forward in theorizing about race because it recognizes ideology as a force that operates at the macro and micro levels. In other words, ideology not only structures society but also produces "raced" individuals. The institutionalization of racial beliefs and racial stereotypes at the *macro-level* of society suggests the way that white privilege becomes a part of the normative operation of the society at-large within groups and institutions. The racial beliefs and stereotypes consist of judgments about the "realities" of racial categorization and operate to explain variations in human nature. The stereotypes held about the occupants of the racial categories help shape the meaning as to their intellectual, moral, and physical and artistic temperaments. At the micro level, racial beliefs, traditions, and stereotypes form a racial etiquette that guides the racial practices of individuals, confirm the "obviousness" of the racial beliefs and racial stereotypes, and thus affect the racial identities of individuals. Racial formation, however, does not explain racism as an aspect of continued racial order and racial structure because the central organizing feature of this racial ideology rests upon the principle of racial group interests and not animosity.

Other theorists examining racial ideologies choose to focus more on racial control arising from white domination of economic, social, and political structures. For example, sociologist Eduardo Bonilla-Silva argues that racism continues to exist in the United States and is concerned with issues of domination and resistance between racial groups. He bases his theoretical approach from the standpoint of racialized social systems. According to Bonilla-Silva (2001, 2006, 2017), racial ideology emerges from a hierarchical racial structure but becomes an autonomous social force in the society. Further, the ideologies of the dominant racial group are crystallized and diffused in society to a greater degree than the ideologies of the subordinate racial groups. Within this understanding, racial ideology is a component of the ideological structure of the social system and operates to define racial notions and stereotypes. Racial ideologies therefore form within a racial hierarchy where there are differing levels of privilege and prestige and different racial interests for each racial category. The different objective interests result in competing ideologies that, in turn, lead to racial contestation.

Bonilla-Silva (2017) explains that racial ideology is the "racially based framework used by actors to explain and justify (dominant race) or challenge (subordinate race or races) the racial status quo" (9). He suggests that, conceptually, racial ideology consists of the following three elements: common frames, style, and racial stories. According to this framework, racial ideologies are about meanings expressed through relations of domination. Moreover, dominant actors, white capitalist males, because of their position in the social system and their superior resources, frame the debates and influence the views of the subordinates. Bonilla-Silva contends that the dominant ideology is effective because it provides the frames to organize differences. In the U.S., the dominant racial ideology is that of white supremacy. It is an autonomous element of the social system and organizes social relations between whites and Blacks. According to Bonilla-Silva, white supremacy provides justification for racial inequality, specifies the rules of engagement that guide social conduct (racial etiquette), shape racial identities, and provide a systemized framework for understanding one's place in society.

Other race-based theories trace the historical emergence of racial ideology to colonization and the colonial model. According to the institutional racism perspective, colonialism led to white domination of the political, social, and economic systems in the U.S. and links racial ideology to these racial structures. There are two main trends of thought within this perspective, institutional racism and the internal colony model. These trends differ on explanations of the relationship between racial ideology and racial structures. From the institutionalized racism perspective, slavery helped to instill the sense of white superiority in the minds of all members of society. Stokely Carmichael and Charles Hamilton (1967) argue that institutional racism placed Blacks in colonized situations and led whites to adopt a group position of superiority. The ideology of white superiority combined with the degrading experiences of Black people led many Blacks to believe in their own inferiority. They further claim that the status of Black Americans was one of constant degradation and dehumanization and the results were a denial of humanity on the part of whites and self-hate on the part of Blacks. Carmichael and Hamilton (1967) believe that the ideology of white superiority emerges from the structure of white privilege and Black disadvantage and helps to unify the system of white power. They posit that, "a sense of superior group position prevails: whites are 'better' than Blacks; therefore Blacks should be subordinated to whites. This is a racist attitude and it permeates the society on both the individual and institutional level, covertly and overtly"

(5). Within this perspective, white privilege is an element of racial structure and white superiority is an element of ideology in the larger society.

On the other hand, the internal colony model piloted by Robert Blauner suggests a theoretical separation of white privilege from white superiority. However, within this perspective, white privilege is an ideology that emerges from the structure of race and fosters the ideology of white supremacy. Here, racial ideology is linked to social control and the origin of racial oppression under global colonialism that spurred the need for labor exploitation and control, including in the United States. The problem of control over a racialized labor force stems from the manner of labor recruitment, as well as differences in culture between dominant and subordinate groups. A labor force recruited through violent means of conquest or physical coercion creates fears of resistance and revolt in the minds of their oppressors. Blauner (2001) argues that there are four basic components of colonization, the first is the mode of entry, the second the colonization of the culture, and the third the social organization of the colonized people. The fourth component of colonization he suggests is racism, which he defines as "a principle of social domination by which a group seen as inferior or different in alleged biological characteristics is exploited, controlled and oppressed socially and physically by a superordinate group" (66). Further, Blauner (1972) believes that one of the most significant mechanisms of racial control is cultural domination. Through cultural domination, appropriate roles and activities for subordinate racial group members are defined and Christianity and other Western values are held as superior to non-Western and non-Christian ways of life. Thus, the United States of America is built on the principle that it would be a white man's country in which Western European values dominate cultural nationalism, educational systems, and social media (31).

In general, both the institutional racism and internal colony approaches contribute to the conceptual development of racial ideology through debates about white privilege and white superiority. From the perspectives of both Carmichael and Hamilton (1967) and Blauner (1972, 2001), the racial ideology of white privilege emerges from the racial structure of colonization and continues to legitimate, organize, and maintain white superiority as the dominant element of the political, economic, and social systems of the U.S. society. Their arguments suggest that the racial ideology of white privilege and the ideology of white superiority exist at different levels of the ideological system with the former more concerned with racial structure and the latter with the nature of the social system. While they have their usefulness, the two perspectives do not systematically develop the concept of ideology and remain incomplete theoretical tools in understanding systematic and persistent racism.

Interestingly, while critical race theory, or CRT, is a theoretical approach that also traces racial ideology to colonization, slavery, and the Jim Crow eras, CRT is based on the understanding that race and racism continue to exist across dominant cultural modes of expression and in recent events in the post–Civil Rights Era. While drawing on several disciplines, CRT developed into its current form during the mid-1970s with scholars like Derrick Bell, Alan Freeman, and Richard Delgado, who were concerned with the dangerously slow progress of people of color following the Civil Rights Movement of the 1960s. CRT grew out of the legal field and, thus, analyzes how law and legal traditions through history and contemporary experiences inequitably impact people of color. Today, CRT is applied to the intersection of race, law, and power, as well as society and culture (Delgado and Stefancic 2001; Matsuda, Lawrence, Delgado, and Crenshaw 1993). Mari Matsuda (1991) defines critical race theory as, "the work of progressive legal scholars of color who are attempting to develop a jurisprudence that accounts for the role of racism in American law and that works toward the elimination of racism as part of a larger goal of eliminating all forms of subordination" (1331).

Importantly, CRT scholars, such as Derrick Bell and others, recognize that racism is embedded deeply within the fabric and systems in U.S. society—that is, social, economic, political, and power systems. Bell (1987, 1992) maintains that the existing power structures in the U.S. depend upon and are built on white privilege and white supremacy, which perpetuate racial inequalities and inequities and marginalize people of color. Although much progress was made during the Civil Rights Era, and important legislation passed, Bell criticizes civil rights scholars' (and activists') endorsement of colorblindness and their focus on intentional discrimination rather than centering their efforts on improving the conditions of racial equality.

In his early CRT scholarship, Bell developed a model of interest convergence, which contends that semblances of justice for people of color hinge on converging interests, ideas, and realities of both people of color and whites. According to Bell (1980, 2004), power dynamics between parties with unequal bargaining power undermines and subverts the subordinate party's interests and can move forward only to the extent that these interests align with the interests (or status quo) of the majority party. Thus, racial "progress" through legislative changes does not necessarily prove changes in racial ideologies and beliefs but rather reveals how changes align with power interests—and, by extension, resources and opportunities. Delgado and Stefancic (2000) posit that CRT advances Bell's conceptualization of interest convergence as a framework for naming subordination and power differentials. The framework identifies relevant and subordinated interests and finds points of convergence among the different interests at stake. Similarly, Matsuda and colleagues (1993) also prioritize the reproduction of hierarchy and shine a spotlight on racial domination and racial oppression.

Primarily, according to Richard Delgado and Jean Stefancic (2000), CRT has six defining properties. First, CRT recognizes that racism is an endemic, permanent feature of American life. Second, CRT expresses skepticism toward dominant claims of neutrality, objectivity, colorblindness, and meritocracy. Third, in challenging ahistoricism, or forms of revisionist history, CRT insists on a contextual and historical analysis of structures and policies. Fourth, CRT insists on recognizing the experiential knowledge of people of color. Fifth, CRT uses an interdisciplinary approach, convening such diverse branches of knowledge as law, economics, politics, and social sciences. And, sixth, as mentioned above, CRT works to eliminate racial and all forms of oppression.

In sum, the different perspectives of racial ideology as portrayed in the "racial projects" described by Omi and Winant, the "racial contestations" theory of Bonilla-Silva, the "institutional racism" approach of Carmichael and Hamilton, Blauner, and others, and the "critical race theory" of Bell and others, further contribute to our understanding of how racial ideology is produced and used. Nevertheless, with the exception of CRT, they are weak in their analyses of the effect of gender, other ethnic groups, and class and status differences within and between hierarchical racial structures. They also, in themselves, cannot adequately explain why race, as both structure and ideology, can vary in form or extremes. Additionally, none of the approaches can escape the circularity between ideology as both the cause and consequence of racialization. For these approaches, it is only hypothetical that in a system of multiple racial groups, some groups may develop divergent racial ideologies and that competing ideologies could develop within one socially classified racial grouping. To understand the change, continuity, and diversity in racial ideologies, in the following sections of this chapter we introduce the role of human agency in the creation, recreation, and variation of racial beliefs during slavery and the plantation society, Jim Crow, and the post–Civil Rights Era, with a focus on the South. Our discussions are founded on the understanding that in the U.S., the idea of white supremacy is the kernel from which racial ideologies developed.

RACIAL BELIEFS AND PRACTICES OF THE OLD SOUTH — SLAVERY AND JIM CROW

For more than three hundred years, the U.S. South was essentially a plantation society, in which the plantation system dominated the economic, political, social and cultural life. During the seventeenth and eighteenth centuries, slavery played a key role in economic development in the Southern economy as well as the social relations between white plantation owners and enslaved Blacks. The racial beliefs that undergirded this rigid system of slavery and plantation society were essentially white supremacy. For instance, C. Vann Woodward (1951, 1974) argues that these dogmas took shape within the context of a white population divided by political, economic, and social conflicts. He identifies beliefs about white supremacy and Black inferiority in the South as falling into three categories—racial extremists, racial conservatives, and racial liberals. According to Woodward (1951), the extremists of the South reached a wider audience in the first decade of the new century through the social media of that time that included novels such as *The Clansman*, *The Negro Beast*, *The Negro: A Menace to America*, and many others, some of which were made into screenplays.

The overarching depictions in these scripts were those of a degraded race characterized as bestial and incapable of improvement. This white supremacy myth over Blacks infected the mainstream collective consciousness and was promoted to young whites in children's books. Donnarae MacCann writes about the characterizations of African Americans in her work on white supremacy and children's literature and reveals the scope of white supremacist ideology. According to MacCann (1998), children's literature did not focus on the brutal aspects of slave labor on the plantations, but rather on the personality of Blacks compared to whites. This included ideas that Blacks were "moved by instinct rather than logic, prone to imitate rather than initiate action, as excitable and immoderate, as self-depreciating and clownish" (83–84). Despite all the anguish of slavery, writers of children's books at that time went to great length to instill in young white minds that plantation life was 'humane' and 'desirable.' Images of savagery mixed in with those of the childish, habitually lazy and happy enslaved Black. MacCann references many writings such as those of Louise-Clarke Pyrnelle's (1882) pieces on *Diddie, Dumps, and Tot* or *Planation Child-Life* where the author's depiction of itinerant camps resembled Sunday picnics in which "negroes were well clothed, well fed, and the great majority of them looked exceedingly happy" (130).

To maintain the racial order of white superiority and Black inferiority, the dominant whites also established certain laws (e.g., Slave Codes or Black Codes) between 1800 and 1866. Slave Codes were used to restrict the movement, freedoms, and livelihoods of African Americans during the slave era. Similarly, Black Codes (modified variations of Slave Codes), which were birthed during the Reconstruction Era, were used to delimit civil rights and civil liberties of African Americans consistent with the dominant racial ideology of that period. Moreover, the racial beliefs emanating from slavery and the Southern plantation society continued well into the Jim Crow period, in spite of changes brought about by the Emancipation Proclamation (1863), the Civil War (1861–1865), Reconstruction (1865–1977), and the increasing integration of the South into the national economy. According to Woodward (1974), the racial belief and doctrines of extreme racism continued after slavery although they were mostly rejected, limiting, and had varying mani-festations.

The Jim Crow Era

There is no doubt that there were economic, political, and social changes at the end of slavery. Emancipation and an unsuccessful attempt at Southern secession during the Civil War created an extraordinary dilemma for South-ern white society. The economic and political infrastructures of the South were in shambles, plantation owners were destitute, and state governments were broke. Further, Southerners did not know what to do with the near 4 million freed slaves. Under slavery, racial order was maintained through imposed contracts of bondage of slaves to slave owners, but following the Civil War, it was unclear what institutions, laws, and customs were necessary to maintain white control. According to Bonilla-Silva (2017), because slav-ery did not always require specific or sophisticated rules or racial ideology to maintain 'social order,' segregationist laws after Emancipation were estab-lished and were explicitly racist. The new laws, known as Jim Crow laws, not only enforced the separation of races and maintained racial order, but also helped in producing a low-paid, submissive labor force. As a result, a new racial caste system emerged that was as repressive as slavery.

Woodward (1974) stresses that the system of Jim Crow was born and matured in the North before reaching the South. Jim Crow laws, like the Black Codes, consisted of both state and local laws. They mandated *de jure* racial segregation in all public facilities in the states of the former Confeder-ate States of America, starting in 1890 with a "separate but equal" status for African Americans. Jim Crow laws continued in force until the segregation of state-sponsored public schools was declared unconstitutional in 1954 by the U.S. Supreme Court decision in the *Brown v. Board of Education* case. Jim Crow laws were finally overruled by the Civil Rights Act of 1964 and the Voting Rights Act of 1965.

White elites considered Jim Crow laws necessary because they feared that, with Emancipation, free Blacks posed a physical, economic, and politi-cal threat to white supremacy and domination. The scope and detail of Jim Crow laws were equal to the Black Codes, reinforcing the conditions of slavery and extended, whether by actual law or custom, to all facets of control over the Black population. These decrees developed slowly as vari-ous state constitutions adopted laws similar to previously developed laws in other Southern states. Racial ostracism was rigidly and legally sanctioned in virtually all institutions and spheres of life for Blacks. Although the Jim Crow laws mandated "separate" but "equal" accommodations, this was al-most never the situation. Thompson-Miller, Feagin, and Picca (2015) ac-knowledge that white officials, and many ordinary whites, unlawfully committed large-scale violence and other atrocities against Blacks for violating the informal norms of Jim Crow.

Woodward (1974) explains that it was a commonly held belief that 'all' Southern whites shared a resolution that the South "shall be and remain a white man's country." Moreover, whites resented the idea that the "negro bred to slavery was typically ignorant and poor" should be given the rights to certain amenities and luxuries afforded to whites (32). One of the shared racial beliefs of whites during this period was that minorities were intellectually and morally inferior and that Blacks and whites should not mix. Blacks, on the other hand, believed that whites hated them because they were Black and avoided direct interactions, including eye contact, because they feared for their lives if they broke the Jim Crow laws or social norms (Thompson-Miller, Feagin, and Picca 2015). The birth of Jim Crow also saw a resurgent militaristic Ku Klux Klan group that fought against Reconstruction governments and leaders and engaged in bombings, lynching, and mob violence.

Without doubt the racial attitudes and beliefs of the Jim Crow Era have their roots in the racial ideology of the slavery period. However, there were variations in racial beliefs among the different groups of whites. Woodward (1974) finds racial beliefs about white supremacy and Black inferiority during the Jim Crow Era to have diverse perspectives similar to those under slavery, including racial extremist, racial conservative, and racial liberal ideological positions. These variations affected how individual states decided to adopt or not adopt Jim Crow laws, as well as in political campaigning to get Black support. There are also examples where any one white political leader adopted more than one racial ideology and used these interchangeably based on circumstances. For example, Georgia Populist Tom Watson, elected U.S. Congressman in 1890, in his famous essay on *The Negro Question in the South* (1892), called for a strategic political alliance and the cooperation between Black and white farmers. However, after the turn of the century he led the efforts to disfranchise Blacks and published demagogic attacks on Blacks as well as on Catholics and Jews. For example, Woodward (1974) found in *Watson's Jeffersonian Magazine* published in 1909, where Watson preached for "*the Superiority of the Aryan* [italics his]" and on the "HIDEOUS, OMINOUS, NATIONAL MENACE [capitalization his]" of "Negro domination" (352).

South Carolina's Democratic senator, Benjamin Tillman, also promoted similar extremist ideas. Between 1901 and 1909, he consistently promoted the idea that Negroes were "akin to the monkey" and were an "ignorant, debased and debauched race." Woodward further cites Simkins in *Pitchfork Ben Tillman* where the senator, in popularizing his racial beliefs, advocated, "to hell with the Constitution, if it interfered with lynching rapists" (352). On March 23, 1900, in his speech before the U.S. Senate, Senator Tillman defended the actions of his white constituents who had murdered several Black citizens of his home state. Purday (1991) also quotes from Tillman's speech where he blamed the violence on the "hot-headedness" of Southern Blacks and on the misguided efforts of Republicans during the Reconstruction Era after the Civil War to "put white necks under Black heels." Tillman also defended violence against Black men, claiming that Southern whites "will not submit to [the Black man] gratifying his lust on our wives and daughters without lynching him" (147)—an evocation of the deeply sexualized racist fantasies of many Southern whites. Some Southern whites who held extremist racial beliefs went as far as to create their own "racial creed." For example, in 1919, Southern educator Thomas Pearce Bailey developed 15 decrees, some of which stated that, "the white race must dominate," "the Negro is inferior and will remain so," and "let the lowest white man count more for the highest Negro." In his view, "this is a white man's country," and there shall be no social and political equality (Woodward 1951, 355–356).

Not all Southern whites professed such harsh and violent judgments for Blacks. Woodward also identified Southerners who were more of the older generation and who held conservative racial beliefs. According to Woodward (1951), white conservatives, like those under slavery, also had a paternalistic viewpoint. For example, Thomas G. Jones, the 28th Governor of Alabama (1890–1894), proclaimed that whites were the "custodians" of Negroes, that Negroes were under the power of whites, and if whites did not lift Negroes up and accord them their civil rights, they will drag whites down (49). Others were sometimes astonished at what they thought were "fierce, ungovernable passions." For instance, William C. Oates, the 29th Governor of Alabama (1894–1896), was bewildered that, "now when the Negro was doing no harm that people wanted to kill him and wipe him from the face of the earth" (352–354). According to Woodward, the primary goal of this group was to conserve money and resources and therefore they believed that "the Negro had something to lose as well as something to gain" (48).

White conservatives of the time acknowledged that Negroes were inferior and subordinate but did not think that they should be segregated or humiliated. These conservative racial beliefs, however, were not common among all state officials, especially those in the South. The more common consensus was that 'the Negro' was not adapting to the new era and was deteriorating as a laborer. This belief also was found in the North where in 1903 it was acknowledged that, "the 'new Negro' in the South was less industrious, less thrifty, less trust-worthy and less controlled than his father and grandfather." Both Southerners and Northerners agreed that, "the transition from the slavery system to the caste system had been accomplished at the cost of grave deterioration in race relations" (353–354). According to Clement Eaton (1966), Southerners alluded that free Negroes were the most vicious members of their race. They contended that these free Negroes tended to corrupt slaves, lead insurrections, sold liquor, and were thieves, idle, and more of them were in jails (257).

Unlike the conservatives, Southern radicals and populists did not believe that they had a paternalistic relationship with Negroes. Instead, they believed that racial hatred was tied to financial despotism and that there were class-based similarities of experiences. For example, they thought that white tenants and Negro tenants and Negro sharecroppers and white sharecroppers, as well as white laborers and colored laborers, shared similar interests. Further, by electing Negro representatives on several committees and in their party, the Populists felt that this would encourage more racial integration. Woodward (1974), however, warns that both the conservatives and radicals gave erroneous signals of racial harmony.

From time to time, liberal ideas and racial beliefs emerged from the various extremist promulgations, conservative, and populist notions. Eaton (1966) reports that now and again whites themselves were "deeply affected" by the violence and the "cavalier attitude toward observance of the laws" (260). Similarly, both W. E. B. Du Bois and Henry James noted that occasionally someone "sympathized" and "struggled" with the perplexity of the race question. In fact, to some degree, Booker T. Washington's work required finding a pragmatic compromise from someone who had some liberal racial beliefs and could possibly help resolve the antagonism, suspicions, and fear of white extremists. According to Woodward (1974), in the North, Washington sought out those considered "friends of the race," those "Christlike philanthropists" (195). Nonetheless, the changed attitudes of some Southerners of the later antebellum period did not necessarily mean that there was a change in the racial beliefs of white superiority and Black inferiority. It simply reflected the variation in racial beliefs.

Interestingly, all three forms of racial beliefs (extremist, conservative, liberal) are also observable in the myriad of urgings among Southern ministers and their Christian followers. Inferences emerged from these groups that suggest that the Negro and the white man are separately created species—an idea that is contradictory with the biblical teachings on the origins of man. Blackford (1954) finds overwhelming evidence that the average Southerner was convinced that the Bible sanctioned slavery. In fact, Eaton (1966) finds that for those who "worried" like W. C. Preston, the ex-senator of South Carolina (1828–1834) and former president of South Carolina College (1845–1851), became convinced that slavery was legitimate according to Christian religions after reading Baptist Minister Reverend Thornton Stringfellow's book on the "rightfulness of slavery" (356). Southerners also believed that religion could improve the morals and spiritual side of the Negro.

Neglected in this categorization of racial beliefs is the recognition of the role of the Black population whose members also held divided political, economic, and social situations. Survival called for some degree of accommodation to the prevailing racial practices during the Jim Crow Era. However, this accommodation aligned with differing positions ranging from acceptance to public and private resistance to white supremacy. Woodward noted that Blacks were aware of the class differences among whites and when Northern liberals and radicals did not support their interests, they turned to the upper class Southern conservatives. A symbiotic type of relationship evolved around practical self-interest on both sides. However, the *Plessy v. Ferguson* 1896 Supreme Court decision (and other similar examples) reminds us that legislation and changes in social relations are inadequate in eradicating racial beliefs of white superiority and Black inferiority. And, as Bell (1980, 2004) argues, these beliefs can be jaded by converging interests. Even further, Michelle Alexander (2010) asks: what has changed since the collapse of Jim Crow since it is no longer socially and legally permissible to use race explicitly to discriminate?

RACIAL BELIEFS AND PRACTICES IN THE POST–CIVIL RIGHTS ERA AND BEYOND

There is no doubt that today, post–Civil Rights America looks different from the eras of slavery and the plantation society, segregation and the Jim Crow period. Great strides have been made and antiracist changes in politics and culture successful. Many of these changes are due to the Civil Rights Movement (CRM) of the nineteenth and twentieth centuries, which encompassed several social movements that ended legal racial segregation in the United States. The goals of the CRM were to eliminate racial discrimination and to secure for African Americans legal recognition and federal protection of the citizenship rights enumerated in the U.S. Constitution and federal laws. The movement was characterized by major campaigns of civil resistance and other forms of non-violent actions. In spite of the successes, many today still challenge the extent that these changes, derived from the CRM, the liberal and post-war Black movements, were able to overthrow the deeply rooted racial belief that the United States is still a "white man's country" (Bonilla-Silva 2001, 2006, 2017; Thompson-Miller, Feagin, and Picca 2015; Winant 2004). They question the idea of white supremacy and the role it plays in structural changes. Scholars, such as Bell, Crenshaw, and others, argue that even though there were some changes, the economic, social, cultural, and political institutions largely still support systemic privileges to whites because deep-rooted racial beliefs and practices prevail.

Intriguingly, when the perspectives of these race scholars are examined, Woodward's three identifiable pattern of racial beliefs, extremist, conservative, and liberal are discerned. Winant (2004) does not use the same labels as Woodward but instead arranges trends in racial beliefs and practices into four white racial projects. According to Winant, the first, *The New Right Racial Project* is a reaction/resistance to the Black movements of the 1950s and 1960s and George Wallace's 1968 presidential campaign based on right-wing populism. The racial belief at the center of this New Right Racial Project was that, "white supremacy was not an excrescence on the basically egalitarian and democratic 'American Creed' but a fundamental component of U.S. society. To destroy it would mean reinventing the country, the social order, the government" (55). The second, *The Neoconservative Racial Project*, also seeks to preserve white advantages but through denying race differences. According to this perspective, it is possible to overcome racial difference politically and culturally. The Neoconservatives appeal to universalism in social policies including educational, literary, and poverty standards, but, in so doing, avoid issues of racial inequality. According to Winant, "it not only argues for a 'color-blind' racial politics but rearticulates formerly antiracist politics in a discourse denying any validity to perceptions of race differences . . . a rationalizing formula" (59).

The third racial project, *The Liberal Racial Project*, "seeks to limit white advantages through denial of racial difference" (59). Winant explains that the liberal perspective centers on social structures as opposed to the culturally focused right-wing racial beliefs. In other words, this perspective requires a racial ideology with racial beliefs that would repudiate the Civil Rights agenda and state-enforced equality, without regressing explicitly to white supremacy, or openly reverting to the policies of Jim Crow segregation. According to Omi and Winant (2015), this type of neoliberal perspective overlaps with, and requires colorblindness. Those who believe in a colorblind view of race also advocate that the goals of the Civil Rights Movement have been substantially met; that we live in a post-racial society; and that overt racism is outdated. Moreover, Omi and Winant argue that in the United States, colorblindness as a racial project is "a rude beast: ineffective, uneven, ungainly, deceptive, and contradictory" (259).

On the other hand, the *New Abolitionist Project*, a fourth racial project identified by Winant (2004), places race at the center of its arguments and racial belief on "the invention of whiteness" (63). Within this understanding, both the gestation and evolution of white supremacy play central roles in U.S. politics and culture. This is observable in the examples of the history of the old South, the Jim Crow period, and in the more recent election of Donald Trump as the 45th president of the United States. Winant suggests that in order to refute white privilege, the "lie of whiteness" must be exposed from intellectual as well as practical measures. This requires believing that there can be no white culture, politics, or whiteness without racially defining "the other" (63–64). This perspective directly challenges the idea of "the invention of the Negro and by extension Blacks" that emanated from slavery and was reinvented through Jim Crow and the post–Civil Rights Eras.

Bonilla-Silva also addresses contemporary racial beliefs but arranges the different viewpoints into racial frames rather than racial projects, but nonetheless comes to the same conclusions as Winant and others. That is, racial beliefs and the practice of racism may be more subtle in the contemporary U.S., but "vulgar" and "explicit" racism still exists. Bonilla-Silva believes that "remnants of the Jim Crow racism are clearly resurgent," but because in this post–Civil Rights Era it is important to maintain the idea of a nonracial, colorblind society, whites adopt a diminutive approach. For example, instead of outright opposition to affirmative action, interracial marriages, and/or the socio-economic plight of minorities, liberal whites express concerns linked to nonracial social variables, or in some cases talk about "reverse racism" as discriminatory. Bonilla-Silva (2014) found in the tales of color-blind racism whites express their beliefs in a nonracial manner to explain away racial inequality—"its economics, not race" or "Blacks are the really prejudiced ones" (118).

He agrees with Winant (2004) that William Julius Wilson's (1978, 1980) argument on the "declining significance of race" is a class reductionist approach to race and a good example of a liberal perspective. Proponents of this kind of "colorblindness" assert that the goals of the Civil Rights Movement are substantially achieved, that overt forms of racism are outdated, and that the United States is well on its way to a "post-racial" society. This idea was prominent in the 1970s and, as Bonilla-Silva explains, it is consistent with the data on white attitudes, as well as studies on racial disparities that suggest a reduction in the social inequality between whites and Blacks.

Bonilla-Silva observes that while old stereotypical racial beliefs are stronger with the older generation, the younger and college educated whites are more likely to use the diminutive approach. Like the less educated, white working class group, they feel a sense of resentment and believe they are entitled to a job or to a promotion over Blacks whom they think are not qualified. Resentment among working class whites is also found because they believe that their federal tax dollars are being spent on Black "welfare queens" or undocumented immigrants. According to Bonilla-Silva (2014), whites believe that "Blacks use discrimination as an excuse to cover up their own inadequacies" (119). Similarly, Thompson-Miller, Feagin, and Picca (2015) note that "many whites today claim that Blacks need to 'get over' the racism of the past and move on" so that they (whites) can be resolved of past racial transgressions" (51). They explain that, today, most whites and other non-black Americans believe that we live in a post-racial, colorblind society and that the Civil Rights Era has fixed many racial and social ills.

Overwhelmingly, critics of colorblindness such as Bell; Bonilla-Silva; Thompson-Miller, Feagin, and Picca; Winant; and others argue that racial inequality is not just about ideology or beliefs, but that race, racism and white supremacy are pervasive and continue to generate inequality through racially biased structures and systems. This includes racial inequality in education, health, housing, the criminal justice system, and in employment and incomes, among others. Bell's (1987, 1992) musings acknowledge progress but still insist on the elusive quest for justice, as Blacks *still* "are not saved" from stringent racial inequities and continue to be relegated as "faces at the bottom of the well." Bell (1992) poignantly assesses that the vestiges of the past are still prevalent today because they are entrenched "along with the deeply embedded personal attitudes" that "supported it for so long. Indeed, the racism that made slavery feasible is far from dead in the last decade of twentieth-century America" (3). Similarly, Thompson-Miller, Feagin, and Picca's interviews with African Americans show that, though hopeful, many still believe that Jim Crow–type racial beliefs and practices still exist— "dressed now in new clothes . . . and that things are better but still not equal" (192).

CONCLUSION

Overall, race theorists agree that right-wing extremist racial ideas, beliefs, and practices co-exist in the contemporary United States along with people who are "compassionate conservatives" and those who believe that we are living in a "colorblind" society. For the latter two groups, the election of President Donald Trump was not based on deep-rooted racial beliefs of white superiority, but that he, Trump, would "deliver" for the working lower- and middle-class whites. According to Bonilla-Silva (2017), modern racial ideology flourishes not on the ugliness of slavery and Jim Crow, but on a "sanitized" ideology of "colorblindness." Increasingly, liberal ideas are espoused where whites believe that Blacks and other minorities (e.g., Mexicans and Native Americans) are not successful because they are not trying hard enough. Much like the old racial beliefs, the inferior position of Blacks in society is still largely based on stereotypes that Blacks are lazy, have a poor work ethic, engage in more criminal activities, and so on. In other words, non-racial factors are to blame for social inequality in a post–Civil Rights, post-racial, "colorblind" United States of America.

Michelle Alexander (2010), in explaining the mass incarceration of Blacks, suggests that in post–Civil Rights America a "new race-neutral language was developed for appealing to old racists' sentiments, a language accompanied by a political movement that succeeded in putting the vast majority of Blacks in their place" (40). She believes that proponents of racial hierarchy have installed a new racial caste system within the limits of the current laws and political discourse. In other words, new tactics are used in the post–Civil Rights Era to achieve the same goals of the colonists and Founding Fathers.

Despite the variance in the racial analytical framing, the scholars all believe that racial ideology manifested as racial beliefs and practices allows the continuation of structured racial inequality. While certain things have changed on the surface, the overarching rationalization of white superiority and Black inferiority remains in post–Civil Rights America. Winant (2004), in a succinct analysis of one hundred years of racial theory, concludes that the world will never get beyond race and racism, but can overcome the hierarchical stratification, injustice, and inhumanity that usually accompanies them. He acknowledges W. E. B. Du Bois and the Chicago School of Sociology for their pioneering work on racial theorizing in the twentieth century and, at the same time, identifies the limits of contemporary social theory and race.

According to Winant (2004), there is a tendency in contemporary racial theorizing of *reductionism* in which the race concept is subordinated to the more "objective" and "real" social structure focused on *ethnicity-based* and *class-based* theories. Winant also describes this trend as a "theoretical crisis" that reflects the "continuing sociopolitical crisis of race," particularly when there is a persistence in racially based distinctions. He concludes that to understand the changing nature of race, racial beliefs, and practices in today's world, there needs to be a more effective theory of race. Such a theory "must address the persistence of racial classification and stratification in an era officially committed to racial equality and multiculturalism" (161–162).

This chapter opens this discussion. Here we have elaborated upon the nature and role of racial ideology, and the persistent creation and recreation of the idea of white supremacy and racial beliefs of white superiority and Black inferiority. The next chapter discusses how racial ideology continues through social relations, practices, traditions, and customs for the same historical periods. It analyzes how racial etiquette and the use of stereotypes support notions of white superiority even with change in the socio-economic and political systems of the United States of America. Moreover, the chapter shows the link between racial ideology and beliefs with racial etiquette and stereotypes.

REFERENCES

Alexander, Michelle. 2010. *The New Jim Crow: Mass Incarceration in the Age of Colorblindness.* New York: The New Press.

Bell, Derrick A. 1980. Brown v. Board of Education and the Interest-Convergence Dilemma. *Harvard Law Review, 93* (3), 518–533.

———. 1987. *And We are Not Saved: The Elusive Quest for Racial Justice.* New York: Basic Books.

———. 1992. *Faces at the Bottom of the Well: The Permanence of Racism.* New York: Basic Books.

———. 2004. *Silent Covenants: Brown v. Board of Education and the Unfulfilled Hopes for Racial Reform.* Cambridge, MA: Oxford University Press.

Blackford, Launcelot Minor. 1954. *Mine Eyes Have Seen the Glory: The Story of Mary Minor Blackford.* Cambridge, MA: Oxford University Press.

Blauner, Bob. 1972. *Racial Oppression in America.* New York: Harper and Row.

———. 2001. *Still the Big News: Racial Oppression in America.* Philadelphia: Temple University Press.

Bonilla-Silva, Eduardo. 2001. *White Supremacy & Racism in the Post-Civil Rights Era.* Boulder/London: Lynne Rienner Publishers.

———. 2006, 2014, 2017. *Racism without Racists: Color-Blind Racism and the Persistence of Racial Inequality in America.* Lanham, MD: Rowman & Littlefield.

Bourdieu, Pierre. 1990. *The Logic of Practice.* Stanford University Press.

Carmichael, Stokely and Charles V. Hamilton. 1967. *Black Power: The Politics of Liberation.* New York: Vintage Press.

Cox, Oliver Cromwell. 1948. *Race, Caste and Class.* New York: Monthly Review Press.

———. 1976. *Race Relations: Elements and Social Dynamics.* Detroit: Wayne State University Press.

———. 2000. "Race Relations." In *Theories of Race and Racism: A Reader*, edited by Les Black and John Solomos, 75–82. London/New York: Routledge.

Dawson, Michael C. and Lawrence D. Bobo. 2009. "Editorial Introduction: One Year later and the Myth of a Post-Racial Society." *Du Bois Review*, 6:2, 247–249.

Delgado, Richard and Jean Stefancic. 2000. *Critical Race Theory. An Introduction.* New York: New York University Press.

Eaton, Clement. 1966. *A History of the Old South,* 2nd Edition. New York: The MacMillan Company.

Fields, Barbara Jean. 1966, 1985, *Slavery and Freedom on the Middle Ground: Maryland during the Nineteenth Century.* New Haven/London: Yale University Press.

Gramsci, Antonio. 1971. *Selections from the Prison Notebooks,* 56. Later printed edition, International Publishers Company.

Jordan, Winthrop, D. 2000. "First Impressions." In *Theories of Race and Racism: A Reader*, edited by Les Black and John Solomos, 37–55. London/New York: Routledge

MacCann, Donnarae. 1998. *White Supremacy in Children's Literature: Characterizations of African Americans, 1830–1900.* New York & London: Garland Publishing Inc.

Mannheim, Karl. 1955. *Ideology and Utopia: An Introduction to the Sociology of Knowledge.* New York: Harvest Books.

Matsuda, Mari. 1991. Voices of America: Accent, Antidiscrimination Law, and a Jurisprudence for the Last Reconstruction. *Yale Law Journal* 100:1329–1407.

Matsuda, Mari, Charles Lawrence, Richard Delgado and Kimberle Crenshaw. (Eds.). 1993. *Words that Wound: Critical Race Theory, Assaultive Speech, and the First Amendment.* Boulder: Westview Press.

Omi, Michael Omi and Howard Winant. 1986, 2015. *Racial Formation in the United States: From the 1960s to the 1980s.* New York/London: Routledge.

Purday, Richard. 1991. Speech by Senator Benjamin R Tillman, March 23, 1900, *Congressional Record, 56th Congress, 1st Session,* 3223–3224. Reprinted in Richard Purday (editor), *Document Sets for the South in U.S. History.* 147. Lexington, MA: D.C. Health and Company.

Thompson-Miller, Ruth, Joe R. Feagin and Leslie H. Picca. 2015. *Jim Crow Legacy: The Lasting Impact of Segregation.* Boulder/New York/London: Rowman & Littlefield.

Todorov, Tzvetan. 2000. "Race and Racism" In *Theories of Race and Racism: A Reader,* edited by Les Black and John Solomos, 68–74. New York/London: Routledge.

Wilson, William. Julius. 1978, 1980. *The Declining Significance of Race: Blacks and Changing American Institutions.* Chicago: The University of Chicago Press.

Winant, Howard. 2004. *The New Politics of Race: Globalism, Difference, Justice.* Minneapolis: University of Minnesota Press.

Woodward, C. Vann. 1951. *Origins of the New South 1877–1913.* Baton Rouge: Louisiana State University Press.

———. 1974. *The Strange Career of Jim Crow.* New York: Oxford University Press.

Chapter Three

Racial Etiquette and Racial Stereotypes

Clarence R. Talley and Theresa Rajack-Talley

The earlier chapters discuss racial structure and racial ideology as coercive social forms imposed upon the population of the United States of America. The arguments show that racial structure and racial ideology were created under slavery and the plantation society, re-created under Jim Crow, and persist in the post–Civil Rights Era around white supremacy and Black inferiority. Specifically, racial ideology is the medium through which people perceive and live their lives as "Same" or "Other." In this chapter, we look at how racial ideology is exhibited through racial etiquette. We examine and discuss the rules of engagement through the same historical periods as in the chapters before on racial structure and racial ideology. We also discuss the role that racial stereotypes play, how they change with socio-economic and political shifts and at the same time continue to support the notion of white superiority and Black inferiority. The link between racial etiquette, racial stereotyping and racial ideology is made clear.

"Racial etiquette" is the term used to describe how social relations between persons, bounded by hierarchical racial classifications, are displayed in the private and public spheres. It is observed through racial practices, traditions and customs and reflects the racial beliefs of individuals and groups. According to Bertram W. Doyle, racial etiquette defines the social conduct between people who are not of equal status. In his work on the etiquette of race relations in the South, Doyle (1937) explains that, "etiquette enables a person to act freely within the limits which the formal rules of personal relations impose and has, perhaps, no higher sanction than the feeling of superiority one feels when one succeeds, or than the sense of inferiority when one fails (5)."

One function of etiquette, then, is to exert control over the relationships between persons and groups. In the United States, racial etiquette regulates the comportment of Blacks with whites as they interact, including the expected and accepted behavior of Blacks by whites. In essence, the practices of racial etiquette, or the code of social usages according to Doyle, "are the forms required by custom and tradition to be observed in contacts and relations of the two races during the period of their association in America; the ceremonial side of race relations" (11). As such, racial etiquette is used to preserve social order and maintain social distances between the two groups. Laws do not dictate racial etiquette but it is, nonetheless, enforced through public opinion. Doyle contends that racial etiquette is the essence of the caste system since the prestige of the superior always involves the respect of the inferior."

Decades after Doyle's publication on racial etiquette, David R. Goldfield (1990) in his writings on race relations and Southern culture, describes racial practices, rituals and customs as "the etiquette of race." Similarly, Jennifer Ritterhouse (2006) in her studies on growing up under Jim Crow notes how Southern children learn race and she links this to what she terms, "the etiquette of race relations." The research of these scholars offers different labeling but they all concede that racial etiquette persists in the contemporary United States. Further, although social relations and economic situations change over time, racial etiquette lives on through re-creations and negotiations. The scholars also agree that racial etiquette is a tool for social control used by the white dominant group to keep Blacks and other minority groups in subordinated situations and positions. Some race scholars may dislike the term racial etiquette because in their view it gives the impression of some kind of interactive agreement and/or equal status, however, they too come to the same conclusions. That is, after slavery, to make up for the end of extreme physical violence and domination, unwritten rules on expected behavior and practices were established as a means of racialized social control (Thompson-Miller, Feagin and Picca 2015).

RACIAL ETIQUETTE IN THE OLD SOUTH: SLAVERY, PLANTATION SOCIETY AND JIM CROW

In the old southern plantation society there were not too many laws regarding racial etiquette, but there were strict observances made in certain situations. However, researchers found that over time an elaborate etiquette developed to regulate race relations during slavery that continued after Emancipation. It consisted of a complicated set of rules and customs that placed individuals and groups in a racial and class hierarchy (Doyle 1937; Goldfield 1990). Further, during the seventeenth, eighteenth and nineteenth centuries, Southern states were mostly agrarian and rural and the codes by which many lived differed somewhat for rural and urban settings as well as for private and public spaces. Nevertheless, the codes, rules and customs were all part of a racial etiquette thought to create an "orderly" means of discourse and amenable behavior in a very chaotic and uncertain Southern environment. It also helped to reinforce white supremacy and domination over enslaved and freed Blacks. According to Goldfield (1990), racial etiquette "bound whites together, though not equally, and it relegated Blacks to a permanent state of inferiority" (2).

Racial Practices, Traditions and Customs during Slavery

There are many illustrations of behavior defined by the racial etiquette of the South during slavery and the plantation society. For example, upon meeting with a white person, a male slave was required to touch or remove his hat and the female slaves bowed or nodded. Slaves kept their eyes on the ground during conversations with whites and replied with "Sir" or "Ma'am" as the situation required, while whites usually addressed slaves as "Boy" or "Girl." Older slaves who were 'dear' to the family might often be given the respected title of "Uncle" or "Auntie"; this was the highest form of respect accorded slaves by whites. Slaves also were referred to as "Nigger" or "Nigger-fellow," these terms were used by whites often to address slaves that they did not know (Goldfield 1990).

The ways that slaves and whites interacted in public social settings were often quite different from the ways in which they interacted in more intimate settings such as in the household or on the plantations. Since slaves and whites usually shared close quarters either in the planter's homestead or in separate housing on the plantation estates, it was necessary to maintain some social distance between them. Etiquette was often more strictly adhered to in these instances. For example, no slave was ever allowed to sit down in the presence of whites, and slaves were not permitted to eat in the same room as whites. Oftentimes, slaves were not permitted to eat the same kinds of food that whites ate. Slaves' food was rationed weekly and usually consisted of a very small meal, some sort of meat (usually pork), and a portion of molasses. On larger plantations, field slaves never ate in the master's house and were rarely allowed past the yard. Contacts with the master and mistress were minimal (Doyle 1937; Goldfield 1990).

The vocabulary, gestures, rituals and manners described above are good examples of the code or etiquette that was enforced in every social setting and both whites and especially Blacks were expected to play their respective roles. Critics of racial etiquette might say that not everyone followed the social guidelines set forth through etiquette as some whites may have crossed boundaries in their relationships with slaves, especially with slave women. These individuals were looked upon as louts and persons of ill-repute. On the other hand, a slave who failed to observe the guidelines of etiquette was considered to be impudent or out of place and was usually punished for such insolence. According to Doyle (1937), there was a relational order within which if one tries to follow the guidelines but fails, he or she was viewed as unfortunate and inferior.

Goldfield (1990) suggests that these manifestations of racial etiquette that were used to control the practices and behavior between whites and Blacks produced the "stage Negro," and most likely whites and almost certainly Blacks knew it. Moreover, this social control reinforced the negative stereotypes of Blacks as "childlike," "stupid," "lazy," "oversexed" and so on, emphasizing Black inferiority. In fact, whites required less of Blacks, expected them to perform stereotypical actions (stealing of chickens, relaxing on the job, etc.), and punished lacks less if they carried out the anticipated actions. According to Goldfield, etiquette required Blacks to live and act down to white expectations. He further suggests that because racial etiquette gave the false impression of "poor," "shiftless" but "happy" slaves, it also made them invisible (3–5). This is observed in several examples used by Ralph Ellison in his 1947 novel, *Invisible Man*, where he explains how Blacks were not perceived as human beings but rather as figments of the white man's imagination when staged to display expected behavior.

These depictions of enslaved Blacks also support the claim by W.E.B Du Bois that racial etiquette helped whites to "discount" the cruelty that they unleashed on Blacks as well as to keep Blacks in a position of inferiority. The racial etiquette and racial stereotypes of the plantation society supported the erroneous idea that slaves were happier and more peaceful and prosperous in the South. In other words, racial etiquette helped rationalize the racial hierarchy and served to legitimate white desires—such as control, status and positioning

The impression that slavery was civil and good for Blacks is heavily critiqued in Donnarae MacCann's (1998) work on white supremacy in children's literature. In her discussions on the social-political context in which such literature was promoted, MacCann accuses the popular British writer, George A. Henry, of treating American slavery as a superior social security system. She exposes Henry, who uses an ex-slave vernacular in his publication *By Sheer Pluck* (1984) to this end:

> Me trabel a good deal, and me think dat no working people in de world are so merry and happy as de slabe in a plantation wid a good massa and missy. De not work so hard as de white man. Dey have plenty to eat and drink, dey hab deir gardens and deir fowl. . . . De slabe hab no care and be very happy. . . . Me tell you dat de life on a plantation a thousand times happier dan de life of a black man in his own country (MacCann 1998, 189).

While the theatrical exchanges between Blacks and whites were used to give the impression that race relations during this period were consensual and harmonious, there were always Black resistances to both the physical and social control of Blacks by whites. Under the plantation system Blacks resented the fact that they had to take their cues from whites, and although some internalized their roles and seemed to accept their assigned places, others practiced avoidance and many more resisted. As a result, plantation slavery often included slave revolts in a labor system, so much so that white overseers were hired not only to maintain production but also to keep order on the plantations. Additional white special-forces policed other spaces for rebellious and/or runaway slaves.

Enslaved Blacks who resisted found that they had their behavior criminalized because it contradicted the racial order and racial etiquette. In particular, they were beaten violently and often lynched. Lynching is an important part of racial violence as it often hinges on dehumanizing Black bodies and creating a spectacle—the strange fruit hanging from the tree—for whites to observe. The resulting coerced performances by Blacks led many visitors to the South to proclaim Southern slaves to be the most courteous set of slaves that they had ever met. The "politeness" of slaves in the South, seen at both private and public events, afforded whites peace of mind (Doyle 1937).

The racial etiquette of slavery and the plantation society has been described as a mode of communication, a code of behavior (Ritterhouse 2006), and a tool for social control (Doyle 1937; Goldfield 1990; Ritterhouse 2006). After Emancipation, racial etiquette continued to be enforced by violence and the threat of violence. Ritterhouse (2006) poses the dilemma that, "precisely how many black men and women died at the hands of whites intent on preserving racial etiquette is something historians can never know" (36).

Racial Practices, Custom and Traditions in the Jim Crow Era

Although racial etiquette continued in the Jim Crow period, it was somewhat modified along with the economic and social transformations resulting from Emancipation and a changing plantation society. As whites and Blacks struggled with morphing economic, social and racial structures, racial ideologies and racial beliefs were challenged and the rules governing their social interactions had to be redefined. Ritterhouse (2006, 37) observes that the code of racial etiquette that "scripted daily life in the post-emancipation South" was flexible and molding slowly to a modernizing region. Small but significant material and symbolic changes were being made. For example, addressing a white person as "Master," "Mistress," or "Missy" was eliminated from the South's racial vocabulary, instead, titles such as "Boss" and "Captain," "Mister" and "Sir" replaced "Master." In addition, prominent Black political leaders were referred to as "Mister" in some white newspapers. Ritterhouse assesses that the title changes not only symbolized a change in the social relations between whites and Blacks, but also the open rejection of intimacy between the two racial groups. She further explains that even with these changes, "the scripted daily life in the post-emancipation South resembled the code of slavery in many ways, but it was flexible enough to adapt as the Region slowly modernized" (37).

With time, the underlying logic of racial practices, traditions and customs during the Jim Crow Era was codified into laws of segregation. Segregation existed in the antebellum period but became prevalent after the Civil War. According to Goldfield (1990), while some promoted segregation as an improvement over the planation society, it was in essence another form of exclusion evident in a retooled racial etiquette. For instance, Dandridge (2010) cites Stetson Kennedy's *Jim Crow Guide: The Way It Was* (1959) on racial etiquette. Accordingly, there were at least seven simple rules of Jim Crow's conventions which stated that Blacks were: (i) never to assert or even intimate that a white person may be lying; (ii) never impute dishonorable intentions to a white person; (iii) never suggest that the white is of an inferior class; (iv) never lay claim to, or overly demonstrate, superior knowledge or intelligence; (v) never curse a white person; (vi) never laugh derisively at a white person; and (vii) never comment upon the physical attractiveness of a white person of the opposite sex (472–73).

The *Jim Crow Guide* reflects the extremists' viewpoint and beliefs, but Goldfield (1990) argues that not all whites of the Jim Crow Era held extremist positions and "perceived their past as immutable." Nor did all whites believe that the past could be used to explain the present. Nevertheless, there were those who held extremist positions and adhered to an extremist racial etiquette. On the other hand, the liberal whites of the 1900s accepted that racial order was sacred. According to Goldfield, "even the most well-meaning, sensitive whites succumbed to the beguiling corruption of white supremacy" (13). Invariably, they linked the disadvantages that Blacks faced to other socio-economic factors such as type of employment (mainly in agriculture) and poverty, but not to race. They did not pose the problems in the South as the "Negro" problem but problems of Southerners and advocated for change to be gradual especially in race relations. The difficulty for liberal whites in negotiating change in social relations and racial etiquette is observed in the irony found in the example given by Doyle (1937) of a Southern white man who explained that, "Now I admire Booker Washington. I regard him as a great man, and yet I couldn't call him 'Mr.' Washington. We were all in a quandary until a doctor's degree was given to him. That saved our lives! We all call him 'Dr.' Washington now" (10). Despite all of Booker T. Washington's accomplishments and the high regard with which he was held, even the most liberal of whites still could not accord him the same respect given to other whites and call him "Mister."

Liberal perspectives under Jim Crow originated mainly in the political arena and within the Christian culture, although churches and Christians in the South held very different positions to those in the North. There were also some slight differences observed in the racial etiquette practiced in rural and urban environments where for example, in towns and cities strict separation was not always the rule. Blacks could shop in certain department stores and Black buyers were treated more politely in urban stores than in rural stores. This was primarily because competition for the Black dollar was stronger in urban locations compared to rural areas where Blacks did more catalog shopping (Ritterhouse 2006). Nonetheless, in both urban and rural spaces Blacks could not sit for a meal among whites in the same store or anywhere else.

Notwithstanding the minor differences between rural and urban racial etiquette, whites controlled the etiquette of race and racial etiquette empowered all whites, whatever their social status and residential location. Whites were convinced that despite the economic and political differences among themselves, they were better than the 'inferior' Blacks were. This white racial solidarity was important and masses of poor whites along with non-poor whites controlled the racial etiquette and, consequently, all Blacks. This was crucial to preserving the racial status quo as changes occurred in the South and North. Segregation and violence were used to convince Blacks to abide by the racial etiquette scripted for the Jim Crow Era.

Ritterhouse (2006) cites Richard Wright's anecdotes about the "ethics of living Jim Crow and how energetically blacks' minds had to work to control their faces and bodies even as they inwardly scorned the performance of racial etiquette" (47). Wright (1940) describes numerous examples of performances and 'hidden transcripts' that Blacks and whites engaged in on a daily basis. These were complex, nuanced and psychologically difficult for Blacks. Whites on the other hand, did not deviate too far from the social script despite the variation in perspectives and racial etiquette. Blacks remained unprotected, vulnerable and forced on many occasions to conform to whites' expectations of them, a situation that remains prevalent in the contemporary United States.

Although racial etiquette continued in the Jim Crow Era, there were modifications in keeping with the economic, social and political changes in the South. The changing economy demanded different social relations between whites and Blacks. However, Ritterhouse (2006) points out that while historians and sociologists debate the extent to which the Southern economy was stable because of factors such as education, migration, the New Deal programs and other developments, racial etiquette as a means of social constraint remained strong during this period. Southerners found social control to be a better mechanism than violence but Goldfield notes that, "the expenditure in funds and effort to maintain this form of racial charade was prodigious" (11).

Conversely, whites believed that maximum productivity occurred when the codes of racial etiquette were followed. This trend of thought infers that not only are racial hierarchies natural, but they are also more efficient. Such thinking, Ritterhouse (2006) argues, minimized the guilt of whites who believed that Blacks accepted their lower status and agreed with whites about their daily performance, deference and domination. Contrarily, Blacks were less concerned about the profits from white-owned farms and businesses and the improvements of the quality of life for whites. Instead, Blacks were preoccupied with following racial etiquette to prevent the harsh violence that historically was unleashed on them. They understood that violation of Jim Crow etiquette placed their lives and the lives and livelihoods of their families and communities at risk.

In spite of the variations and nuances in the racial etiquette, there are unifying aspects of the white perspectives. This is best expressed by James Baldwin who, in his 1955 collection of essays, *Notes of a Native Son,* argued that, "segregation has worked brilliantly in the South. . . . It has allowed white people, with scarcely any pangs of conscience whatever, to create, in every generation, only the Negro they wished to see." This image of the "Negro" Goldfield suggests was "designed to block out unpleasantness from white southerners' lives," and that "even the most well-meaning, sensitive whites succumbed to the beguiling corruption of white supremacy" (13).

In reality, generations of both whites and Blacks were socialized into accepting the negative stereotypical images of Blacks and the racial etiquette of Jim Crow. Whites did not recognize how the systematic denial of opportunities in education, employment, health and all aspects of human rights for Blacks made it difficult for Blacks to accomplish equality. The lack of progress by Blacks was believed by those who held extremist ideas to be innate, natural and a reflection of inferior abilities and personhood. This belief continues to exist today despite the fact that the image and behavior dictated by racial etiquette was always and continues to be fictional.

Today, in the post–Civil Rights Era, economic, social and political changes continue. Consequently, race relations are constantly adjusting as they struggle every day to be racially conscious and politically correct when it comes to racial issues. The extent to which there is still racial etiquette and what this looks like, in terms of racial practices, traditions and customs, is more difficult to discern. Moreover, current scholarship rarely addresses racial etiquette directly; some authors prefer to assess social interactions between whites and Blacks using different frameworks or conceptual lenses. Nevertheless, most agree that vestiges of Jim Crow's social etiquette linger on through racial beliefs and practices.

RACIAL PRACTICES, CUSTOM AND TRADITIONS
IN THE POST–CIVIL RIGHTS ERA

Without a set of written codes such as those practiced during the Jim Crow Era, it is difficult to distinguish racial etiquette in the post–Civil Rights United States. Moreover, it has become easier for most whites (and some Blacks) to argue that American society is no longer racist, the playing field is now level and the significance of race is declining in comparison to social class disadvantages. It is also common for most whites to not intentionally think, discriminate or use negative language against Blacks. The impression that we live in a post-racial society was furthered when whites and Blacks elected a Black president, Barack Obama, for two terms. This idea of a post-racial America however, is continuously challenged by the findings from data disaggregated by race and social class, social unrest and the ensuing debates on the impact and representation of white supremacy in President Donald Trump's campaign, government and policies.

Eduardo Bonilla-Silva (2017) contends that sometimes when whites and Blacks interact, it can be strained and uncomfortable for whites who may feel they are losing their position of superiority. Some of Donald Trump's white male supporters expressed this view when they proclaimed that "white lives matter." On the other hand, some African Americans felt a sense of betrayal because they were hopeful that things would have gotten significantly better for Blacks under President Obama. Thus, in important ways, the national political landscape creates and influences our perceptions, understandings, and thoughts about racial happenings—and in how we interact across racial, ethnic and cultural groups.

Goldfield (1990) explains that though segregation and discrimination are no longer official, race relations and patterns of racial etiquette built up over the years enable subtle (and sometimes not so subtle) residuals to continue. He cites several instances in the history of the South where daily practices of segregation were adhered to even after the passing of Civil Rights legislation. For example, Blacks could purchase alcohol in any shop but it was understood that they could not consume the liquor in the store with whites. Similarly, all around the South, separate seating arrangements continued to occur in courtrooms, political meetings and other public spaces. Goldfield suggests that in post–Civil Rights America, wariness rather than accommodation characterizes race relations. He gives the canny example of difference between the past and present where a Black man, waiting outside a building to which he had gone to seek employment, confessed that a trooper threatened to shoot him for loitering. But, ten years earlier, the trooper would have shot him (207). Ironically, not everyone thinks that the present is so much different from the past with the high number of unarmed Black men, women and children being shot by the police and others on a weekly basis in contemporary America for 'suspicious' behavior.

Goldfield believes that many Southern cities still cling to racial traditions whereby Blacks remain closed out of economic and social life. Blacks are oftentimes relegated to menial, low paying city jobs, framed by racial discrimination but not disclosed as such. He is, however, cognizant that Blacks have become too much of an economic and political force, especially in the South, to not benefit from racial progress. Thus, while remnants of the old racial etiquette still hang around, there has been change and in most public spaces, whites and Blacks treat each other cordially. He quotes sociologist John Shelton Reed whose research is on the contemporary American South and who suggests that in public spaces increasingly "Southern whites seem disposed to treat black Southerners as sort of honorary white folks . . . Southern blacks seem willing to return the favor" (272).

While this emergent racial etiquette in the South gives the impression that white-Black relations are more cordial, Goldfield also sees the advancement and growth of a Black middle class as problematic for white supremacy. Under segregation, all blacks had to share a demeaning racial etiquette. According to Goldfield (1990), "Southern culture placed great significance on public behavior, and affluent blacks sought to comport themselves in a manner that differentiated them from white stereotypes of blacks" (221). He identifies the great Civil Rights leader, Martin Luther King, Jr. as an excellent exemplar of this; a man who identified with the plight of the poor but exhibited middle-class behavior and appearance because he felt that these were important to his work and a reflection of who he was. Goldfield believes that in the struggle for racial equality, Blacks never sought to overturn Southern culture but to remove white superiority as a barrier to the beneficial operations and social relations between whites and Blacks.

For a long while after the Civil Rights Movement, few scholars and activists focused on racial etiquette. Elisabeth Lasch-Quinn (1999, 2001) points out that, in the 1990s, there was some renewed interest in issues of race and etiquette. She utilizes film and commentary to discuss racial and cultural etiquette and the variations in beliefs and practices among whites. For example, the classic 1967 movie *Guess Who's Coming to Dinner?* exposes the persistence of the old racial etiquette of segregation when a young white woman (Katherine Houghton) introduces her Black boyfriend (Sidney Poitier) to her white liberal parents. This is a good example of how the use of fiction, including satire, helps to articulate race relations through social etiquette. Lasch-Quinn found Tom Wolfe's commentary, "Radical Chic: that Party at Lenny's," another example of the white liberal position in the 1970s. In this article, the author notes that the white liberal organizers of a fundraiser for the Black Panther Party were perplexed about hiring Black servants for an event and thought they had solved the sensitivity by hiring white South Africans.

Lasch-Quinn (1999) follows the trend of the white liberals through the 1980s in the movie *Six Degrees of Separation* made in 1993. Paul Poitier, played by Will Smith, "enters the liberal elite's social world, through a mastery of its etiquette—including its racial complex" (409). Lasch-Quinn's examination of films and other social media depictions of white-Black interactions leads her to conclude that etiquette in the post–Civil Rights Era serves up images that show it is important "to be correct according to one's inner circle; correctness in etiquette is what proves one is authentic, genuine, the real thing" (411). Using the lessons of the films, Lasch-Quinn (1999, 2001) proposes that when the Civil Rights Movement ended segregation in the 1950s and 1960s, many Americans tried to shrug off the rules of engagement between whites and Blacks but failed to sever the connection between race and etiquette. She believes that what we see in contemporary times is a great effort of "politeness" and "proper comportment" in public interracial encounters.

On the other hand, Joe Feagin (2000, 2010, 2014) examines public interactions between whites and Blacks in real life contemporary settings. He refers to these as responses to racial framing and expressions of racism. According to Feagin (2010), centuries of racial framing and counter-framing maintain and rationalize systemic racism. Further, central to the white frame is "its persistent interpretative and motivating power in generating everyday actions, which is one way we know the shape it takes in human minds" (123). This takes the form of routine performances and discriminatory behavior based on stereotypes, images, narratives and emotions. He agrees with Eduardo Bonilla-Silva (2001, 2006, 2017)) and Howard Winant (2004) that everyday forms of racism are normalized in this post–Civil Rights Era.

Feagin does not mention racial etiquette but argues that the perpetuation of systematic racism involves a dominant white-created framing of society that includes racist stereotyping and ideology, as well as emotions, interpretations, visceral images, language and other elements that legitimize discrimination. Feagin explains that whites frequently take material from centuries-old racial framing and use it creatively in racist art, music, narratives and jokes. These practices differ based on backstage and frontstage settings.[1] Blatant racist thought, commentary, and performance are comfortably carried out backstage in all-white audiences, sometimes amongst close friends and families and at other times in public settings—but in all cases amongst whites only. Racist expressions are not performed in public or private spaces when a more diverse population is present—an understood component of racial etiquette.

Corresponding variations in racial beliefs and racial etiquette patterns to those of the plantation society and Jim Crow Era are observed in contemporary American society. In his research conducted on white college students, Feagin (2010) describes white actors and participants as protagonists or dissenters. Protagonists are more like the extremists that Goldfield refers to in that they feel no remorse for the negative framing of Blacks and may or may not openly self-identify as being racist. On the other hand, dissenters are more like the liberals and are somewhat uncomfortable in situations where racist comments, jokes and performances occur, but do not confront the individual or oppose the actions. As a whole, Feagin found that many whites still either enjoy or tolerate the racial framing of Blacks as inferior and condone negative new and/or age-old stereotypes. They often defend the racist individual or try to rationalize why he/she is not racist with the excuse that the person has Black friends. Some report that they did not fully support the anti-Black diatribe of their friend but hung out together because their friend was "fun."

Feagin's research confirms that whites know "how" and "where" it is appropriate to speak and perform racist-based narratives and actions. That is, whites today are still using a set of codes or etiquette that is embedded in a racial ideology that affects the everyday living of African Americans and extends to other minority groups in America. Bruce A. Jacobs (1999) describes some of the common practices and behavior of whites' interactions with Blacks in public spaces, including age-old habits such as avoidance, no eye contact, awkwardness and a sense of uncomfortableness and even paranoia and fear. Though not written or spoken of in public among diverse groups, Blacks also have a set of codes or racial etiquette that they adopt in their interactions with whites. While there are variations based on social class, urban-rural, Southern or other, there are shared understandings and responses. For example, Feagin suggests that Black urban youth have adopted certain behaviors and manners (walk, clothes, gestures, loud talk, etc.) as a way to command recognition and respect of whites and Blacks.

Ritterhouse agrees with Feagin's analyses that the social interactions of whites and Blacks involve public and private or hidden scripts. She makes the connection between children's racial learning and the larger social, economic and political trends in society. For example, in the Jim Crow South, white parents used racial etiquette to teach their children how to perpetuate the racial inequality that was rooted in economic oppression, political disfranchisement and discriminatory laws. Thus, a white girl growing up in Virginia in the 1910s learned "she must always 'talk a little down' to Black people while insisting that they talk 'up' to her" (2006, 1).

Today, Ritterhouse claims, fewer parents want their children to grow up to be racist like those in the Jim Crow era, but children still learn race relations by interacting with the world around them. Similarly, Edward Morris's (2005) research shows that teachers and school administrators negatively interpret and respond to the way Blacks and other students of color dress (e.g., tuck in that shirt) and act (interpreted as threatening) and thus reproduce race (as well as class and gender) biases in education. Assumptions guiding bodily discipline differ for different groups of students because they are learned from the racial etiquette passed on in different generations over the years.

In general, studies show that explanations of inequality between races in post–Civil Rights America are being diverted to non-race factors that result in blaming the racialized individual/child, family or cultural group. George Lipsitz (2011) explains that most people believe that there were legitimate grievances in the past under slavery and Jim Crow, but equal opportunities now exist in post–Civil Rights America. Consequently, unequal outcomes between whites and Blacks are assumed to be the result of shoddy values and beliefs and the dysfunctional behavior of individuals or families. Lipsitz points out that currently there are people who believe that, "the problems that Black people confront today are of their own making." What was once done to them by white racists, this line of argument contends Blacks are now doing to themselves" (2000, 1). Racial inequality is reframed so that the disadvantages that African Americans experience in the contemporary United States of America are linked to their individual or family poor practices, values judgments and culture—a cultural etiquette associated with race, class and inner city life.

Thus, in post–Civil Rights contemporary American society, cultural etiquette is used to blame the victim, individual and/or group, rather than consider the racially biased structural and ideological frameworks that have hindered their progress over time. Consequently, although the problem of race hangs on like an old scent, many are afraid to talk about race in the public sphere. Jacobs (1999) believes that the topic of race is "toxic" as racial hostility and stereotyping have intensified and both whites and Blacks cannot see past a racial panic. While Jim Crow signs of segregation are not physically present, the myths and expectations of what it is to 'be' and 'act' as white and Black in public, remains. In particular, Jacobs calls race in contemporary America "strange" with several "racial traffic signals" (10). Further, assumptions about the causes of the inferior circumstances of Blacks are supported by the creation, re-creation and propagation of racial stereotypes. While it is safe to conclude that stereotypes do not determine day-to-day behavior, their existence as a social and ideological norm reflect the ideology of their era. Moreover, racially based stereotypes of African Americans were conceived from a position of white power and white supremacy, which, according to Scott Plous and Tyrone Williams (1995), is a continuing legacy of slavery.

RACIAL STEREOTYPING

The word "stereotype" emerged in the English language in the late 1700s to describe a printer's metal plate used to produce identical copies of a page. Later it was adopted by a journalist and political commentator to mean "pictures in our heads" portraying all members of a group as having the same attributes (Banaji and Greenwald 2013, 72–73). The creation of the term is not necessarily problematic but, over time its usage, accuracy and purpose has become increasingly disturbing. Moreover, stereotyping has become an everyday practice and everyone uses stereotypes. But, who uses stereotypes and who is stereotyped? According to Banaji and Greenwald, stereotypes are not distributed equally and when unfavorable can have damaging effects. For example, in the United States racial stereotypes of Black men as dangerous criminals have serious life and death implications for all Black males and some women.

Racial stereotypes are linked to prevailing racial beliefs and perceptions of racial differences. Stereotypes, however, can undergo change due to the contestation of racial beliefs as well as political, social and economic change. As John Hartigan (2010) puts it:

> Stereotypes may come and go as people become more aware of their racial biases, but unless we are able to think about and engage the larger society of cultural valuation that generates them in the first place, they will likely simply be replaced by other representations—new code words, perhaps—that reproduce similar racial oppositions but in different registers (38).

Racial Stereotypes in the Old South and the Plantation Society

Racial stereotyping began with the early contact between Europeans and Africans between the sixteenth and eighteenth centuries. Savage or brute were the first stereotypical images that were imposed on Africans (Brantlinger 1985; Pieterse 1992; Pratt 1985). These stereotypes were based on Europeans' perceptions that Africans were "uncivilized" and "heathen" in nature and traditions. The ideas of white superiority and Black inferiority were fixed beliefs and although stereotypes of Blacks had to change somewhat to accommodate the changing conditions of the eighteenth and nineteenth centuries, the same racial discriminatory thinking persisted. As a result, many whites in Europe and the United States still judged African descendants as inhuman and uncivilized but through a different set of stereotypes.

According to Plous and Williams (1995), during the days of American slavery, many whites held stereotypes that, "blacks were mentally inferior, physically and culturally unevolved and ape like in appearance." This viewpoint was widely accepted and reported as "facts" where for example in the 1884 edition of the *Encyclopedia Britannica* on page 316 the "Negro" was described as being the lowest form on the human scale. The physical charac-teristics of African descendants were exaggerated and linked to characteris-tics thought to be suitable for slavery, such as being less sensitive to physical pain and less able to think abstractly (795–96).

Feagin (2010) reminds us that the reality of slavery in the late Colonial Era had a great impact on how Blacks were stereotyped in what he calls the "white racial framing," particularly by those in power. While in later years—the post-slavery eras—stereotypes are found in popular culture and social media, during the period of the plantation society stereotypes were mostly found in newspapers, flyers, pamphlets and speeches by judges, slaveholders, ministers and politicians. Here again, while variations of the white perspec-tive are expressed, white superiority and Black inferiority remain common denominators.

The more extremist and conservative stereotyping of slaves is found in the earlier periods of slavery. For example, Feagin (2010) talks about the writings of a Jamaican slaveholder, Edward Long, who in the 1700s de-scribed the enslaved African as "natural sloth" with "bestial or fetid smell." Long also propagated stories of "ape like" slaves with low intelligence and "having amorous intercourse with apes." Other slaveholders espoused simi-lar descriptions referring to their slaves as "Dam'd dogs, Black ugly devils, idle Sons of Ethiopian Whores" (54). During this period, ordinary, non-slave-holding whites also shared the stereotypical ideas about Black speech, behavior and humanity. Feagin points out that, in the North, both white ministers and intellectuals alike held comparable extremist conservative views. He cites Cotton Mather, a New England minister, who argued in the 1706 treatise for the "Christianization of Negroes" in order to save the souls of these "lowly, brutish, stupid creatures" and "barbarians" (2010, 55).

On the other hand, the liberal stereotyping of whites during slavery and the plantation society are noticeable in the speeches and writings of many of the Founding Fathers, including Benjamin Franklin, Thomas Jefferson, James Madison and George Washington. Over their lifetimes and careers, these white men were leaders, slaveholders, liberals and abolitionists. How-ever, as they moved through their different ideological, social and political positions they never ceased promoting negative stereotypes, imageries and racialized beliefs of Blacks because of their desire to keep "their America" a "lovely white." They adopted the same stereotypes of the early colonial days to support the racial belief of Black inferiority. Feagin (2010) cites Thomas Jefferson's book *Notes on the State of Virginia* (1785) in which Jefferson is quoted saying, "Black Americans smell funny, are natural slaves, are less intelligent, are physically ugly, are lazy, are oversexed, are ape-linked and animalistic, are musically unsophisticated, cannot think well, and cannot if freed ever be socially integrated into white American society" (68–69).

The stereotypes of Blacks represented the racist ideas produced and promoted to justify slavery in the United States by slaveholders, their associates and those in power. Most other whites adopted the same views and stereotypical beliefs and used these to sustain white supremacy and slavery throughout the mid to late nineteenth century. Feagin (2010) reports that politicians such as Senator John C. Calhoun advocated that Southern slavery was a "positive good" for Blacks because Blacks were physically and intellectually inferior and freed Blacks were predisposed to be insane (72). Overall, the common trend of the liberal whites who claimed to oppose slavery was to perpetuate similar racial beliefs and stereotypes as those of the extremist and conservative whites. That is, the idea that enslaved Africans were animalistic, violent and prone to criminal behavior, culturally and intellectually inferior with despicable morals including having promiscuous tendencies. As a result, they were adamant that if slavery ended there should be laws to prohibit interracial marriages and relationships, and even loitering (unemployment). As a rule, it was felt that Blacks and whites should not live together in a free society.

Specific characters emerged from the plantation society and slavery that represented the racial beliefs and stereotypes of this era. These included certain typescript personas such as the Sambo, Tom, Coon, Brute and Buck for Black men and the Mammy, Jezebel and Sapphire for Black women. The Sambo was the typical plantation slave who, according to Stanley Elkins (1968), "was docile but irresponsible, loyal, lazy, humble but chronically given to lying and stealing; his behavior was full of infantile silliness and his talk with childish exaggeration. His relationship with his master was one of utter dependence and childlike attachment" (82). While the Sambo was entertained by food and avoiding work, the Tom characterization was conceptualized as a "good negro," submissive, stoic, selfless and with an impenetrable loyalty to the master even when insulted and flogged (Bogle 2001; Larson 2006).

These controversial descriptions of the plantation slave have generated much discussion centered on whether the Sambo was a "mere stereotype" or whether the character truly existed. George M. Fredrickson (1971) asks which of the very "unstable compound of opposites" the lazy, savage and murdering brute or the more "happy, childlike Negro" was a true depiction of the American slave. Far from the cunning Sambo, or somewhat smart, divisive Uncle Tom, the coons were another stereotype often presented as unintellectual either through their mispronunciation of words, stuttering, or pseudo-philosophical rants (Bogle 2001, 2005; Larson 2006). The coons according to Donald Bogle (2001) are depicted as "unreliable, crazy, lazy, subhuman creatures good for eating nothing but watermelons, stealing chickens, shooting crap, or butchering the English language" (8).

The stereotypes of Black women also consist of "unstable compound opposites." On one hand, there is the Mammy who possesses a "nurturing" demeanor, but lacks femininity and is overweight (Kowalski 2009; Larson 2006; Pieterse 1992). Then, there is the Jezebel character who represents a completely different notion to the Mammy and who is portrayed as an extremely sensuous and promiscuous individual. She represents slave women's reproductive capabilities and historically, was often displayed and "handled" on the auction block in a fashion that was derogatory and controlling of women's bodies (White 1985). Sapphire, yet another offshoot of the Mammy character, is fierce but with a proclivity for being headstrong and contentious (Jewell 1993, 2003).

Patricia Hill Collins (2005) argues that these stereotypes were endemic to chattel slavery and that Black women's sexuality presented opportunities for exploitation and sexual slavery. Black female characters were created in white minds as polar opposites of white (Victorian) women's physical characteristics and behavior. For example, Black women were cast in roles suitable to serve white women and white families. As the "Mammy," she was strong, asexual, and ugly compared to white women believed to be beautiful, fragile and dependent. The Mammy was considered a symbol of nurturance to the white family for whom she worked; safe to be around the white mistress and sexually safe (unlike the Jezebel) around the master.

Interestingly, the Black female was not only stereotyped with different gender roles from white women but also in her own group. For example, the Mammy was depicted as a controller of the males in her own society, a brute within her own household. Sapphire, on the other hand, was also deemed emasculatory because her character required having a "weak" and "corrupt" Black male to ridicule, trick and insult (Bass 2016; Jewell 1993, 2003; Kowalski 2009; Larson 2006). Contrarily, the Jezebel was cast as a direct opposite to the asexual Mammy as she had an excessive sexual appetite and desire for sex just as a man stereotypically does. Collins contends that white slave owners used the Jezebel image as a justification for forced procreation under the pretext that the women possessed a heightened desire for sex. As such, sexual intercourse with enslaved women could not be considered rape.

Fredrickson (1971) suggests that any publically sanctioned stereotype (Sambo, Tom, Coon, Mammy, Jezebel, etc.) is a social and ideological norm that legitimizes the status of one group over the other and can become volatile if the subordinate group is perceived to be "getting out of place" (370–371). In this case, stereotypes of inferior, unevolved Black Africans were used to rationalize and justify the economic and social exploitation of slavery and that of the brute to endorse violence and white nationalism. These stereotypes may have had their beginnings in slavery and the plantation society but as the economic structures, social conditions and race relations in society changed, stereotypes were reconfigured in the Jim Crow and the post–Civil Rights eras. However, the content of Black images and the purpose and outcome of negative racial stereotyping did not. According to Christopher Sewell (2013), negative racial stereotypes of Blacks continue to be an integral part of the American landscape and are particularly important when race relations are at their worst.

Racial Stereotypes in the Jim Crow Era, the Civil Rights Era and Beyond

The continuance of the morphed negative caricatures of African Americans serves the same structural and ideological purposes of the past through different modes. During the Jim Crow era, negative and offensive images of Blacks were disseminated through several media, including in advertising cards where sometimes even Black children were sketched with animal-like characteristics.[2] There are also numerous disparaging representations of minorities in music, literature, children's books and comics. In writing about Negro stereotypes, Edgar Rogie Clark (1948) makes the accusation "the history of mankind has been threatened by a mendacious band of scholars who have concentrated in distorted texts" (545). The patronizing work by these scholars molded patterns that continue to produce and sustain racial stereotypes.

A close examination shows that while racial stereotypes varied they consistently communicated the same message, that of Black inferiority. For example, the emergence of the Minstrel, played by blackface white men after the Civil War and Reconstruction, attempted to reconstruct life on the plantation. Parodies of the Negro as comical, carefree, lazy, a buffoon whose only interests were to eat watermelon, drink gin, steal chickens and carry a razor, distorted the image of the African American. Mathew Desmond and Mustapha Emirbayer (2010) see this as "blackness under complete white control" (353). They also argue that although minstrel shows died out after the early twentieth century "Minstrelsy"—white control of the representation of Blackness (ignorant and silly)—has continued through songs, film, radio and other media.

Clark (1948) alludes that the promotion of stereotypes as entertainment became popular with the minstrel performances, but also, soon after "Coon" songs flooded the country. He lists several examples, such as "New Coon in Town" (1883), "Whistling Coon" (1888), "Little Alabama Coon" (1893), "All Coons Look Alike to Me" (1896), "Mammy's Little Pumkin Colored Coon" (1897), "The Coon's Trade Mark" (1998), "Every Race Has a Flag but A Coon" (1899). Clark concludes from his research on Negro stereotypes that "constant repetition of racial stereotypes were exaggerating and perpetuating the false notion that this is a white Protestant Anglo-Saxon country, in which all other racial stocks and religious faiths are definitely of lesser dignity" (545).

In the more contemporary periods, stereotypes are easier to observe through popular culture and social media. J. Stanley Lemons (1977) suggests that popular culture, which fully developed in the late nineteenth century, gives exceptional insights into what the masses of people are thinking. He also warns that one of the dangers in popular culture is that the images and performances presented become so familiar and oftentimes comedic, that there can be a pervasive lack of sensitivity. For instance, the image of the Mammy and Tom became acceptable characters that gave the false notion that the now "freed" slaves—African Americans—could integrate in the larger society. Mammies could be servants and babysitters in white middle class homes so that white women could retain their "lady-like" roles as the home administrators. The Mammy's ability to cook and manage the kitchen was further commercialized as the "Aunt Jemima" on food products; and, the male equivalent as "Uncle Ben."

Eventually, the screen image of the Mammy evolves in movies such as *Show Boat* (1936), *Gone with the Wind* (1939) and *Pinky* (1949), as well as on the radio with the iconic Beulah in *The Beulah Show* (1945–1954). She eventually becomes the modern day Black matriarch figure in the 1960s, such as in the female characters depicted in *The Flip Wilson Show*. She was both popularized and demonized by the infamous 1965 Moynihan report, *The Negro Family: the Case for National Action*. Today, she continues to head her family that is now urban, but also, is now described as "dysfunctional." The Black youth from these single Black female-headed families are stereotyped as deviant juveniles who are drawn to drugs, gangs and violence. Christopher J. P. Sewell (2013) explains that, "due to their differences, white people looked down on African American habits and tended to disregard their families as "disorganized" or incapable of positive performance" (313). Similar to the plantation society period, economic and structural features are linked to ideological thoughts of white superiority and Black inferiority and deviance.

Black feminists and sociologists offer another perspective of the issue. They assess that the plantation society Mammy has transitioned to the contemporary "strong black woman"—the stereotypical Black matriarch. The Jezebels and Sapphires are now stereotyped as the "welfare queens" with the same negative connotations (Collins 2005, hooks 2015, Jewell 2003). While today's image of the matriarch does not necessarily have the same physique as the earlier Mammy, the idea of the domineering and controlling woman in Black families remains. Ironically, this is also reflected in Tyler Perry's "Madea" character, which can be interpreted as a modern depiction of the "new and improved" Mammy. Here, the physical persona returns along with a comedic and working class social status.

In sum, stereotypes are reiterated in newspapers, movies and films, books, jokes, conversations, radio and all forms of social media and cultural depictions. And, after a while, they form (and inform) deep-seated attitudes and racial thinking. This not only perpetuates the perceived inferiority of Blacks, but also normalizes white aesthetics. Such is the power of the white dominant group. With the use of stereotypes in traditional and social media, history is whitewashed, Blacks misrepresented and the pretention that institutional racism does not exist continues. Feagin (2010) sees this as "white obsession with white purity" where stereotypical images of African Americans evolve, but continue to retain many of the same deleterious characteristics and meanings (75). Moreover, Fredrickson's (1971) concept of "unstable compound opposites" persists with qualities of servitude and incompetence juxtaposed against violent, brutish mannerisms and the hypersexuality of African American men and women.

The continued reinvention and use of the stereotypes reflect how a dominant culture can preserve racial superiority thinking and structural control. Feagin (2010, 2014) is convinced that mass media remains central to the perpetuation of racial stereotypes. He cites Don Imus, a radio personality, who in 2007 referred to the winning Rutgers University women's basketball team as "nappy headed hoes"—a century old depiction of Black women. Feagin also points out that today, whether conscious or unconscious, white fear of Black men is not based on biology or environmental factors but is socially constructed in a white racist framing. He is firm that even in post–Civil Rights America, the popular culture, the media and stereotypes are filtered through a white frame. Bonilla-Silva (2001, 2006, 2017) reminds us that whites' cultural explanation of Blacks also affects how Blacks think about stereotypes. His research found that while few Blacks agree with the racial stereotypes, Blacks as a whole do not support or agree with white superiority and Black inferiority and often resist being placed in this position.

BLACK RESISTANCE

Human agency dictates that where there is domination and oppression, there is resistance. It is, therefore, not surprising that evidence of Black resistance to racial oppression is discerned from the past to the present. Feagin (2010, 2014) maintains that any theory of systematic racism must acknowledge resistance strategies of African Americans and others, and their impact on structural and ideological racism. Such resistance began in the early days of slavery through many different forms. These ranged from violent insurrections and attacks on slaveholders and their property, to non-violent actions such as running away. Talley (2009) also attributed enslaved and free Blacks seeking an education as a form of resistance to domination and oppression.

Similarly, during the Civil Rights era, Black resistance included sit-ins, freedom rides, non-violent protest and demonstrations among other methods. In addition, many civil rights organizations were established, legal battles occurred and victories won with the passing of the 1964 Civil Rights Act. Strategies varied from Black community control or separatist schemes to wanting to assimilate as "just Americans." Both approaches demand equal rights and the same access to opportunities and resources as white Americans. These demands were carried forward in the Black Power uprisings of the 1970s and many are still heard in contemporary protests.

Including in the acts of resistance for economic and political racial equality are Blacks' responses to racial beliefs and racial etiquette. Not only did Blacks resent having to perform white imaged/imagined roles during slavery and the plantation society as well as in the Jim Crow era, but today there is still animosity and resistance to the current forms of racial etiquette. In an interview with Feagin (2010), a Black professional admits that, "I have very little tolerance for white people who expect me to change my behavior to make them comfortable. They don't change their behavior to make me feel comfortable. I am who I am" (274). On the other hand, there are those who admit that they are more tolerant and take the time to explain their concerns to their white colleagues, friends and family when the latter make racist statements. According to Feagin, Blacks have a lifetime of experience with whites; many have developed a counterframing to the white racial frame as well as strategies to fight against white racist beliefs, attitudes and practices. We believe that these survival strategies are forms of Black resistance and are practiced by African Americans and other minority groups across gender, social class and geographical locations within the United States.

African Americans and their white allies have always advocated for inclusion and the ideals embodied in the U.S. Declaration of Independence that "all men are created equal." The fight for equality occurs at the structural level in calls for equal material and political rights, as well as, at the ideological level in the fight against white supremacy and the idea of Black inferiority. It was precisely against the racially biased physical and social ways of life that leaders such as Malcolm X fought to improve the lives of African Americans; Martin Luther King, Jr. and other Civil Rights activists appealed for human rights and dignity as enshrined in the U.S. Constitution. Similarly, those of the Black Power Movement sought Black liberation, self-determination and self- respect. However, Lasch-Quinn (2001) insists that new racial protocols constantly emerge in attempts to steer the improvements brought about by the Civil Rights Movement off track.

CONCLUSION

Today, the emergent position to managing race relations in contemporary society is to adopt "diversity training" and/or engage in "cultural competency" discourse. This, however, requires new types of etiquette and separate etiquettes for interactions among different groups of people. Lasch-Quinn (2001) explains that such etiquettes are based on a "heightened awareness of differences construed as cultural facts, which clearly relies on simplistic, stereotypical renderings of the groups involved" (190). She believes that there is not enough research on racial etiquette in post–Civil Rights America. Feagin (2010, 2014) on the other hand, chooses to focus more research on the on-going racial frame used by hate-based extremist and white supremacist groups. He believes that this racial frame overlaps somewhat with those used by other white conservatives and liberals, where, for example, whites of different backgrounds periodically use the same negative stereotypes and images of Blacks.

While racial etiquette and racial framing allow us to have a better understanding of race relations, they do not directly address the reasons for persistent racial inequality. Bonilla-Silva (2001, 2006, 2017)) fervently argues that historical institutional racism, racial inequality, segregation and white control continues, but many whites in contemporary society have learned to mask their prejudice by using veiled language. He explains the notion of color-blind racism as to why people can make disparaging remarks about race without appearing to sound racist—or even expressing race-based views in the backstage in some of the anonymous and abstract spaces of social media (like Yik Yak). In other words, the racial etiquette of a "supposed" color-blind society is to express racial progressiveness while supporting white economic, political and social gains. Bonilla-Silva refers to this as "white color-blindness"; "racism without racists"; or the "new kinder, gentler and smiling racism."

This chapter, like the ones before, helps in illuminating the complexity and nuances of how racial beliefs, customs and practices change but persist. Moreover, the chapter argued that continued racial etiquette and racial stereotyping are integral to the perpetuation of racial inequality and racial ideology, but are steadily negotiated and resisted. We explained how racial etiquette, that is, rules of engagement between whites and Blacks, guide social conduct, shape racial identities and provide a systemized framework for understanding one's place in society along a hierarchy of racial supremacy and racial inequality. Further, the chapter clarified how racial stereotypes, shaped by racial ideology and racial beliefs, are used to inform racial etiquette, make judgments about racial categorization and "explain variations in human nature." In other words, how individuals and groups are arranged along a social hierarchy based on stereotypes about racial categories that were created and refashioned by the white ruling class over three important epochs in U.S. society. This includes their perceptions of the intellectual, moral, physical and artistic temperaments of Blacks. Based on the analyses racial etiquette and racial stereotypes can be seen as tools used for social control of Blacks by whites

NOTES

1. See also Goffman 1959 book *The Presentation of Self in Everyday Life.*
2. See Plate 1: Trade cards sold by McLoughlin Company, New York

REFERENCES

Baldwin, James. 1955. *Notes of a Native Son.* Boston, MA: Beacon Press (reprint 2012).

Banaji Mahzarin R. and Anthony G. Greenwald. 2013. *Blind Spot: Hidden Biases of Good People.* New York: Delacorte Press.

Bass, Rachael, Traveshia. 2016. "When the Silver Screen Fades to Black: An Analysis of Black Faces in Films." Thesis submitted to the University of Louisville.

Bogle, Donald. 2001. *Toms, Coons, Mulattoes, Mammies, and Bucks: An Interpretive History of Blacks in American Films.* New York: Continuum.

———. 2005. *Bright Boulevards, Bold Dreams: The Story of Black Hollywood.* New York: One World Ballantine.

Bonilla-Silva, Eduardo. 2001. *White Supremacy & Racism in the Post–Civil Rights Era.* Boulder, CO: Lynne Rienner Publishers.

Bonilla-Silva, Eduardo. 2006, 2014, 2017. *Racism without Racists: Color-Blind Racism and the Persistence of Racial Inequality in America.* Lanham, MD: Rowman & Littlefield.

Brantlinger, Patrick. 1985. *Victorians and Africans: The Genealogy of the Myth of the Dark Continent.* Chicago: University of Chicago Press.

Clark, Edgar Rogie. 1948. "Negro Stereotypes." *The Journal of Negro Education* 17:545–49.

Collins, Patricia Hill. 2005. *Black Sexual Politics: African Americans, Gender, and the New Racism.* New York, NY: Routledge.

Dandridge, Nicole. S. 2010. "Racial Etiquette and Social Capital: Challenges Facing Black Entrepreneurs." *Western New England Law Review* 32:471–82.

Desmond, Mathew and Mustafa Emirbayer. 2010. *Racial Domination, Racial Progress: The Sociology of Race in America.* New York: McGraw-Hill.

Doyle, Bertram. 1937. *The Etiquette of Race Relations in the South: A Study in Social Control.* Chicago: The University of Chicago Press.

Du Bois, W. E. B. 1903. *The Souls of Black Folk.* Chicago: A.C. McClurg & Co.

Elkins, Stanley. 1968. *Slavery: A Problem in American Institutional and Intellectual Life.* Chicago: University of Chicago Press.

Ellison, Ralph. 1947. *Invisible Man.* New York: Vintage Books (reprint 1972, 1995).

Feagin, Joe R. 2000, 2014. *Racist America: Roots, Current Realities, and Future Reparations.* New York/London: Routledge.

Feagin, Joe R. 2010. *The White Racial Frame: Centuries of Racial Framing and Counter-Framing.* New York/London: Routledge.

Fredrickson, George M. 1971. *The Black Image in the White Mind: The Debate on Afro-American Character and Destiny, 1817–1914.* New York: Harper & Row.

Goffman, Erving. (1959). *The Presentation of Self in Everyday Life.* Norwell, MA: Anchor Press.

Goldfield, David R. 1990. *Black, White, and Southern: Race Relations and Southern Culture, 1940 to the Present.* Baton Rouge: Louisiana State University Press.

Hartigan, John. Jr. 2010. *What Can You Say? America's National Conversation on Race.* Stanford, CA: Stanford University Press.

hooks, bell. 2015. "Eating the Other: Desire and Resistance." In *Black Looks: Race and Representation*, 44–72. New York: Routledge.

Jacobs, Bruce. 1999. *Race Manners: Navigating the Minefield between Black and White Americans.* New York: Arcade Publishing.

Jewell, K. Sue. 1993. *From Mammy to Miss America and Beyond: Cultural Images and the Shaping of U.S. Policy.* New York: Routledge.

Jewell, K. Sue. 2003. *Survival of the African American Family: The Institutional Impact Of U.S. Social Policy.* Westport, CT: Praeger.

Kowalski, Jenifer. 2009. "Stereotyping of History: Reconstructing Truth and the Black Mammy." In *transcending silence* (e-journal). Available at http://www.albany.edu/womensstudies/journal/2009/kowalski/kowalski.html

Larson, Stephanie G. 2006. *Media & Minorities: The Politics of Race in News and Entertainment.* Lanham, MD: Rowman & Littlefield.

Lasch-Quinn, Elisabeth. 1999. *How to Behave Sensitively: Prescriptions for Interracial Conduct from the 1960s to the 1990s.* Paper published by the Woodrow Wilson Center, 1999.

———. 2001. *Race Experts: How Racial Etiquette, Sensitivity Training, and New Age Therapy Hijacked the Civil Rights Revolution.* New York: W.W. Norton and Company.

Lemons, Stanley J. 1977. "Black Stereotypes as Reflected in Popular Culture, 1880–1920. *American Quarterly* 29:102–16.

Lipsitz, George. 2011. *How Racism Takes Place.* Philadelphia: Temple University Press.

MacCann, Donnarae. 1998. *White Supremacy in Children's Literature, Characterizations of African Americans 1830–1900.* New York & London: Garland Publishers, Inc.

Morris, Edward W. 2005. "Tuck in that Shirt! Race, Class, Gender and Discipline in an Urban School." *Sociological Perspectives* 48:25–48.

Moynihan, Daniel Patrick. 1965. *The Negro Family: the Case for National Action.* Washington, DC: United States Department of Labor.

Pieterse, Jan Nederveen. 1992. *White on Black: Images of Africa and Blacks in Western Popular Culture.* New Haven: Yale University Press.

Plous, Scott and Tyrone Williams. 1995. "Racial Stereotypes from the Days of American Slavery: A Continuing Legacy." *Journal of Applied Social Psychology* 25:795–817.

Pratt, Mary Louise. 1985. "Scratches on the Face of the Country; Or, What Mr. Barrow Saw in the Land of the Bushmen." *Critical Inquiry* 12:119–43.

Ritterhouse, Jennifer. 2006. *Growing Up Jim Crow: How Black and White Southern Children Learned Race.* Chapel Hill: The University of North Carolina Press.

Sewell, Christopher J.P. 2013. "Mammies and Matriarchs: Tracing Images of the Black Female in Popular Culture 1950s to Present." *Journal of African American Studies* 17: 308–26.

Talley, Clarence. 2009. The "Race Concept and Racial Structure." In *Racial Structure and Radical Politics in the African Diaspora.* 61–79. *Journal of Africana Studies*, Vol.3.

Thompson-Miller, Ruth, Joe R. Feagin and Leslie H. Picca. 2015. *Jim Crow Legacy: The Lasting Impact of Segregation.* Lanham, MD: Rowman & Littlefield.

White, Deborah Gray. 1985. *Ar'nt I a Woman: Female Slaves in the Plantation South.* New York: W.W. Norton.

Winant, Howard. 2004. *The New Politics of Race: Globalism, Difference, Justice.* Minneapolis: University of Minnesota Press.

Wright, Richard. 1940. *Native Son.* HarperCollins Publishers (reprint 1993).

Chapter Four

Black Male Mentorship

Derrick R. Brooms

ON MENTORING AND MENTORSHIP

Mentoring relationships play an important role in students' schooling experiences, their personal development, and their success efforts. Sociologist James E. Blackwell has contributed much to our understanding of and need for mentoring Blacks. Blackwell defines mentoring as a process, which persons of superior rank, status, or prestige serve in roles to instruct, guide, and facilitate the development of persons identified as protégés. Additionally, Blackwell argues that mentoring hinges on the quality of social supports and these supports—such as mentors or role models—significantly impact students' ability to complete educational programs. Importantly, mentoring can take multiple forms, such as formal and informal, and they are critical in various stages in a person's development. Thus, given the impact of race and racism and the needs of students, mentoring can prove to be a valuable resource in helping individuals meet their goals.

Extant research continues to reveal, and reaffirm, the importance of Black teachers, faculty, and staff members (all here considered institutional agents) in the schooling experiences and successes of Black male students (Bonner and Bailey 2006; Dancy 2011; Strayhorn 2010). Without a doubt, the contributions of Black teachers and faculty members help enrich academic learning environments, personal development, and school/campus climate. Important in their efforts are the teaching pedagogy and praxis as well as relationships and engagement with students that institutional agents interface with. Necessarily, as is evidenced in the men's narratives in this chapter, is that these engagements, relationship building, and interactions occur both during in-class and out-of-classroom spaces. In fact, as has been argued, interactions and engagements outside of the classroom can be even more important than in-class experiences, given a particular students' overall experiences, skills, expectations, and needs (see Bonner and Bailey 2006; Brooms and Davis 2017). As an example, Bonner (2003) contends that students across the academic spectrum, from high-achieving students to those with greater needs, benefit from their meaningful relationships with faculty members (or institutional agents). In addition, as the evidence in this chapter makes quite clear, a number of Black males feel empowered for self-discovery and identity development through their interactions and relationships with faculty (Brooms 2014, 2016; Moore and Toliver 2010; Palmer and Gasman 2008).

Given the needs of students to develop and enhance their skills, faculty members/mentors play a critical role in how they develop, persist, and experience the schooling culture and environment. Thus, developing faculty-student relationships, both formally and informally, can influence and impact Black males' academic, social, and personal development. Most importantly, developing a community that brings together faculty/institutional agents and students offers alternative images of what it means to be Black men, provides a space for self-expression and development, and contributes critical support for Black males' academic efforts and intellectual abilities (Brooms 2016, 2017; Brooms, Goodman, and Clark 2015; Strayhorn 2008).

As part of our work in preparing this book, each of the authors, as well as other former students of Dr. Clarence Talley offered reflections on their living experiences as young Black men as well as their learning with Dr. Talley and other Black males. Their contemplations focus on two specific areas: living racism and male mentoring. We share the men's reflections here to offer their own authentic voices, as a window to better understand who they are, and as a way to appreciate the role of mentoring. First, we explore their experiences in living racism. This section is important because it not only helps provide a context for the role of mentoring in Black men's lives, but it also provides important connections to the foundational chapters of this book on racial ideologies and racial structures. Additionally, the men's narratives provide valuable insights into the background of their own higher education pursuits as well as their research interest on race and social inequality, which they offer in the remaining chapters of this book. Thus, the current chapter serves as both a bridge and as a window. In the former sense, this chapter bridges the early theoretical chapters and the substantive studies in the second half of the book. In the latter sense, the men's narratives help us: (a) see how their lives and experiences are racialized; and (b) better understand the particular trajectories and engagements that they have engaged in their educational and professional pursuits. In many ways, these men offer us their unique epistemological standpoints from which to learn.

In the remainder of this chapter, the men's narratives are divided into two main sections: (1) living racism, which encompasses their own experiences with racism; and (2) mentoring reflections, which includes their reflections and meaning making on their male mentoring experiences.

LIVING RACISM: EXPERIENCING AND NAVIGATING RACE AND RACISM

As a way to provide a context to the men's experiences with mentoring, and as a measure to align with the focus of this book project, the men reflected on their experiences with racism. As opposed to offering an analysis of each of the men's individual experiences, I offer the men's collective narratives so that readers can focus on the full range of what they share. A brief synopsis is offered at the end of the two main sections, before I turn to a more robust discussion in the conclusion.

Former Student

Beyond the conversations that I would hear my father and his friends having while I was young, I can remember in the third grade, there was two other Black males and myself who stayed fairly tight in school and out. While we were not the only group of three or more friends who were constantly together, we were the only all Black male group. After a while I started to realize that we were seen differently due to our race. While that was my first experience, it was definitely not my last.

Overt racism, I first experienced right outside of my school. I couldn't have been in any higher grade than the sixth. On my way to the TARC (public transportation) stop, right after school, just trying to get home, I spit on the sidewalk. It just so happened, that as I was spitting, a white cop was coming down the street. The cop immediately placed their lights and siren on me and pulled up alongside of me. Not knowing the cop was trying to get to me I kept walking—which I am to assume made the cop furious. So here I am, eleven or twelve years old, being sequestered to a cop's window. Once there, the cop used aggression trying to intimidate me, informed me that they can lock me up for spitting on the sidewalk and that I best watch myself in the future.

For some, it is hard to navigate race and racism due to them seeing themselves as the one to blame or the one in the wrong when issues of race and racism come up. With me, I quickly realized that the issues that I experienced surrounding race and racism were things that I couldn't control and the ones acting upon me were indeed the ones to blame.

Contributing Author

My initial experiences with racism were as a child. I can distinctly remember being likened to a character from the film *The Jungle Book*. The character, of course, was an orangutan. Though I did not know about the word "racism," I knew how it made one feel. In that instant, I responded by leveling my classmate with a blow that sent his glasses and his body to the floor. I remember a distinct sense of satisfaction in having hurt and embarrassed him in front of the entire class—consequences be damned. Though I am not averse to physical forms of self-defense, these days many of my challenges to white supremacy and racists, be they in the general public or in academia, happen by way of my research, my writing, and my affiliations with various political organizations.

More often than not, I navigated racism by fighting the racists who offended me. Now, I excel.

Contributing Author

My experiences with racism have almost always come from being in academia surrounded by (mostly) white students and teachers. I remember being in middle school and I was in a literature class that required us to write a persuasive piece on anything we wanted. I wrote a piece about how King Tut was murdered (instead of dying naturally, I don't remember the full details of the piece since I wrote it some time ago). Long story short, my literature teacher, who was a white woman, assumed I had plagiarized the piece—presumably because of how well-written it was. Now, keep in mind, I worked hard on that piece for days. My mother helped me write it and even went to the library to help find sources, as if she were a student. We worked on that piece enough to drive us both crazy . . . just to have this white woman assume that I didn't actually do it. She tried to sweeten the assumption by saying "Now, be honest, did you copy this? A lot of students cheat, you know." "A lot of students" was probably code for Black and brown students. I assured her that I did not cheat and, at the time, I had no idea how to respond beyond that because I did not understand racism, but looking back on it, it still makes me mad how white teachers will openly (mis)treat students of color.

The next incident occurred in high school in a physics class in which I was one of three Black students in a class full of mostly white and Asian students. I was enrolled in a magnet program centered around the STEM fields and I immediately felt out of place and unwelcome because I was usually one of a few Black kids in a class and I always felt that I was at a disadvantage being surrounded by so many highfalutin, pompous white middle-class nerds and snout bands who truly thought they knew it all and showed open confusion when people (like me) didn't just understand things they believed were "easy" and "simple," ignoring socioeconomic differences and (racial) inequalities in education. Anyway, I was in a physics class and I had no idea what I was doing—ever. I didn't understand the concepts, the math, or the point in understanding physics, on top of being a Black student in a white space with an older white male teacher who did not have the best record of dealing with Black students. When I did group projects, I would always work with the two other Black students in class—we sat together and supported each other as if we were the last of our species. We struggled together, studied together, often at a distance from the rest of the class. There was one project where we just couldn't figure out what we were doing, even though the teacher had explained the assignment, and we went to ask for his help. He greeted us with, and I kid you not "Well, let's see how my remedial group is doing." "Remedial." He labeled us as remedial, of course, the only "remedial" students in his class just so happened to be the only brown people in class. Coincidence? Probably not; he was known for showing microaggressions. Throughout my academic life, I carry the weight of that label "remedial" because that's how a lot of my white peers have treated me.

I navigated the aforementioned experiences, and others, by using cool-pose—although I was never, *ever*, the cool kid. I was a goober, a nerd, but I felt like one of the only ways to survive school around my peers was to be the "cool Black friend." It was a way for me to distance myself from my struggles as a Black male in mostly white spaces. I often tried to fit into groups of people who were white and I performed for whites as a way to gain some social capital among peers in order to avoid the pitfalls of stereotype threat and other racial trapdoors and labels. I also went out of my way to overachieve. My mother made it a point to make sure I achieved a lot, which was nice of her, but that often required doing so in white spaces where I had to overachieve just to be seen as "equal" to the white students who just barely achieved or met expectations.

Contributing Author

In thirty-three years of life, I've never been called a *nigger* in the way it's depicted in films and popular culture as the go-to/short-hand expression of bigotry where there is no question who the racist is. You know the kind—the dispossessed white male with some version of a southern accent confronts a Black person or group of Black folks and hurls the word in the direction of his target—an adult or child, male or female—as a single-word, two syllables, as a reminder, an assertion to the target and himself where each of them "belong" in the social order. I know people who have experienced this; it has simply never happened to me.

In the second semester of my freshman year at Western Carolina University, I took an elective course, "The Bible as Literature." The course was taught by a former nun from Arizona (how she came to lose the habit and teach this course must be an interesting story in and of itself). This was the first time in my academic career my intelligence was questioned in a way that could only be traced back to racism, this micro-level manifestation about what I was capable of as a Black male sitting in a university classroom. She returned my first writing assignment to me in class. As I flipped through the pages looking for her comments in margins, looking for feedback, I saw individual words circled in red ink. There were comments in the margins that raised the question of how I knew these words. There was an accusation of plagiarism laid at my feet. I was shocked at first but the shock soon gave way to danger. How did she arrive at this conclusion? It was insulting. And I needed to defend myself. It's clear she hadn't seen my writing before.

I took the issue to her office hours, meeting her on her terrain. She invited me to take a seat but I refused the offer; standing up in front of/on the other side of her desk allowed me to communicate to her that I would be standing up for myself; I would not take this insult, this accusation sitting down. I think my insistence on standing caught her off guard. The meeting was brief. She explained why she circled the words and I defended myself, using my pedigree as a shield: I've been taking Gifted English classes since the seventh grade (when we read George Orwell's *Animal Farm*); I'm taking English Composition for honor's credit in the English Department—you can meet with her if you have questions about my writing style and use of language. I told her/reminded her that an accusation of plagiarism was serious enough to get me kicked out of school. I told her I found it insulting.

At some point, she decided to retract any speculation regarding the originality of my work and I left the office convinced I had won this battle. She seemed cautious about her interactions with me and in her comments on my assignments moving forward. I won the right to have my work taken seriously in her class. Or, at the very least, to be free of such flippant accusations.

Almost fifteen years removed from this incident, I see it with a somewhat different lens. I see her challenging my work based on a notion of who she thought I was and what she believed I should be capable of. She probably hadn't expected that this young Black man would push back and defend himself, that he would assert a strong sense of self and integrity. However, I also see the larger issue. My work wasn't accepted as my own and I was forced to defend myself, to legitimize my intellectual capability. I was forced to defend myself, to list my credentials, to justify my intellectual capabilities to a woman who wasn't capable or willing to accept that a then-nineteen-year-old Black male would know words she didn't think I should know. She might as well had called me a nigger and gotten it over with. This is the precarious condition of navigating an institution of higher-ed. Black intelligence is subject to questioning/scrutiny from the jump. Would my work have been questioned had I walked into class a young white man or woman, someone who looked the part of an "intelligent" university student?

Over the years, I developed a layman's algorithm, mental calculus for situations like these. Instead of numbers, I'm computing interpersonal dynamics to determine how much of what is happening to me is informed by racism. There was the time in graduate school when a white sociology professor openly stated on the first day of class in front of our small and mostly white seminar class that I may need to do some extra reading to "keep up" in class because I was coming from another discipline. And later, at the opening of my PhD program when a sociology professor initially refused to accept my assignment in front of class only to later accept it in private. In these situations and others, the mental calculus kicks in. What is happening? Who is doing this? Why might this be happening? Navigating my daily life means regularly calculating the weight of these interactions to determine how much racism is at play here.

I talk about them sometimes with my wife, with my parents, or I may run a situation by a mentor to help unpack any lasting feelings or thoughts I have about the situation. Often, these conversations aren't to indict anyone's behavior. They help me process my feelings and validate my experiences in ways that let me know that my responses to these racist moments aren't unfounded.

Former Student

Growing up in the Southwest, I was surrounded by family, friends, and teachers as well as a community of people, of different ethnic backgrounds, who encouraged me, loved me, and put their very best into me. My mother moved to the Southwest because my sister felt it would provide a better education for my siblings and I. It was here that I grew into a teenager, and as teenagers do, I began to explore my city. My peers and I rode further out on our bikes than usual, we caught the bus to the shopping malls, arcades, skating rinks, and we began to hang out with peers from different high schools and in different neighborhoods; noticeably more affluent neighborhoods. When at home we began to stay out later at night. It was during this time period that I began to experience racism. I didn't experience the overtly racist attitudes and policies that, say, my mother spoke of when she described growing up in the Deep South. Racism, as I experienced it, in my city, was more subtle, diffuse, and as I would come to learn, structural. Whether in a large group or even when I was with a peer, I was followed around convenience stores and then ushered out. Over time, I was questioned increasingly to open my bag by mall staff while others were not. When riding around exploring other neighborhoods, we were followed, stopped, questioned by police officers, asked to leave, and then ushered out.

However, my most pointed experience with racism was when I was charged with "assault by threat." I was expelled from high school the second day of my senior year. To explain, an assistant principal harassed me while waiting in line to receive my textbooks. Despite being new to the school, he was aggressive, physical, short-tempered, and disrespectful. He shoved me out of the line and told me I needed to go to class. I told him that I had been waiting in the line for over thirty minutes and that I just wanted to get my textbooks as I had a class and an assignment I needed to complete. As a student-athlete, and as a senior, I knew all too well how important it was to stay ahead in my studies. After a few exchanges, he radioed to our campus police officer and I thought it was probably time to leave, so I walked off. The officer ran over, made me face the brick wall, patted me down, handcuffed me, and walked me over to his office. I soon found out that I was under arrest and was being charged with "assault by threat" and that my behavior caused the staff member to be fearful. My version of the story was never heard, my mother's tears and pleas were not considered, and despite having an outstanding history at the school, as a contributor in various areas of school life, I was made to leave the school.

"Assault by threat," lack of accountability or due process, being handcuffed at school when I was violent in no way, my mother's lack of knowledge about her rights as a parent is racism in its subtle and diffuse form. The collective assumption that I was a "threat," the arrogance and lack of humility on behalf of these two staff members, and most insulting of all, the benign neglect on behalf of the other teachers and the school with regard to my well-being is racism in its structural form. It was after this injustice that I began to become more aware of others' perception of myself and my peers, not just African and not affluent, but other minorities as well. The next high school I attended was a predominantly African American and Hispanic one, whereas my previous school was comprised of middle class students of sizeable Anglo, Indian, Asian, and continental African descent. The teachers, leaders, and staff members at my new school were predominantly minority, as well. The staff at this school took an active interest in me being African American, a minority, and male. Similar to my previous school, politics, English, history, psychology, and science were taught to a high standard, but they were taught by teachers who expressed daily that we would need more than curriculum to navigate the challenges to be successful. We needed to be critical thinkers, great writers, good researchers, and stand-up individuals.

How did I navigate through racism? Mentorship; both male and female. Male mentorship first entered my life when I started working as a dishwasher at a pizza restaurant in my home city. How symbolic! The entire kitchen staff, the delivery drivers, and the owner were male. For the first time in my life, I was surrounded by fathers, brothers, sons, husbands, and professionals; faithful and unfaithful, happy and not, fulfilled, or in transition. During our breaks, I began to take an active interest in their lives, their challenges, and their dreams. I was drawn to their stories and they were drawn to mine. These men, young and elderly, African, Black, Hispanic, and Italian, each poured the best of themselves in me. In two years I was closing that restaurant as an assistant manager. By the time I was expelled from my first high school I had gained a value in learning and sharpening my skills and I learned the importance of being timely. Most of all I had developed an insatiable appetite for mentors and so I began to seek them out.

As can be heard through the men's narratives, they have experienced and endured racism in a number of different ways. Consistently, their narratives speak to the challenges they've faced "simply because they're black men" (Brooms and Perry 2017). In their study of Black men's experiences and responses to the killing of Black men, Brooms and Perry (2017) found that their respondents believed that black men faced deleterious fortunes precisely because of their Black maleness (their racialized and gendered identities) and because of the lack of value for Black life. In this chapter, the men speak directly to how Black males are diminished, denigrated, and marginalized in schooling spaces. As previous research reveals, Black males often are made to be "bad boys" in school; thus, they receive a disproportionate level of disciplining practices and labels (Ferguson 2001). In addition, Black males also are projected as deficient often, experience stereotype threats, and endure a number of racial battles (Hall 2001; Hotchkins 2016; Robertson and Chaney 2015; Smith, Allen, and Danley 2007; Steele 1997). Thus, as education scholar Michael Dumas (2014) maintains, schools have become and continue to be sites for Black suffering.

REFLECTIONS ON EXPERIENCES AND POSSIBILITIES OF MALE MENTORING

In their reflections on mentoring, the men share their stories about how they have experienced mentoring in their lives and how mentoring has mattered. In the narratives that follow, the men express specific moments in their lives where they recall with great detail their male mentoring experiences. As can be expected, the men offer understandings of male mentoring from their own situated standpoints and epistemologies. While some may have questioned the need for mentoring earlier in their life, they acknowledge the benefits of it later. Interestingly, each of the men speaks to how mentoring helped inform their abilities to navigate educational spaces. Missing from the calls for more Black males to serve as teachers and role models for Black males, are specific understandings *from* Black males about their needs, wants, and desires. That is, all too often mentoring has been mapped onto Black males' experiences, thus centering Black males as "the problem" in need of fixing (see Butler 2013; Dumas 2016). The men's experiences speak directly to culturally relevant and critical mentoring approaches (see Weiston-Serdan 2017). Here, we provide the men with a wide canvas to discuss their mentoring experiences.

Former Student

The truly interesting part about male mentoring is that as soon as one steps into the public sphere without the physical protection of one of their parents, they're Black males that will attempt to guide you. So, the original realm of Black male mentoring is something that takes place by those in the community in an attempt to steer one in the right direction. However, for my mentoring to be in a consistent place such as it is now, that didn't take place until I arrived on UofL's (University of Louisville's) campus as a college freshman. Prior to me taking a class with a Black male professor, upperclassmen would reach out in an attempt to guide me. Unaware that I needed the guidance, it was not until I almost flunked out and began to take classes that better suited me, that I began to see more Black professors. Those Black professors were majority men and they began to first reach out to me through using me or my name in their examples. As to say that, "Yes, I see you in here," and "Yes, I know your name, but it's up to you to come for the additional aid."

With Dr. Clarence Talley, he showed me how to operate inside of a PWI (predominantly white institution), and within a predominately white field. We both shared a passion for sociology, which is heavily dominated by whites. His mentoring showed me how to operate in class, and how to educate others in the class, even the teacher if they were wrong or off target.

Without the mentoring that I received, I would not understand myself as a Black man, the different facets of Black men, how to maneuver within a space of scholarship, nor how to operate in society at large freely as my own man.

I have started to volunteer at my daughter's school with "The Men of Quality," which is an organization started by Omega Psi Phi Fraternity, Inc., that works with middle and high school minority youth in a mentoring effort. Some of their components are community volunteering and an education requirement also. I have consistently taken the time out to speak with my extended family youth and neighborhood kids whenever I am in that public sphere. While on campus whenever I am able to catch the attention of an underclassman I take the time out to speak with them in passing on or off the campus.

The possibilities of mentoring depend on the level of the individual that is getting mentored. You have to meet them in a comfortable space for them.

Beyond that I believe that the individual getting mentored has to also be in the right place in their mind where they're ready to listen and take the advice that is given to them.

Former Student

Midway through undergrad, I was both a recipient and steward for mentorship. When I met Dr. Clarence Talley as a graduate student of Pan-African Studies at the University of Louisville, I believe I had experienced a shift in my relationship with mentoring. Before, I was learning from men and women, but now I was learning *from* and *through* visionaries. Both who and how I was learning shifted. Differently, I was no longer just learning how to be a man in the world I was living in, I was now learning how to change the world I was living in. In his garden, Dr. Talley talked incessantly about "carving a space" for ourselves. I began to see my future, my purpose, my wants as malleable. As he talked about the garden, his ambitions for the room outside leading to the garden, hiring help and doing the work himself, I began to look at him and life differently. For the first time in my life, I looked around the house and began to locate what it was that I wanted in life, in a profession, and in a partner. As I watched him and Dr. Rajack-Talley cook together almost seamlessly, I begin to long for a wife that I could share that dance with. On weekends, as me and other students moved furniture into and around the house, I started to take notice of their reading room, their chairs, the dining room. It was no longer a home they lived in; it was the home they created. As Dr. Talley discussed the projects that he and Dr. Rajack-Talley were working on, I began to see the research skills, people skills, and love they developed for the Diaspora as a set of tools that they were using to transform the African experience. I remember the toil in the heat helping to decorate, organize, and repair the garden, I know now that it was 'our' garden and as PAS students we often used it to host our parties. Through Dr. Talley, I learned the value of reciprocity, love, and family. Through Dr. Talley, I learned how important it is to establish the ingenuity and skills necessary to develop a vision, realize that vision and, most importantly, to value equipping others with these skills.

Today, I am a psychologist and an educator. I currently direct an all-boys school and I have accepted an offer in a different location doing similar work next year. Also, I founded an organization for adolescents and adolescent educators. I train and mentor young men and women in the skills necessary for them to be effective change agents in their lives and in the lives of others. I also train teachers and school leaders how to establish a school culture, a classroom culture, and a peer culture which fosters collaboration, student agency, personal excellence, and social justice in teenagers, teachers, and in the various other stakeholders associated with the school and the community.

Mentoring flourishes most in a space that it is malleable, when those involved are ready to receive and listen willingly and passively; rather than when it is forced. Mentoring is sharing. Mentoring is optimal when it is shown/revealed through the telling of stories, through constructing meaning from one's own story, and when we provide the opportunities for others to locate themselves in that meaning. Mentoring should be personal and lived rather than be done. We need more mentors and less mentoring.

My advice for Black males is to learn about who you are. Become more self-aware. Find the courage to ask and listen to your teachers, parents, and peers, discuss how they see you, your strengths, and your weaknesses. Locate what you agree with and be honest with yourself. Then work on being a better version of yourself. Attach yourself to men and women alike who strive to better versions of themselves, better Africans, better husbands, better men, better fathers, and better friends. Challenge yourself to be a better boyfriend and a better son. Explore how these mentors do it now and how they have done it in the past. Explore where they were and what they attribute to where they are now. Make their best practices your best practices, thus making you a better man. My advice to Black males is to do what it takes to become a mentor and the mentoring will have already taken place.

Contributing Author

Mentoring has been significant to my life since a child. Whether it was my father, my uncles, or older cousins, I have always had male role models willing to assist in my growth. As I became an adult, mentors became even more important, particularly as I moved further away from home. Such was the case when I moved to Louisville, Kentucky. There I was fortunate to encounter a number of male mentors. These included Drs. Clarence Talley, J. Blaine Hudson, and Professor Jan Carew. As co-chair of my thesis committee and the only Black faculty in the Department of Sociology, Dr. Talley showed me both how to conduct worthwhile and solid scholarship, and how to navigate the college and the discipline. Each of these men provided examples of strength, scholarship, and dedication to the betterment of the Black Diaspora.

The form of mentorship I received from Dr. Talley and others exceeded the university and their offices. Viewing me as more than a student, but as a future colleague, these men, and their spouses, welcomed me and countless other graduate students into their homes, all the while, instilling in us a more comprehensive model of mentorship. Dr. Talley, in particular, did as such through dinners at his home, sharing work in his backyard garden (a passion of mine), and by introducing me to other elderly Black men in and around Louisville whom he respected. It goes without saying that I am forever indebted to him. My work is a testament to his impact on my life.

Mentoring has been key to my growth both inside and outside of academia. The time and energy given to me by men and women that are my seniors—be that chronologically or professionally—has helped me navigate many hurdles. Mentoring has been instrumental in my academic advancement.

In fall 2017, I will begin my first faculty position as an assistant professor. As I embark on my academic career, one that will no doubt, include the counsel of undergraduate and graduate students, I am reminded of the ways I was mentored. I hope to be as challenging and as careful with my students as were the mentors I was fortunate to inherit.

In thinking about spaces for male mentoring to flourish, I found, after completing a master's degree in Pan-African Studies and joining a majority white doctoral program in geography that I had to create the spaces I needed. Therefore, during my first year, I actively took classes beyond my discipline. It was while taking courses in sociology and anthropology that I met other Black men who are my friends and colleagues to this day. Without taking the initiative to create the space I needed—knowing full well that the university had a paucity of such spaces—my social and academic development would have suffered. These colleagues—Drs. Orisanmi Burton, Robert L. Reece, Adam Bledsoe, and Brian Foster—are part of the next generation of Black male scholars who will further their respective disciplines and break new ground for young Black scholars and other scholars of color to follow.

Contributing Author

I never had a Black male mentor until college, specifically in graduate school. Prior to that, I had a Black female mentor who was supposed to help me as a freshman handle the stress of transitioning from high school to college, but we stopped talking when she graduated. Prior to that, my mother was always my "mentor" who made sure I knew what I was supposed to know to succeed. So I had always been mentored by Black women and I gravitated toward Black women for guidance. I remember when I was in elementary school and I was mentored by a Black female teaching assistant and our school had what I think was something akin to a social worker come in (the school I went to was majority Black/brown) and she took an interest in me, probably because I was one of the more . . . open students she dealt with. I was more emotional and insightful than most other students. (I'm not bragging here, I really was a thinking-man at a young age and that certainly didn't make me superior. That insight often made things difficult for me, emotionally.) So, I had only ever known the mentorship and guidance of Black women, and I grew up being in some ways isolated from and afraid of other Black men because I was often teased by Black boys. Not until I had to develop a thesis in graduate school did I actually have a Black male mentor, partially because he was the only person in my department who was Black, eligible to be on my committee, and understood the nuances of race/racism, which is what I studied. I was in my early twenties when I got his mentorship.

I honestly don't fully know the full extent of the roles mentoring has played in my life. I took a year off from grad school to explore myself and my options, so the mentoring I received almost felt like wasted potential. Now that I have returned to school, for the time being, I have had the opportunity to publish with my mentor. So, I guess I can say that my mentor has become a networking and publishing nexus, and that is a valuable connection to have, at least professionally. Personally, I'm not entirely sure how his mentorship has or will impact me beyond helping me come to a greater understanding of the radicalized (and racialized) world we all live in; that insight into whiteness has been important to my understanding of myself as a Black man. But, I truly believe I have yet to learn my greatest lessons and I think I have only just begun my journey toward true self-understanding.

I incorporate male mentorship in academia, ironically after all of my struggles in school. I am a teaching assistant at a university and part of my job is to mentor students when they ask for it. I'm also open to helping other classmates with understanding social theory and race/racism.

One place for male mentoring to flourish is in school. I think school is one of the more powerful spaces to meet other Black male mentors, be they teacher or counselor, and learn. I was mentored in school and I think I am better for it. Another space I think is helpful is the home. I think, above all else, the home is one of the most important spaces for people. I know growing up that I was always asked, by family members, if I was willing to tutor/mentor their children—there was always this trope that I was the "smart" one in the family. I always playfully rejected those advances, but I think it is important for Black males to mentor others in their homes and among family, as those tend to be the most common and enduring tropes in Black male development.

Contributing Author

I never thought about mentoring as a thing that people do. Rather I've never viewed the relationships I had with older men and other Black men closer to my age from the perspective of mentorship. The men in my life—my stepdad, some teachers, my brothers, or older guys in the neighborhood—just looked out for me.

Mentoring felt like a thing I began to recognize when I got to college. I was the first member of my immediate family to pursue education beyond high school and I looked for other students I could go to with questions about navigating the university experience. I cultivated healthy and supportive relationships with other Black males in college as a member of a fraternity. When I transferred to Georgia State, I adopted a number of faculty members as informal mentors who helped show me the way through my undergraduate career.

In regards to specific experiences, Dr. Talley always had a way of making students feel seen and heard. He came through our hallways in the Pan-African Studies Department, stopped to talk with us about our ideas and the papers we were working on. He also talked with us about the world and how our work as thinkers was connected to improving the conditions facing Black folks. He never tried to make his students replicas of who he was as a scholar. He was there to nurture our growth as scholars and as people.

Mentors helped me understand what kinds of opportunities were available to me and encouraged me to pursue them. Many of the mentors I encountered in the last decade have been in the realm of academia. I transferred to Georgia State University after my first two years at college; I also started the voyage into my interest in academia. Former undergrads from the Department of African American Studies turned grad students at the university were my teaching assistants in my Intro to African American Studies class. They became the first Black graduate students I developed personal relationships with. I also found the first cohort of mentors at Georgia State University. This group of professors challenged my intellectual development in class and supported our, mine, and other students', willingness to engage our communities beyond the classroom. They helped create the vision in my mind about what I could become: a scholar, a professor. They created a vision in my mind that there was a space for me, for us, in the academy, and a need for us to be there despite how hostile this institutional space can be for Black people (students, faculty, and hourly workers included). My interest in pursuing a PhD was supported by Dr. Akinyele Umoja. He responded to my interest in learning about research by encouraging me to apply to the Ronald E. McNair program, designed to increase the presence of underrepresented groups who attain PhDs. He also supported my application for graduate school. The faculty at Georgia State University collectively prepared me to go on to the next level and many have continued to offer their support now.

I feel that it's necessary to look for opportunities to help others move forward with their goals. I know that each bit of support along the way makes a difference because it happened that way for me. This hasn't translated into long-term formal mentoring relationships as yet. However, I talk with students candidly about pursuing graduate school in my role as a graduate student and instructor. I try to be intentional about passing along information and opportunities that may help them achieve their goals.

In my research at the recreation center, I volunteered with a male mentoring and tutoring program. I'm there to help kids improve their math and reading skills, and play pick-up games with teenagers who are trying to stay busy and off the streets with something productive. I've helped guys write resumes to get part-time jobs, talked with them about college, and listened to them when they needed an ear. My presence is a small contribution to their lives but I hope that our relationship can have a positive impact on them as they grow and develop into young men.

I think that in any space or opportunity males can feel comfortable sharing their inner world with another male without fear of ridicule or that these ideas will be used against him is fertile ground for mentorship. This can happen in any number of places adults or older males are willing to listen to what younger males have to say about themselves or the world around them and validate their perspectives.

Contributing Author

Unlike the other contributors to this volume, I am white.

Dr. Clarence Talley taught me to "hate" my whiteness. This—perhaps more than anything else we ever spoke about—has stuck with me over the years. What he meant by this was not to hate myself, or be fearful or angry about being white, but instead to "hate" what whiteness meant. Whiteness—the color of my skin—refers to a system of ideological thinking that attached specific beliefs and values to genomic variations; not my history, culture, or family lineage. Instead, "whiteness" in this context refers to the ranking of peoples' bodies based on shades of color. As a white male, I can embrace my background and still hate my whiteness. Dr. Talley had a way of reaching students and broaching these topics without making anyone feel put off.

As I reflect upon these types of conversations, I think these experiences speak to the importance of having a Black male mentor. We—not just whites, but all of us—are presented with myths about race, and particularly myths and stereotypes about Black males. Many white students may not interact with a Black male mentor until they reach college. As a result, myths about race, about crime and discipline, about Black males, are likely the sole source of information that white college students begin their academic careers with. It's not that Black male mentors are the only ones who can strike down these stereotypes that are so enmeshed within the public consciousness, but for me, having a Black male mentor made a difference.

So why is it important for white males to have a Black male as a mentor? Though we face similar social pressures and expectations due to our maleness, our racial experiences are unique. The status quo won't change on its own and white males have to be part of the change; to challenge the established racial hierarchy in the United States and to challenge the stereotypes that define us and others. As a white male, if you aren't working to change the status quo, you are helping the status quo remain. In this sense, inaction is action. We can learn from Black males and, in addition, mentorship from Black males on issues related to race and to maleness is inherently strong.

On a more personal level, having Dr. Clarence Talley as a mentor motivated me to actually do something about race in the United States. He was able to inspire me about racial issues in ways that no other professor (almost all white) was able to do. It's not that white professors can't discuss racial issues (they should!), but in my experience it was certainly different. Dr. Talley had a level of authenticity; he didn't just discuss racial issues during class time and then turn it off at the end of the day. You could tell it was something he carried with him and it made you want to do the same. That's the importance of having a Black male mentor.

As the men's narratives attest, the role of male mentoring has been critical in their development, academic aspirations, and their successes. Brooms and Davis (2017) argue that, in a number of instances, the similarities in educational experiences between Black male faculty members and students "can serve as potential road maps to help students navigate college" (322). This sentiment was expressed most strongly by each of the men. Additionally, a number of men also spoke through their masculine identities as well. Researchers note that a number of male students lack quality help-seeking behavior when they enter college. As a way to improve in this area, it is imperative for these students to be aware and willing to reach out to others. Communicating a need for help is not a weakness but rather should be seen as an opportunity to strengthen one's efforts. For instance, Strayhorn (2008, 2010) found that Black and Latino male students benefitted greatly from meaningful and supportive relationships with peers and other institutional agents. As such, the experiences that these men share in the current chapter are clear lessons for future students about ways to navigate colleges more effectively. In a number of critical ways, mentoring matters in both what Black males experience and how they experience schooling environments, social encounters and relationships, and personal development (Brooms 2016, 2017; Brooms and Davis 2017; Dancy 2011; Moore and Toliver 2010).

CONCLUSION

This chapter explored the lived experiences with racism of a select number of men as well as their mentoring experiences through their self-narrated reflections. As was discussed in chapters 1 through 3, racism, and all of its antecedents, is part of our social structure. As such, our identities matter a great deal in how we experience and navigate the social environment and social institutions. A burgeoning question from these men's experiences is: what are the costs of navigating white spaces and the constant barrage of racialization? According to noted sociologist Elijah Anderson (2015, 10), "wider society is still replete with overwhelmingly white neighborhoods, restaurants, schools, universities, workplaces, churches and other associations, courthouses, and cemeteries, a situation in which Black people are typically absent, not expected, or marginalized when present." These settings, Anderson notes, often are referred to by Blacks as "the white space"—a perpetual category—and generally approached with care. Similarly, psychologist William Smith finds that these spaces, routinely, are racial battlefields that Blacks must navigate in order to negotiate and navigate society. Smith and colleagues (2007) assert that Black males' race, gender, and other factors intersect to create unique conditions that often disadvantage them in various settings. They note, at minimum, as they move through society, Black males carry the burden of two negative social identities, "one as a member of the African American race (i.e., anti-Black racism) and the other as a Black male (i.e., Black misandry or anti-Black male attitudes and oppression)" (Smith et al. 2007, 553).

The men expressed a range of ways that they faced anti-Black racism and discrimination in school settings, in the public sphere, and in various social settings. The everydayness of these experiences should not be overlooked but rather understood as the ordinary, mundane, and contiguous elements of racism in all of its many forms. Some of the actors in the experiences that the men shared expressed a variety of racial beliefs, relied on a number of racial stereotypes, and contributed to structures that denigrated these men. Importantly, institutions and structures must have actors. In a variety of the cases that the men shared, these actors included a number of institutional agents—from teachers to administrators—across a number of schools in different locations. Additionally, racial ideologies and beliefs informed the practices and actions of these institutional agents. Ultimately, given the constancy of the men's narratives, these experiences cannot be written off as isolated incidents. Instead, they reaffirm a variety of ways that Black males are repositioned as outsiders in school settings. And, of course, these are not new phenomena. Dumas (2016, 14) writes,

> And this is the broader challenge posed by a theory of antiblackness: There is no clear historical moment in which there was a break between slavery and acknowledgement of Black citizenship and Human-ness; nor is there any indication of a clear disruption of the technologies of violence—that is, the institutional structures and social processes—that maintain Black subjugation.

Maintaining black subjugation and subjectivity relies on active agents, controlling images, and structures to support these practices. Within and across white spaces, people of color face a barrage of racial microaggressions, mini assaults, and questions about their character, worth, work, and belonging. The torrent of challenges and under-appreciation of Black men's abilities and skills force some to engage in prove-them-wrong coping strategies and leave some feeling as if they need to defend their intellect (see Brooms 2017).

Importantly, even as they face a number of challenges, Black men continue to achieve in spite of, not because of, school culture, climate, or the obstacles they face. Additionally, Black men's ways of knowing along with their continuous pursuit of knowledge, degree attainment, and unwillingness to succumb to the deficit rhetoric all are active ways that they resist. In addition to their own individual efforts, as the men shared above, is the support system that the men have at their disposal. As the men attest, mentoring can play a significant role in their schooling experiences and personal development. Individually and collectively, each of the men cited the need for or the benefit of mentoring in their lives. The men's stories and experiences are important because they speak to the role that mentoring can play in enhancing one's life journey.

All of the men shared stories of receiving guidance that was academic, intellectual, social, and personal. LaVant, Anderson, and Tiggs (1997) argue that mentoring continues to be a viable tool in supporting Black men's retention in college. At the same time, Fries-Britt and Snider (2015) maintain that traditional mentoring approaches fall short in supporting the needs of underrepresented populations in higher education and, instead, encourage a "mentoring outside the line" approach—which highlights the importance of authenticity, transparency, and vulnerability in effective mentoring relationships. These authors, much like the men whose voices inform this chapter, assert that *how* they were mentored matters. A number of the men's narratives reflect their familial capital—"those cultural knowledges nurtured among family (kin) that carry a sense of community history, memory and cultural intuition" (Yosso 2005, 79) and that men do matter in Black males' lives (see Richardson 2009). As Dixon-Reeves and Brooms (2017) assert, it is critical for mentees and protégés to recognize their own agency in acquiring the information that they need in order to pursue and achieve their goals. They offer three critical points in this regard: (1) the importance of communicating one's needs; (2) see your area of need as an area of growth; and, (3) accept the responsibility of identifying your needs.

In many ways, the men recounted professors' intentionality in reaching out and building a relationship with them. A critical insight was the ways in which these professors, and mentors, created opportunities for these men to be "visible" in academic and non-academic spaces—thus, pushing the boundaries of mentoring well beyond the classroom. The mentoring they received connected well with their goals and aspirations. Even further, the mentoring informed and strengthened the men's resolve to pursue excellence and aspire to excellence. In learning how to navigate college campuses, academic disciplines, and various venues, the men found a number of individuals who were willing to assist in their growth, serve as role models and mentors, and offer tutelage and guidance in their efforts. Additionally, these mentors helped break down myths about race, helped deepen the men's own understanding, and helped them learn even more about themselves and their possibilities.

The importance of Black institutional agents, many of whom were identified as faculty for these men, in the lives and development of students cannot be understated. These mentoring relationships provide fertile ground to build on students' own cultural wealth while also developing and enhancing intellectual knowledge and skills. Beyond the classroom experiences, these relationships speak to the holistic development of students as opportunities for planting seeds that might harvest their own desires to guide and mentor others. Not only can the strong bonds developed in student-faculty relationships play a key role in students' college years (see Brooms and Davis 2017), but they also can be critical in enhancing students' social and cultural capital that can be applied to or deployed in their future endeavors.

The men's experiences and narratives provide an outline of what high quality, student-centered mentoring looks like in action: (1) make Black males visible in academic and non-academic spaces—helping students feel that "there is a space for us"; (2) assist, support, and nurture in students' growth and development; (3) provide examples, from one's own life and behavior, of sense of self, engagement, scholarship, and dedication; (4) expose students to a greater range of individuals—or other institutional agents—and be intentional in sharing information and resources; (5) help students develop a collective consciousness; (6) help students better understand how their race and gender matter; and (7) be willing to listen to students about their world, their understandings, and their perspectives. According to Weiston-Serdan (2017), a number of these are the characteristics of critical mentoring, which help youth construct powerful identities and gain valuable experiences while at the same time challenging deficit-based notions of protégés and engages in liberatory processes. Paying closer attention to how Black males experience the world, perceive themselves, and make meanings of both can help inform us of ways to help Black males, as well as others, be and become who they are, develop healthy identities, and navigate society with greater clarity, commitment, and fortitude.

REFERENCES

Anderson, Elijah. 2015. "The White Space." *Sociology of Race and Ethnicity* 1 (1): 10–21.
Bonner, Fred A. 2003. "To Be Young, Gifted, African American, and Male." *Gifted Child Today* 26 (2): 26–34.
Bonner, Fred A. and Kevin W. Bailey. 2006. "Enhancing the Academic Climate for African American College Men." In *African American Men in College*, edited by Michael J. Cuyjet, 24–46. San Francisco, CA: Jossey-Bass.

Brooms, Derrick R. 2014. "Mapping Pathways to Affirmative Identities among Black Males: Instilling the Value and Importance of Education in K-12 and College Classrooms." *Journal of African American Males in Education* 5 (2): 196–214.

———. 2016. "'Building Us Up': Supporting Black Male College Students in a Black Male Initiative Program." *Critical Sociology*, 1–27. doi: 10.1177/0896920516658940

———. 2017. *Being Black, Being Male on Campus: Understanding and Confronting Black Male Collegiate Experiences.* Albany, NY: State University of New York Press.

Brooms, Derrick R. and Arthur R. Davis. 2017. "Staying Focused on the Goal: Peer Bonding and Faculty Mentors Supporting Black Males' Persistence in College." *Journal of Black Studies* 48 (3), 305–26.

Brooms, Derrick R., Joseph Goodman, and Jelisa Clark. 2015. "'We Need More of This': Engaging Black Men on College Campuses." *College Student Affairs Journal* 33 (1): 105–23.

Brooms, Derrick R. and Armon R. Perry. 2016. "'It's Simply Because We're Black Men': Black Men's Experiences and Responses to the Killing of Black Men." *Journal of Men's Studies* 24 (2): 166–84.

Butler, Paul. 2013. "Black Male Exceptionalism? The Problems and Potential of Black Male-Focused Interventions." *Du Bois Review* 10 (2): 485–511.

Dancy, T. Elon. 2011. "Colleges in the Making of Manhood and Masculinity: Gendered Perspectives on African American Males." *Gender & Education* 23 (4): 477–95.

Dixon-Reeves, Regina and Derrick R. Brooms. 2017. "Perspectives from First-Generation Minority Academics on Mentoring." In *Reflections on Academic Lives: Identities, Struggles, and Triumphs in Graduate School and Beyond,* edited by Shannon Orr and Staci Zavattaro, 212–14. New York: Palgrave-McMillan Press.

Dumas, Michael J. 2014. "Losing an Arm: Schooling as a Site of Black Suffering." *Race, Ethnicity and Education* 17 (1): 1–29.

———. 2016. "My Brother as 'Problem'; Neoliberal Governmentality and Interventions for Black Young Men and Boys." *Educational Policy* 30 (1): 94–113.

Ferguson, Ann A. 2001. *Bad Boys: Public Schools and the Making of Black Masculinity.* Ann Arbor, MI: University Of Michigan Press.

Fries-Britt, Sharon and Jeanette Snider. 2015. "Mentoring Outside the Line: The Importance of Authenticity, Transparency, and Vulnerability in Effective Mentoring Relationships." *New Directions for Higher Education* 171, 3–11.

Hall, Ronald E. 2001. "The Ball Curve: Calculated Racism and the Stereotype of African American Men." *Journal of Black Studies* 32 (1): 104–19.

Hotchkins, Bryan K. 2016. "African American Males Navigate Racial Microaggressions." *Teachers College Record* 118 (6): 1–36.

Lavant, Bruce D., John L. Anderson, and Joseph W. Tiggs. 1997. "Retaining African American Men through Mentoring Initiatives." *New Directions for Student Services* 1997: 43–53.

Moore, Penelope J. and Susan D. Toliver. 2010. "Intraracial Dynamics of Black Professors' and Black Students' Communication in Traditionally White Colleges and Universities." *Journal of Black Studies* 40 (5): 932–45.

Palmer, Robert T. and Mary Beth Gasman. 2008. "It Takes a Village to Raise a Child": The Role of Social Capital in Promoting Academic Success of African American Men at a Black College. Journal of College Student Development 49 (1): 52–70.

Richardson, Joseph B. 2009. "Men Do Matter: Ethnographic Insights on the Socially Supportive Role of the African American Uncle in the Lives of Inner-City African American Male Youth." *Journal of Family Issues* 30 (8): 1041–69.

Robertson, Ray V. and Cassandra Chaney. 2015. "The Influence of Stereotype Threat on the Responses of Black Males at a Predominantly White College in the South." *The Journal of Pan African Studies* 7 (8): 20–42.

Smith, William A., Walter R. Allen, and Lynette L. Danley. 2007. "'Assume the Position . . . You Fit the Description': Psychosocial Experiences and Racial Battle Fatigue among African American Male College Students." *American Behavioral Scientist* 51 (4): 551–78.

Steele, Claude M. 1997. "A Threat in the Air: How Stereotypes Shape Intellectual Identity and Performance." *American Psychologist* 52 (6): 613–29.

Strayhorn, Terrell L. 2008. "The Role of Supportive Relationships in Facilitating African American Males' Success in College." *NASPA Journal* 45 (1): 26–48.
———. 2010. "When Race and Gender Collide: Social and Cultural Capital's Influence on the Academic Achievement of African American and Latino Males." *The Review of Higher Education* 33 (3): 307–32.
Weiston-Serdan, Torie. 2017. *Critical Mentoring: A Practical Guide*. Sterling, VA: Stylus.
Yosso, Tara J. 2005. "Whose Culture has Capital? A Critical Race Theory Discussion of Community Cultural Wealth." *Race, Ethnicity, and Education* 8 (1): 69–91.

Chapter Five

Risky Bodies

Race and the Science of Crime and Violence

Oliver Rollins

The state of New York is currently debating the potential adoption of a new forensic technique, what some journalists have called "genetic stop-and-frisk" (Lewis 2017; Silverstein 2012; Whitford 2017). The phrase stop-and-frisk should be familiar given the media coverage and legal challenges of the highly contentious practice in African American and Latinx communities.[1] The reason for the qualifier genetic is less straightforward. The growing reliance upon genetics, and increasingly neuroscience, in forensic science, criminology research, and policing practices is neither apolitical nor neutral. Genetic science is associated most clearly with advancements in health; however, scholars have become more attuned to the way such knowledges are actively shaping larger societal ideas around difference, governance, and identity (Clarke et al. 2010; Duster 2003a; Krimsky and Gruber 2013; Richardson and Stevens 2015; Rose 2007). In addition, there is a troublesome and unsettled racial history underpinning biological approaches to crime and violence (Duster 2004; Gabbidon 2015; Gould 2006; Rafter 2008), which raise serious concerns about the intent and use of technoscientific practices like genetic stop-and-frisk in an already racialized criminal justice system.

Historically, research programs like *bio*-criminology made race an integral part of research. In this context, racial characteristics represented biological proof of distinct population differences in the occurrence and rate of criminal behavior. This use of race is demonstrated in the work of late nineteenth century *bio*-criminologist Cesare Lombroso—the Italian physician often recognized as the founder of modern criminology. Lombroso (2006, 91) provided a succinct summary of his stance on race in the final chapter of his seminal book *Criminal Man*, writing that "those who have read this far should now be persuaded that criminals resemble savages and the colored races." Lombroso, like other scientific racists of the late nineteenth century, purposely tethered "defective" biological material to race, which aligned well with social discourses and practices of racism throughout much of Europe and the United States (Simon 2006).

Lombroso's overall thesis about the "born criminal" was rejected following World War II due to the Nazi regime's use of biocriminology to justify racism and genocide (Rafter 2008). Nevertheless, the ontological principles, and often the racist underpinnings, of Lombroso's legacy persist in many of the contemporary reformulations of the research program.[2] Biocriminology was revived in the 1960s through the publication of Hans Eysenck's *Crime and Personality*. This reformulation said little about the research program's racist foundations or how it would address questions of racial differences in crime. What was clear, however, is that the question of race was not discarded in this era. While most researchers avoided directly linking race to crime, others have relied on *proxies* for race, such as IQ performance (Herrnstein and Murray 1996; Hirschi and Hindelang 1977) or evolutionary histories (Rushton 1995), to strengthen racist stereotypes about Black men being inherently more dangerous and to justify the seemingly natural over-involvement of African Americans in criminal activities. These contemporary biological theories of crime, therefore, continued to operate as *racial projects* (Omi and Winant 1994), essentially *bio*-criminalizing the concept of race itself by threading racist understandings of crime through a lens of biology.[3] New optimism about the biological study of violence came in the late 1980s, when the epistemological focus of the research program shifted to genetics and neuroscience (e.g., Brunner et al. 1993; Fishbein 2000; Raine 1993; Rowe 1986).

Genetic and neuroscientific practices lend a new sense of confidence in biological research on crime, seemingly inoculating science from biological determinism, technical shortcomings, and cultural bias that plagued past biological research. This optimism stems from a common narrative about science, which incorrectly assumes that "errors" from the past can be corrected simply through the natural progression of scientific thought and technological advancements (Fleck 1981; Kuhn 1996). However, problematic scientific claims from the past were not errors or accidents, but the results of the *coproduction* (Jasanoff 2004) of knowledge. Science and Technology Studies (STS) scholar Sheila Jasanoff (2004, 3) coined the term coproduction to "call attention to the social dimensions of cognitive commitment and understandings, while at the same time underscoring the epistemic and material correlates of social formations." Scientific knowledge, then, is not just an investigation to uncover objective facts about the natural world, but at once a synthesis of the practices to 'know' nature *and* a reflection of socio-political interests and cultural discourses of power. Thus, it is shortsighted to automatically grant immunity to newer biological techniques for crime or to view them as instinctively devoid of racial meaning or intent. Social and political values are already embedded within these new technologies, and I argue, made visible through their application in society.

In this chapter, I take a closer look at the resurgence of biological approaches to crime and violence, and specifically how such understandings enact a specific *biopolitics* of race, which helps configure new(er) lines of connection among measurements of biological processes, criminal predictability, and racial bodies.[4] My concern is with the authoritative assumptions undergirding the practice of biocriminality. Specifically, the *biopolitics of race*, which empower biological knowledges and measures to operate as vital passage points through which accurate, or more complete, understandings of crime can be discovered. Through the veneer of objectivity and truth, these technologies, like those of the past, threaten to reinforce and/or exacerbate racial inequalities in society.

This chapter starts with a brief outline of the key findings from contemporary genetic and neuroscientific research on crime to show how race has been taken up in today's biological models of crime. This section centers on the "disappearance" of race in biological research on crime and the adoption of "race-neutral" positions to help guard against criticism of racial insensitivity or scientific racism. I then examine the use of these new knowledges about genes, brains, and crime in the social worlds of criminology and law enforcement. Examining the resurgence of bio-criminology, I critique the efforts by biosocial criminologists to *re*-inscribe race as a biological trait. This move allows biosocial criminologists to defend the use of race as a predictor of crime. Finally, I return to the question of "genetic stop-and-frisk," examining the growing use of genetic science in forensic practices and its racial significance in society. In a less direct way, such technoscientific practices also proscribe a racialized belief of risk, in which certain racial bodies are targeted because they are deemed inherently riskier.

CONTEMPORARY SCIENCE OF VIOLENCE

Since the late 1980s, increasing authority of genetic and neuroscientific knowledges are actively reshaping how we think about and "know" health, behavior, identity, and overall "life itself" (Clarke et al. 2010; Duster 2003b; Rose 2007). In terms of crime, the use of genetic and neuroscientific approaches grew exponentially through psychological research that links genes and brains to anti-social and aggressive behavior. Psychological approaches to anti-social behavior focus on the influence of biological (genetic) factors that affect mental (brain) functioning and especially the way such biological processes increase the risk for deviance in certain individuals. Such efforts have positioned the psych-sciences as the undoubted engine for the "new biology of control" (Rose 2000). Sociologist Nikolas Rose (2007, 248) explains that the new biology of control is, "not concerned with the control of population groups *en masse*, but with the identification of specific individuals where a biological or familial predisposition may, in certain developmental or social circumstances, lead them to violence or anti-social conduct." This is made clear through the relationship between the construction of criminal biomarkers and the epistemological assumptions about risk.

Bio-markers of Risk

Biomarkers are defined as unique biological characteristics that can be objectively measured and used to reliably indicate the operating state (i.e., normal or abnormal) of a biological process or condition (Strimbu and Tavel 2010). However, biomarkers are increasingly being used to predict future behavior or the mental states (Singh and Rose 2009). In terms of genetic biomarkers for crime, researchers are less interested in finding *the* gene for crime, and most insist that no single gene exists. Instead, their focus is on correlations between specific gene(s) and an individual's risk or propensity for criminal behavior. A gene like the monoamine oxidase A (MAOA), the so-called "warrior gene," is one of the most popular biomarkers for antisocial or violent behavior (Buckholtz and Meyer-Lindenberg 2008; Lea and Chambers 2007). MAOA is a gene that helps control the quantity of neurotransmitters important for the brain's function and development. A deficiency in MAOA inhibits the brain's ability to control behavior, thus increasing the chance that an individual will engage in violent or aggressive behavior (Buckholtz and Meyer-Lindenberg 2008; Caspi et al. 2002). Importantly, the MAOA gene was one of the first biomarkers associated with environmental stressors, as demonstrated by Avshalom Caspi and colleagues' (2002) well-known study on genetics and childhood maltreatment. Caspi and colleagues find that the MAOA gene is moderated by childhood maltreatment, and the presence of certain versions of the gene increases the risk that an individual mistreated as a child will display antisocial or violent behavior as an adult.

Neuroscientific biomarkers for antisocial behavior, on the other hand, are related to abnormal brain patterns that increase the risk for antisocial or violent behavior. Using neuroimaging technologies that help researchers "see" the inner-workings of the brain, neuroscientists correlate the morphology and function of specific brain regions to antisocial behavior (Blair 2010; Raine 2008). Neuroscientific understandings of violence essentially reduce antisocial or criminal behavior to *inabilities* in decision-making and emotional processing. These technologies hold the promise to help better screen for signs of criminality, but the specific focus on the individual-level causes also renews questions about biological determinism and the potential public policy shift away from sociological forces toward personal choice (Duster 2003b, 2006a). Therefore, the production of biomarkers for criminality goes hand and hand with the construction of risky bodies.

Genetic and neuroscientific biomarkers for crime denote more than bodies at-risk; they also promote, and even require, the development of technologies and policies to manage the potential futures of those at-risk (Rose 2007, 2010). Constructing the risk for crime requires a seemingly unquestionable belief in the ability to conceptualize, calculate, and predict outcomes. While these epistemic commitments help ensure more confidence in biological models of crime, they also allow researchers to collapse or reduce complexity, essentially erasing the uncertainties that challenge or undermine the logics of behavior made possible through the models (Pickersgill 2009; Spallone 1998). Risky bodies in the biological sense, are co-constructed through our societal perceptions and management of safety, violence, and health; societal perceptions that are deeply connected with discourses and practices of race and racialization. This practice is not purely biological nor statistical, but an exercise in biopolitics, in which biological measurements or observations are privileged as a way to establish, fix, or renew existing norms of society (Agamben 1998; Foucault 1990; Lemke 2011). The construction of a body at-risk, then, is not a simple extension of biological determinism, but a way to shape how behaviors matter and which bodies are suitable for study, management, and disciplining.

Racial Science without Racist Scientists?

To paraphrase sociologist Eduardo Bonilla-Silva, can there be "racial science without racist scientists"?[5] The management of risky genes and brains generate important questions about race, and especially the possibility for the new biology of control to produce new(er) forms of scientific racism. Biological researchers studying crime today are aware of the research program's history as an explicit racial science, but have been less attuned to the ways that today's social practices of race get absorbed into the science indirectly through research practices and technologies (Rollins 2014). Troy Duster observes that geneticists studying crime scrupulously avoid the issue of race, and I have documented a similar trend with neuroscientists studying violence and antisocial behavior (Duster 2006b, 10; Rollins 2014). This move toward *race-neutrality*, as Duster (2006b) notes, is in response to shifting social and political environments and the hypersensitivity about race and violence in our society. The race-neutral tactic in the study of biology and crime manifests as the: (1) absence of any mention of race in publications, (2) restriction of research to racially congruent study populations to control for race differences, and/or (3) limiting any discussion about racism to the classroom, and only then in a historical perspective (Rollins 2014).

In justification of their research, some scientists have defended the turn to race-neutrality as a more comprehensive and objective scientific practice that will even help end racist interpretations of criminal behavior. Criminologist Diana Fishbein (2000, 94), writes that "defenders of [biological research on crime] deny that it must be captive to our racial history, and argue that it will ultimately do far more to *alleviate* than exacerbate racial tensions." Similarly, neuroscientist Adrian Raine (1993, 315) adds that "blocking research that aims to understand and control crime and violence may prove to be a major disservice to selective minority groups . . . [and] could even be constructed as racially biased itself." The adoption of race neutrality, however, does little to quell the tangible threat that this knowledge will be used to exacerbate existing racial inequalities (Duster 2006a; Rollins 2014). Race is a social process, a dynamic that is continually relied upon to understand, ascribe, and order social experiences and worth. It is already embedded within the ways we "know" criminals and think about violence, due to our social engagements with and practices of racialization and racial ideology. In a paradoxical way, the efforts to avoid race are reshaping the types of research practices, questions, and potential uses for biological science in ways that do not necessarily resolve the longstanding race/crime conundrum associated with the research program.

Biological framings of crime and violence, which again privilege the application of novel "objective" biotechnologies, overlook the deeply entangled associations between race and crime and the racialized consequences that are systematically reconstituted through our social institutions and relations. Contemporary biological research on crime may operate in a seemingly neutral manner, but the socio-political consequences of these practices are illuminated through their application in our society. Arrest records, for example, are commonly used as part of the evaluation for psychological disorders related to antisocial and violent behavior, yet the racialized impact of these records—that they often are the results of racially unequal policing practices—often goes unmentioned. Genetic and neuroscientific practices help wash these records clean of their racial underpinnings, essentially obscuring the actual lived effects and consequences of race. When used to help calculate and predict which bodies are at risk for crime, researchers miss the way that sociopolitical dynamics, and not just individual variants, disproportionately shape the interactions between the criminal justice system and some racial groups more than others. Where sociologists may interpret differences in criminal rates as racial bias (Hawkins 2003), contemporary biocriminologists instead opt for race-neutral biomarkers that seemingly allow them to elevate above such social milieu. The issue, however, is that such race-neutral biomarkers are not a remedy for the social consequences of race, but instead a way to sidestep the tenacity and complicated functioning of racialization in society. Thus, this type of *color-blind* logic of crime can actually harden socially forged bonds between race and crime even more.

BIO-CRIMINOLOGY AND RACE IN THE TWENTY-FIRST CENTURY

Since the turn of the twenty-first century, *biosocial criminology* has sought to resurrect the study of biology in American criminology.[6] Biosocial criminology is skeptical of traditional sociological theories of crime, and insists that sociological ideas of crime alone lack the empirical power to understand completely the underpinnings of crime. Traditional criminology theories are instead reframed through the language of genetics, neuroscience, and especially evolutionary biology to capture better the causes of crime (Beaver 2009; Beaver, Barnes, and Boutwell 2014a; Walsh and Beaver 2008).

Conversely, biosocial criminology faces much skepticism itself. The subdiscipline is often described as a renewed *Lombosian* project (Carrier and Walby 2014). Critics argue that biosocial criminology research promotes biological reductionism by advantaging the identification and pathologization of biological material as the most salient etiological agent of crime. Biosocial researchers do not outright dismiss social/environmental factors, but often center biological factors over sociological ones as the origin of crime in their models. This is demonstrated well through biosocial criminology writings about race and crime.

Biosocial criminology treats race as a biological trait—an innate marker of immutable distinction that evidences a person's susceptibility and probability of criminal behavior. Publications from some of the most influential biosocial criminologists mirror the illogical and dangerous conceptions of race promoted by past biocriminology, and illustrate the research program's utility as a racial project in the twenty-first century. For example, biosocial criminologists John P. Wright and Mark Morgan (2014) state that biosocial criminology, unlike more sociological-focused criminology, provides space to explore a biological understanding of race and its role in explaining differences in crime rates. The reason for this spate of biological theorizing was clear for Wright and Morgan (2014, 69), as they explain, "blacks, tend to have significantly higher levels of self-esteem, more narcissistic traits, and score significantly lower on measures of intelligence and intellectual functioning . . . [and] each of these phenotypes is moderately to highly heritable across all races but appear expressed more often in blacks."

This reading of race reflects biosocial criminology's affinity for evolutionary biology. Evolutionary conceptions of race, which have been thoroughly refuted, recapitulate the troublesome idea that race captures a natural hierarchical arrangement of ability, worth, and humanness, and most often places African ancestry at the bottom of this order. In this way, *Blackness* is rendered a pathology that self-perpetuates its own social inabilities. Wright's (2009, 151) article "Inconvenient Truths: Race and Crime" clearly establishes this viewpoint:

> Evolution provides a powerful mechanism to understand the development of human races and the distribution of traits and the behaviors within and across races. It helps explain why races would appear and under what condition races would appear. It helps to explain why certain traits would be beneficial and why these traits, such as higher IQ, would be unequally distributed across races. Moreover, evolutionary theory helps explain why race-based patterns of behavior are universal, such as Black over-involvement in crime. No other paradigm organizes these patterns better. No other paradigm can explain these inconvenient truths.

According to Wright, race has little to do with the aim of his essay on inconvenient truths. The goal is supposedly to defend the purest of truth and science. The idea is that science provides many "truths" about race that sociologists neglect to take up due to biased political ideologies and an obligation to social constructionism. However, Wright's treatise on race really seeks to shape what kinds of "truths" should matter in the study of crime. Moreover, this so-called pursuit for scientific truth is severely compromised by his use of evolutionary claims about race, heredity, and IQ, which have been debunked and discarded by contemporary genetic and anthropological research (Fuentes 2012; Gould 2006; Marks 2003).

Biosocial criminology's approach to race analysis is driven by a conservative racial ideology, and demonstrates what sociologist Ruha Benjamin (2015, 131) calls the "dexterity" of biological sciences. Biological sciences are not inherently racial or racist, but their diagnostic appeal empowers specific authoritative claims about group dynamics, boundaries, and value (Benjamin 2015). As such, the research program's promotion of biological race yields two vital consequences. First, the commitment to evolutionary ideas of crime helps frame race as a constituent element of criminality, which provides a sense of warrant for the fallacious claim that race is a valid and useful predictor of crime. Secondly, it places biosocial criminology in an authoritative position to excuse and even justify systemic racism and its effect on criminality in society.

Race as a Predictor of Crime

Biosocial criminologist Anthony Walsh argues for the usefulness of race as a predictor in models of crime. According to Walsh, evolution is the strongest indicator of behavior, and it causes specific cultural deficiencies that limit some groups' abilities to behave and achieve properly in society. Framing socially aberrant values as hereditary components is vital to the argument that race is a useful predictor of crime, as is evident in Walsh's (2004, 111, emphasis added) description of "parental versus mating efforts":

> Given the roots of the modern African American family in African practices, the experiences of slavery, and the persistently low Black sex ratio, it is difficult to see how inner-city mating strategies can be brought into conformity with the demands of modern society. To do so, however, is imperative if we are to see a decrease in Black crime rates. *Children born out of wedlock are both genetically and environmentally handicapped from the beginning.*

Walsh's assumption fuels conservative beliefs that trace the root cause of criminal behavior to the problematic culture of the African American family. This idea is not new, as it echoes the "culture of poverty" thesis of the late 1960s.[7] However, Walsh's idea that race produces crime may be even more dangerous because he filters it through a language of *biosociality*.[8]

Biosocial research attempts to mend the nature/nurture divide by focusing on the interaction of the biological and social factors for behavior and health. As Walsh (2004, x) states, "after all, our genes are our genes, and they are activated according to our needs as we confront environmental challenges." However, recent epigenetic research makes clear that genes do not simply respond to environments, but also respond to the cumulative effects of an array of social inequalities, including racism (See Meloni 2017). That is, genetic expression may also be interacting with the way we experience social ideologies and practices that push the effects of race under the skin. Walsh's view neglects the dynamic forces that make environmental spaces unequal or unequally experienced, and it closes off any reading of race as social practice. Therefore, Walsh's take on biosociality subverts a biosocial interactionist approach into a biological deterministic reprise, which simultaneously privileges biology (read biological race) as the preserver and transmitter of deleterious traits and reduces environments to simply by-products of an inferior genetic code.

In addition, other biosocial criminologists, who are ostensibly more agnostic in their analysis of race and crime, still assent to the usefulness of race as a predictor of crime. Biosocial criminology research on the correlation between the monoamine oxidase A (MAOA) gene and weapon use exemplify this problem. Using data from the National Longitudinal Study of Adolescent Health, biosocial criminologists Kevin Beaver and colleagues (2010) argue that young men with the low variant MAOA gene are more likely to join gangs and use weapons. Most of the population in the study self-identified as "white" and the authors state that race was not significant to the findings. However, in a more recent publication, Beaver, Barnes, and Boutwell (2014b) now find that race is a significant factor when looking at MAOA and shooting and stabbing behaviors. In this article, Beaver, Barnes, and Boutwell (2014b) contend that the 2-repeat allele of the MAOA gene influences shooting and stabbing behaviors that are *independent* of environment—a claim that seems to work against the biosocial philosophy promoted by the research program. The authors note that the 2-repeat allele of MAOA is the most significant predictor of criminal behavior, and in a somewhat predictable manner, they find that this rare allele is more common in African American young men. These findings raise questions about the utility of the gene in predicting shooting or stabbing behaviors, as the authors admit that the 2-repeat allele is extremely rare in the general population and present in less than six percent of the African American population.[9] Furthermore, and regardless of intent, the Beaver, Barnes, and Boutwell article reconstitutes a racialized vision of criminal risk, and reaffirms the use of race as a useful predictor of crime.

Erasing Racism

Biosocial criminology's employment of race, as a direct biological calculation of evolutionary progress and proxy measure for one's proclivity for bad social traits, also positions the research program to contest the role of racism in society. Walsh (2004, 71 emphasis added), for instance, calls racism a "distant past," explaining that:

> African Americans certainly had solid grounds for fearing white society in the past, and while a little paranoia may have served them well in former times, the current problem with conspiratorial rumors is not so much their falsity but in their role in perpetuating distrust between the races. . . . The rumors and sense of injustice they must generate, may lead to "Black rage" or "angry aggression" and to increase defiance of the "white man's" law. *It is this rejection of the law that has forged a subculture that embraces violence and celebrates ignorance, and that is what is eating at the soul of Black America.*

As a result, Walsh notes that racism is not the problem. Instead, he suggests that crime control should focus on the inheritance of faulty genes that place African American's at greater risk for criminal behavior. Walsh's logic both reframes disparities as a product of a group's own inability to assimilate properly into American society, and minimizes systemic forms of racism. Moreover, Walsh reduces the inability to achieve in society to subpar biological traits that give rise to pathological socio-cultural behaviors. This allows biosocial criminologists to tap into the larger social anxieties and attitudes about race, as a stable marker of group identity and worth, and use biological language to further naturalize the seemingly disparate differences between racial groups.

In a recent publication, Beaver, Wright, and DeLisi (2011) aim to challenge current research about the impacts of racism and student behavior by investigating how teachers evaluate the social skills of their African American students. The group finds no evidence that racism impacts how teachers evaluate academic or behavioral performances of African American students. They instead suggest that social skill deficits by African American children are the result of a greater (seemingly innate) propensity for antisocial behavior, inadequate parenting, disinterest in learning or attaining good grades, and an overall pattern of Black over-involvement of crime. At best, the article demonstrated that a teacher's official report of a student's social skills does not vary by race. However, the broader claim that there is "no evidence suggesting that teachers are biased against black students" is a reach.

The article does not capture the actions or attitudes of teachers (intentional or not) toward their students, or an appraisal of how students interpret or respond to such actions or emotions. Moreover, linking measurements of social skills to racial differences in behavioral problems, as the group does throughout the article, requires consideration of the way students are disciplined by their teachers, and not just an evaluation of behavior. Beaver's group admits that they did not have data on disciplinary sanctions, thus it is unclear how these teachers treat any of their students deemed to have disciplinary problems or if there were differences in these actions based on race. Thus, it is questionable if the article captures racism in any actual sense. Beaver and colleagues' article does not take a biosocial approach, but it does blame African American children, or their supposed prior or innate disciplinary problems, for any perceived discrimination they may experience in school. Ultimately, this explanation of African American behavior aligns seamlessly with the troublesome racialized findings outlined above from other biosocial criminology research.

THE BIOLOGIZATION OF POLICING

In this final section I return to the issue of *genetic* stop-and-frisk, or the collection of DNA during these problematic police encounters. Stop-and-frisk is a controversial, yet constitutionally legal, policing tactic that permits law enforcement officers to stop and detain individuals for questioning or search (Gelman, Fagan, and Kiss 2007; White and Fradella 2016).[10] The tactic is not new, but is the result of the 1968 *Terry v. Ohio* Supreme Court decision that ruled police officers, regardless of probable cause, have the authority to perform reasonable searches of individuals for safety reasons. However, stop-and-frisk tactics have come under increased scrutiny since the late 1980s due to links with racial profiling, especially in New York City. In 2013, *Floyd v. City of New York* ruled that the practice of stop-and-frisk by the city's police department violated the Fourth Amendment rights of

African American and Latinx populations. The court deemed stop-and-frisk unconstitutional in this capacity, and ordered that the tactic undergo drastic modification if it were to continue (Rosenfeld and Fornango 2017). As politicians, criminal justice officials, and researchers continue to wrestle with the fallout of this ruling, the state is now considering the formal adoption of the so-called *genetic* stop-and-frisk practice.

Genetic science has transformed the way police departments make and utilize identification in their investigations. National DNA forensic databases, like the Combined DNA Index System (CODIS), are composed of two different indexes, one that contains DNA evidence from crime scenes and another that stores the DNA profile of individuals who have been convicted or charged with crimes (Greely et al. 2006). Forensic scientists collect DNA samples from crime scenes or potential suspects to test against existing profiles and attempt to reveal or confirm the identification of the unknown sample. On the one hand, the expansion of forensic DNA databases assists in missing person cases, paternity and maternity testing, and victim identification. On the other hand, the adoption of genetic practices intensifies law enforcement's authority to monitor, search, and prosecute citizens.

The Expansion of Forensic Databases

Police departments' authority to collect DNA was expanded by the 2013 Supreme Court ruling in *Maryland v. King*. The ruling ostensibly authorized police departments to use collected DNA samples from a person charged, but not convicted, of one crime to test against DNA samples in unsolved crimes without warrant. DNA collection in this case was viewed as synonymous with existing protocols for identification like mugshots or fingerprints, yet the ruling opened the door for DNA to be used in "suspicion-less searches" for crimes that go far beyond the scope of identification (Joh 2013; New York Times Editorial Board 2013; Roth 2013). Following this ruling, there have been reports that some police departments have instructed their officers to stop and "ask" certain individuals, who are not suspected of criminal activity, for "volunteer" DNA samples (Murphy 2016). These samples are not eligible to be added to national DNA databases, but instead are added to privately run databases for the department or state. This troubling trend raises ethical concerns about collection tactics and the assemblage and usage of DNA databases.

Law enforcement officers wield a specific authority that, knowingly or not, can influence individuals to "volunteer" samples in order to avoid or minimize further stigmatization or punishment (Gordon 2013). In other words, providing DNA to prove one's innocence or identification may be interpreted as a demand, and not just a request. This is especially relevant in states along the southern border where politically charged policing practices have targeted immigrant groups for minor traffic violations to justify the collection of DNA (Murphy 2016). These are communities that have a history of mistrust for law enforcement, and it is not improbable to envision similar surveillance tactics being used in African American and other marginalized communities. Thus, it is justified to question the optics of volunteerism that are assumed through genetic stop-and-frisk.

Furthermore, the practice of collecting DNA during routine police encounters is compounded by the promise that advancements in genetic technologies will be able to rapidly collect and analyze DNA using portable handheld devices (Duster 2004; Jobling and Gill 2004). These devices would allow collected genetic information to be transmitted to central databases where it could be quickly compared against known DNA profiles. Portable DNA devices are not in official use at this time, but there is certainly a desire for these technologies to decrease the time needed to analyze and match DNA material. Sociologist Troy Duster (2004) notes that prototype devices have already been tested in the early 2000s by police departments in New York.[11] Duster agrees that these technologies may improve the efficacy of criminal DNA analysis, but he also warns that they will inevitably expand the potential for officers to target specific populations and resuscitate antiquated and dangerous ideas that link biological make-up to innate criminality. Indeed, Duster's caution seems to be justified given claims by some forensic scientists to identify the "race" of the forensic DNA samples.

The ability to detect race from forensic DNA material relies on new research about genetic ancestry. Bioethicist Pamela Sankar (2010, 49) remarks that forensic DNA uses genetic ancestry to "locate genotypes linked to ancestry and physical appearance, such as eye color, and uses these genotypes to assign race and predict appearance." These racial descriptors are utilized by police departments to help narrow searches for suspects, a practice that is not uncommon using other types of evidence. Race is much more than descriptions about eye or skin color. Therefore, commercial forensic companies, like now defunct *DNAWitness*, that promise to infer race from genetic material ignore the ways that such traits overlap racial classifications. This begs further investigation into the question that anthropologist Duana Fullwiley (2008) poses "can DNA 'witness' race?"

Genetic technologies that try to predict race provide a rationale for misguided biological understandings of race. The science of genetic ancestry uses biomarkers, such as Ancestry Informational Markers (AIMs), to identify and trace population frequencies of a person's genome to specific geographical regions (Fujimura and Rajagopalan 2011; Fullwiley 2007).[12] Supporters of this genetic technique are careful to note that ancestral frequencies are not race, but critics warn that genetic ancestry can give the impression that race is something located in genetic heritage and therefore operates as a proxy for race and ethnicity (Duster 2015; Fujimura and Rajagopalan 2011; Fullwiley

2007; Shim et al. 2014; Yudell et al. 2016). In the context of crime and violence, the threat of remaking race into a biological construct is even more pressing.

Forensic DNA *phenotyping*, as Sankar (2010) labels the practice, uses of ancestry research to reconstruct and naturalize the nexus between race and crime. In this way, DNA is not just a "silent witness" of criminal activity, but an active player in the reinforcement of difference via genes, a process that anthropologist Amade M'Charek (2008) argues is wholly based upon processes of racial classification. According to M'Charek (2008), attempts to reconstruct race through forensic DNA collapse distinctions between individual and group identity, which complicates the legal decision in *Maryland v. King* that defined DNA as another form of identification. While the Court's decision found the ability to makes claims about individual identity using DNA, it is now clear that such practices can also discursively map racial classifications onto DNA evidence. These concerns about DNA collection and interpretation should raise alarms about the use of this tactic in racially marginalized communities, yet New York State's debate about genetic stop-and-frisk adds an even more troubling layer of complexity to this story.

The ensuing debate in New York that some dubbed genetic stop-and-frisk is actually about the state's proposal to expand DNA collection and databases to *familial DNA*. Familial DNA raises interrelated concerns about privacy, surveillance, and identification, and importantly threatens to further instantiate a racialized vision of risky bodies and criminal communities. The forensic use of familial DNA operates in a slightly different way than traditional DNA. As noted above, the goal of DNA analysis in criminal investigations is identification, which relies on the premise that everyone's DNA is unique at distinct stretches known as short tandem repeats or STRs. U.S. crime labs concentrate on a set of thirteen STRs in order to match or eliminate an unidentified sample of DNA from crime scenes with a sample from a potential suspect (Greely et al. 2006). It is nearly impossible for two unrelated persons to share the same set of thirteen STRs. However, related individuals may share up to half of these markers, as is the case of first-degree relatives, and this is at the heart of the growing interest in familial DNA forensic searches (Greely et al. 2006).[13]

Familial DNA Searches

Familial searches look for *partial* matches between crime scene DNA and existing profiles from convicted individuals. A partial match implies that the DNA sample in question is from a first-degree relative (e.g., a sibling, child, or parent) of the convicted individual (Greely et al. 2006; Rohlfs et al. 2013). This evidence is then used to construct a list of potential suspects for the crime in question, meaning the DNA evidence becomes a lead to find a person who is outside the DNA database. Not all police departments use familial DNA searches—the practice is outlawed in Maryland and the District of Columbia—but the desire for better investigative leads has helped popularize this method as a more effective policing tactic. Moreover, the practice of identifying close relatives using familial DNA seems to work.

Rori Rohlfs and colleagues (2013) recently tested the efficacy of familial DNA protocol for California, one of the handful of states that uses the tactic. They find a high probability that the technologies will locate correct matches for crime scene DNA if a close relative's DNA profile is in the database. Nevertheless, the group also warns that the reliability of the familial searches is severely limited if the sampled DNA is matched to a more distant relative. Familial searches assume that partial matches denote a correlation between very close relatives, but it is possible that a more distant relative in the database may match the sample and be misidentified as a first-degree relative (Rohlfs et al. 2013). This compromises the confidence that police will find the right person, as the comprised list of suspects likely will be confined to first-degree relatives. Moreover, the practice of familial DNA searches expands the scope of such investigations to innocent family members, which disproportionally effects African American and Latinx communities because they are over-represented in national DNA databases (Duster 2004; Greely et al. 2006; Rohlfs et al. 2013).

The racial consequences of forensic genetics are complex and not always straightforward. For example, African Americans are most likely to be *both* targeted for forensic DNA databases and benefit from DNA exonerations— the use of forensic analysis to prove innocence of a crime. It is clear however, that both outcomes are the result of disproportional targeting of racially marginalized communities. African Americans make up less than thirteen percent of the US population, yet it is estimated that the group may account for up to forty percent of the DNA profiles in CODIS (Greely et al. 2006). This disparity is not simply the outcome of higher rates of criminal activity, but largely the result of systematically biased policing and judicial practices that profile, arrest, and incarcerate African American, Latinx, and poor individuals at an inequitable scale (Alexander 2010; Duster 2004; Loury 2008; Wacquant 2009).

DNA technologies and DNA databases are inextricable parts. If one piece of this puzzle is produced systematically through racist mechanisms it is logical to expect that the practice will at least help rationalize racially biased policing and at worst even intensify such behavior. Furthermore, the use of forensic DNA practices reignites questions about the biological basis of violence, and its racial import. Forensic DNA is unique because it is based on non-coding genetic regions, meaning it does not provide information about preexisting health conditions, mental state, or appearance. Therefore, it cannot be used to screen individuals for genetic biomarkers of crime, like the previous mentioned efforts with the MAOA gene. Yet, this has not prevented law enforcement departments from drawing racialized conclusions about the genetic material they use in criminal investigations, as mentioned above in the practice of DNA phenotyping.

In the debate about genetic stop-and-frisk in New York, the New York Civil Liberties Union (NYCLU) stresses similar concerns, along with other worries about privacy and the lack of oversight for both forensic labs and police departments handling forensic DNA (New York Civil Liberties Union 2017). Many states permit innocent individuals to remove their DNA from national and state databases, but it is often a convoluted and expensive process and the onus is usually placed upon the individual to initiate expungement (Joh 2015). These concerns led some legal scholars, like law professor Erin Murphy, to call for a ban on such genetic practices. Murphy (2010, 304) argues that:

> Familial searches should be forbidden because they embody the very presumptions that our constitutional and evidentiary rules have long endeavored to counteract: guilt by association, racial discrimination, propensity, and even biological determinism. They are akin to adopting a policy to collect and store the DNA of otherwise database-ineligible persons, solely because they share a blood relation with a convicted person, while deliberately sheltering similarly situated individuals from similar genetic exposure.

I agree that the expanding use of genetic DNA databases engenders greater challenges for individual privacy and normalizes racial profiling even further. Additionally, I argue that this process also biologizes race as it blurs the lines among societal representations of difference, American fears of crime and terror, and genetic identification. In this way, genetic-stop and frisk does not explicitly call for the biologization of racial crime, but it does articulate a need to control and manage risky (racialized) bodies as a commitment to social safety, freedom, and justice. DNA databases then, are part of a larger assemblage of criminal justice technologies that essentially help, in the words of historian Khalil Muhammad (2010), "write race into crime."

CONCLUSION

This chapter demonstrated how the making of risky criminal bodies reproduces racialization in our society. Genetic and neuroscientific technologies imbue a sense of authority and reliability, but can also help obscure the way "blackness" gets repurposed as an innate property of criminality in biological research. Legal scholar Dorothy Roberts (2010, 261) argues that we "cannot apply the same old sociocritiques or paste the same label of eugenics on contemporary biopolitics, nor can we uncritically assume that the new *biocit-*

izenship necessarily fosters individual life and choice and necessarily intervenes on the consequences of inequality, rather than legitimizing inequality." These thoughts echo the sentiment of Troy Duster, who has spent the last nearly thirty years emphasizing the consequences of the increasing molecularization of race. Following Roberts and Duster, this chapter demonstrated how the troublesome racial legacy of biological research on crime has been extended, in more discursive ways, through contemporary genetic and neuroscience research.

The revival of bio-criminology demonstrates the dangerous return of biological race in the study of criminality. This fallacious argument promotes race as a reliable biomarker for criminal and violent behavior; that is, a *real* criminal type exists along the supposed hierarchal axis of biological (racial) heritage. Importantly, however, biosocial criminology's logic of racial difference is *not* based on contemporary biological research, but antiquated evolutionary biology arguments that have been debunked. This research program represents a crude attempt to legitimize these well-worn biologic notions of race through the language of genetics and neuroscience. The purpose of this research program, at least in terms of race, is to promote a conservative criminology that minimizes the role of systemic racism in favor of individualized, and especially innate, causes of crime. This essentially targets racial bodies as the most suitable for criminality research, and thus rationalizes disproportionate and destructive criminal justice policies and practices toward African American and Latinx groups in U.S. society.

These new technoscientific practices have produced new types of race configurations that are made visible through the application of this biocriminological knowledge. That is, the contention that "being related to a convicted offender in itself suggests that a person is more likely to be a perpetrator of crime" helps justify, scientifically, the social value of racial profiling and stop-and-frisk techniques (Murphy 2012, 3). The role of forensic DNA poses a unique set of racial challenges. Existing policing practices affect the lives of African American, and Latinx, communities in prejudicial and unequal manners, which has led to a greater proportion of DNA profiles in our national forensic databases from these communities. This means when DNA matching "works," there is a greater likelihood that the suspect pool will target African Americans populations. This process does not make risky bodies, as much as it provides the forensic "proof" to justify some racial groups as more violent, dangerous, and/or at-risk. DNA databases, then, not only replicate racial disparities, but effectively help sanction such stratifications as an effective and convenient method to keep society safe.

There is no doubt that biological research will continue to play a role in ways we think about and approach crime and violence, as demonstrated by the recommitment to biological models of violence via genetic and neurologic biomarkers. Nevertheless, it is socially irresponsible to adopt biological research or technologies of crime in an uncritical manner given the historic role that such research has played in reinforcing deterministic, eugenic, and racial philosophies. Today's biological research builds upon the concept of *risk* to help minimize these hazards, but biomarkers of crime, like the MAOA gene, demonstrate how seemingly objective biological research can make and reinforce its own biopolitics. Such logics of criminality necessitate the need to expose the ways that biological approaches to crime repurpose race as biologic fact. Instead of elucidating the underpinnings of crime, biomarkers for crime simultaneously ascribe which and whose body requires discipline and management. The production of these biomarkers blind researchers to the deeply entangled social associations between race and violence that go to the very heart of the way crime research and prevention are performed and deemed valuable for society.

NOTES

1. The term *Latinx* is used here as a more intersectional and inclusive term for all genders of the population, in lieu of the masculine term *Latino* as a descriptor for the entire group.
2. Lombroso's theory of the "born criminal" was an extension of social Darwinist arguments of inherent inferiority. Lombroso argued that certain individuals were born with specific psychological traits (e.g., skull shape, skin tone, ear size) that supposedly marked their increased criminal propensity.
3. Michael Omi and Howard Winant (1994, 56) define racial projects as "simultaneously an interpretation, representation, or explanation of racial dynamics, and an effort to reorganize and redistribute resources along particular racial lines."
4. Biopolitics can be defined in a simplistic way as the governance of human society through the optimization, disciplining, and standardization of the body, or bodily measurements, and increasingly molecular processes (See: Agamben 1998; Foucault 1990; Lemke 2011; Rose 2007; Rabinow and Rose 2006).
5. Here I am drawing from Bonilla-Silva's (2006) influential book on the operation of color-blind racism in society, *Racism without Racists*.
6. Biosocial criminology's recognition as a contributing section in criminology and its presence at national criminology conferences has expanded, the number of undergraduate criminology textbooks devoted to the topic has increased, and there has been a steady rise in the number of undergraduate and graduate courses in biosocial criminology (DeLisi 2012; DeLisi and Piquero 2011; Wright and Cullen 2012).
7. The culture of poverty thesis essentially argued that poverty is self-perpetuating due to the individuals being subjected to such conditions (e.g., Moynihan report; Oscar Lewis 1966).
8. Biosocial research is attempts to mend the nature/nurture divide by focusing on the interaction of the biological and social factors for behavior and health.
9. The authors note that the research sample was limited to African Americans because of "low base rate of Caucasian males carrying the 2-repeat allele" (2014b, 262). The gene is said to be carried by 5.5 percent of African Americans. However, it is not clear how the authors estimate this distribution of the allele in the designated racial populations.
10. See also *Terry v. Ohio*, 392 U.S. 1 (1968) which ruled that regardless of probable cause, police officers have the authority to permit reasonable searches of individuals for safety reasons.
11. See also Batt et al. (2009), a summary of the grant application (Award Number: #2004-DN-BX-K001) for a DNA based hand-held forensic tool through the U.S. Department of Justice. It also documents their testing of a prototype device through the New York State Police Forensic Investigation Center in 2005.

12. Genetic ancestral testing has been popularized by commercial businesses that have promised to help reconstruct genealogical histories and unveil the true ethnic and racial makeup of their clients (See: Bolnick et al. 2007).

13. The exception here is identical twins, who do match at all thirteen markers because their genetic makeup is identical.

REFERENCES

Agamben, Giorgio. 1998. *Homo Sacer: Sovereign Power and Bare Life*. Translated by Daniel Heller-Roazen. 1 edition. Stanford, Calif: Stanford University Press.

Alexander, Michelle. 2010. *The New Jim Crow: Mass Incarceration in the Age of Colorblindness*. New York: The New Press.

Batt, Carl A., Scott J. Stelick, Matthew J. Kennedy, Clarissa S. Lui, and Adam J. Lowe. 2009. "A Hand-Held DNA-Based Forensic Tool." Grant Reward (Award # 2004-DN-BX-K001) 227499. Washington DC: US Department of Justice.

Beaver, Kevin M. 2009. *Biosocial Criminology: A Primer*. 1 edition. Kendall Hunt Publishing.

Beaver, Kevin M., J. C. Barnes, and Brian B. Boutwell. 2014a. *The Nurture Versus Biosocial Debate in Criminology: On the Origins of Criminal Behavior and Criminality*. SAGE Publications.

———. 2014b. "The 2-Repeat Allele of the MAOA Gene Confers an Increased Risk for Shooting and Stabbing Behaviors." *The Psychiatric Quarterly* 85 (3): 257–65. doi:10.1007/s11126–013–9287-x.

Beaver, Kevin M., Matt DeLisi, Michael G. Vaughn, and J. C. Barnes. 2010. "Monoamine Oxidase A Genotype Is Associated with Gang Membership and Weapon Use." *Comprehensive Psychiatry* 51 (2): 130–34. doi:10.1016/j.comppsych.2009.03.010.

Beaver, Kevin M., John Paul Wright, and Matt DeLisi. 2011. "The Racist Teacher Revisited: Race and Social Skills in a Nationally Representative Sample of American Children." In *Classrooms: Management, Effectiveness, and Challenges*, edited by Rebecca Newley, 115–32. New York, NY: Nova Publishers.

Benjamin, Ruha. 2015. "The Emperor's New Genes Science, Public Policy, and the Allure of Objectivity." *The ANNALS of the American Academy of Political and Social Science* 661 (1): 130–42. doi:10.1177/0002716215587859.

Blair, R. J. R. 2010. "Neuroimaging of Psychopathy and Antisocial Behavior: A Targeted Review." *Current Psychiatry Reports* 12 (1): 76–82. doi:10.1007/s11920–009–0086-x.

Bolnick, Deborah A., Duana Fullwiley, Troy Duster, Richard S. Cooper, Joan H. Fujimura, Jonathan Kahn, Jay S. Kaufman, et al. 2007. "The Science and Business of Genetic Ancestry Testing." *Science* 318 (5849): 399–400. doi:10.1126/science.1150098.

Bonilla-Silva, Eduardo. 2006. *Racism without Racists: Color-Blind Racism and the Persistence of Racial Inequality in America*. 2 edition. Lanham: Rowman & Littlefield Publishers.

Brunner, H. G., M. Nelen, X. O. Breakefield, H. H. Ropers, and BA van Oost. 1993. "Abnormal Behavior Associated with a Point Mutation in the Structural Gene for Monoamine Oxidase A." *Science* 262 (5133): 578–80. doi:10.1126/science.8211186.

Buckholtz, Joshua W., and Andreas Meyer-Lindenberg. 2008. "MAOA and the Neurogenetic Architecture of Human Aggression." *Trends in Neurosciences* 31 (3): 120–29. doi:10.1016/j.tins.2007.12.006.

Carrier, Nicolas, and Kevin Walby. 2014. "Ptolemizing Lombroso: The Pseudo-Revolution of Biosocial Criminology." *Journal of Theoretical and Philosophical Criminology* 6 (1): 1–45.

Caspi, Avshalom, Joseph McClay, Terrie E. Moffitt, Jonathan Mill, Judy Martin, Ian W. Craig, Alan Taylor, and Richie Poulton. 2002. "Role of Genotype in the Cycle of Violence in Maltreated Children." *Science (New York, N.Y.)* 297 (5582): 851–54. doi:10.1126/science.1072290.

Clarke, Adele E., Laura Mamo, Jennifer Ruth Fosket, Jennifer R. Fishman, and Janet K. Shim, eds. 2010. *Biomedicalization: Technoscience, Health, and Illness in the U.S.* Durham, NC: Duke University Press Books.

DeLisi, Matt. (2012). "Genetics: L'Enfant Terrible of Criminology:, in *Journal of Criminal Justice,* 40(6): 515-516. DOI: 10.1016/j.jcrimjus. 2012.08.002

DeLisi, Matt, & Piquero, Alex. R. (2011). New frontiers in criminal careers research, 2000–2011: A State-of-the-Art Review. *Journal of Criminal Justice, 39*(4), 289–301.

Duster, Troy. 2003a. *Backdoor to Eugenics.* New York, NY: Routledge.

———. 2003b. *Backdoor to Eugenics.* 2 edition. New York: Routledge.

———. 2004. "Selective Arrests, a DNA Forensic Database, and Phrenology." In *DNA and the Criminal Justice System: The Technology of Justice*, edited by David Lazer, 315–34. Cambridge, MA: MIT Press.

———. 2006a. "Behavioral Genetics and the Link between Crime, Violence, and Race." In , edited by Erik Parens, Audrey R. Chapman, and Nancy Press, 150–75. Baltimore: John Hopkins University Press.

———. 2006b. "Lessons from History: Why Race and Ethnicity Have Played a Major Role in Biomedical Research." *The Journal of Law, Medicine & Ethics* 34 (3): 487–96.

———. 2015. "A Post-Genomic Surprise. The Molecular Reinscription of Race in Science, Law and Medicine." *The British Journal of Sociology* 66 (1): 1–27. doi:10.1111/ 1468–4446.12118.

Fishbein, Diana. 2000. *Biobehavioral Perspectives on Criminology.* 1 edition. Australia ; Belmont, CA: Wadsworth Publishing.

Fleck, Ludwik. 1981. *Genesis and Development of a Scientific Fact.* Edited by Thaddeus J. Trenn and Robert K. Merton. Translated by Frederick Bradley. Chicago u.a: University of Chicago Press.

Foucault, Michel. 1990. *The History of Sexuality, Vol. 1: An Introduction.* Translated by Robert Hurley. Reissue edition. New York: Vintage.

Fuentes, Agustín. 2012. *Race, Monogamy, and Other Lies They Told You: Busting Myths about Human Nature.* Berkeley: University of California Press.

Fujimura, Joan H., and Ramya Rajagopalan. 2011. "Different Differences: The Use of 'genetic Ancestry' versus Race in Biomedical Human Genetic Research." *Social Studies of Science* 41 (1): 5–30.

Fullwiley, Duana. 2007. "The Molecularization of Race: Institutionalizing Human Difference in Pharmacogenetics Practice." *Science as Culture* 16 (1): 1–30. doi:10.1080/ 09505430601180847.

———. 2008. "Can DNA 'Witness' Race?: Forensic Uses of an Imperfect Ancestry Testing Technology." *Genewatch* 21 (3–4): 12–14.

Gabbidon, Shaun L., ed. 2015. *Criminological Perspectives on Race and Crime.* New York & London: Routledge.

Gelman, Andrew, Jeffrey Fagan, and Alex Kiss. 2007. "An Analysis of the New York City Police Department's 'Stop-and-Frisk' Policy in the Context of Claims of Racial Bias." *Journal of the American Statistical Association* 102 (479): 813–23. doi:10.1198/ 016214506000001040.

Gordon, Scott. 2013. "Drivers Stopped at Roadblock Asked for Saliva, Blood." *NBC 5 Dallas-Fort Worth*, November 18. http://www.nbcdfw.com/news/local/North-Texas-Drivers-Stopped-at-Roadblock-Asked-for-Saliva-Blood-232438621.html.

Gould, Stephen Jay. 2006. *The Mismeasure of Man.* W. W. Norton & Company.

Greely, Henry T., Daniel P. Riordan, Nanibaa' A. Garrison, and Joanna L. Mountain. 2006. "Family Ties: The Use of DNA Offender Databases to Catch Offenders' Kin." *The Journal of Law, Medicine & Ethics* 34 (2): 248–62. doi:10.1111/j.1748–720X.2006.00031.x.

Hawkins, Darnell F., ed. 2003. *Violent Crime: Assessing Race and Ethnic Differences.* Cambridge University Press.

Herrnstein, Richard J., and Charles Murray. 1996. *Bell Curve: Intelligence and Class Structure in American Life.* 1st Free Press pbk. ed edition. New York: Free Press.

Hirschi, T., and M. J. Hindelang. 1977. "Intelligence and Delinquency: A Revisionist Review." *American Sociological Review* 42 (4): 571–87.

Jasanoff, Sheila. 2004. "The Idiom of Co-Production." In *States of Knowledge: The Co-Production of Science and the Social Order*, edited by Sheila Jasanoff, 1–12. London & New York: Routledge.

Jobling, Mark A., and Peter Gill. 2004. "Encoded Evidence: DNA in Forensic Analysis." *Nature Reviews Genetics* 5 (10): 739–51. doi:10.1038/nrg1455.

Joh, Elizabeth E. 2013. "Maryland v. King: Policing and Genetic Privacy Term Paper." *Ohio State Journal of Criminal Law* 11: 281–94.

———. 2015. "Myth of Arrestee DNA Expungement." *University of Pennsylvania Law Review Online* 164: 51–60.

Krimsky, Sheldon, and Jeremy Gruber, eds. 2013. *Genetic Explanations: Sense and Nonsense*. Cambridge, MA: Harvard University Press.

Kuhn, Thomas S. 1996. *The Structure of Scientific Revolutions*. 3rd edition. Chicago, IL: University of Chicago Press.

Lea, Rod, and Geoffrey Chambers. 2007. "Monoamine Oxidase, Addiction, and The 'warrior' gene Hypothesis." *The New Zealand Medical Journal* 120 (1250): 5–10.

Lemke, Thomas. 2011. *Biopolitics: An Advanced Introduction*. Biopolitics. New York: NYU Press.

Lewis, Allison. 2017. "Don't Allow Genetic Stop-and-Frisk." News. *Newsday*. March 23. http://www.newsday.com/opinion/commentary/don-t-allow-genetic-stop-and-frisk-1.13302422.

Lewis, Oscar. (1966). "The Culture of Poverty." In G. Gmelch and W. Zenner, eds. *Urban Life*. Long Grove, IL: Waveland Press.

Lombroso, Cesare. 2006. *Criminal Man*. Translated by Mary Gibson and Nicole Hahn Rafter. Durham, NC: Duke University Press Books.

Loury, Glenn C. 2008. *Race, Incarceration, and American Values*. Cambridge, MA: The MIT Press.

Marks, Jonathan. 2003. *What It Means to Be 98% Chimpanzee: Apes, People, and Their Genes*. New Ed edition. Berkeley: University of California Press.

M'charek, Amade. 2008. "Silent Witness, Articulate Collective: DNA Evidence and the Inference of Visible Traits." *Bioethics* 22 (9): 519–28. doi:10.1111/j.1467–8519.2008.00699.x.

Meloni, Maurizio. 2017. "Race in an Epigenetic Time: Thinking Biology in the Plural." *The British Journal of Sociology*, March, n/a-n/a. doi:10.1111/1468–4446.12248.

Moynihan, Daniel P. (1965). *The Negro Family: The Case for National Action*, Washington, D.C., Office of Policy Planning and Research, U.S. Department of Labor.

Muhammad, Khalil Gibran. 2010. *The Condemnation of Blackness: Race, Crime, and the Making of Modern Urban America*. 1st THUS edition. Cambridge, Mass.: Harvard University Press.

Murphy, Erin E. 2010. "Relative Doubt: Familial Searches of DNA Databases." *Michigan Law Review* 109 (3): 291–348.

———. 2012. "Familial DNA Searches: The Opposing Viewpoint." *Criminal Justice*.

———. 2016. "DNA in the Criminal Justice System: A Congressional Research Service Report* (*From the Future*)." *UCLA Law Review Discourse* 64: 340–71.

New York Civil Liberties Union. 2017. "Comments Regarding Familial DNA Searching." *New York Civil Liberties Union*. February 15. https://www.nyclu.org/en/publications/comments-regarding-familial-dna-searching.

NY Times Editorial Board. 2013. "The Supreme Court Rules on DNA and Suspicionless Searches." *The New York Times*, June 3. http://www.nytimes.com/2013/06/04/opinion/the-supreme-court-rules-on-dna-and-suspicionless-searches.html.

Omi, Michael, and Howard Winant. 1994. *Racial Formation in the United States*. 2nd edition. New York: Routledge.

Pickersgill, Martyn. 2009. "Between Soma and Society: Neuroscience and the Ontology of Psychopathy." *BioSocieties* 4 (1): 45–60.

Rabinow, Paul, and Nikolas Rose. 2006. "Biopower Today." *BioSocieties* 1 (2): 195–217.

Rafter, Nicole. 2008. *The Criminal Brain: Understanding Biological Theories of Crime*. New York: NYU Press.

Raine, Adrian. 1993. *The Psychopathology of Crime: Criminal Behavior as a Clinical Disorder*. 1st edition. San Diego, CA: Academic Press.

———. 2008. "From Genes to Brain to Antisocial Behavior." *Current Directions in Psychological Science* 17 (5): 323–28.

Richardson, Sarah S., and Hallam Stevens. 2015. *Postgenomics: Perspectives on Biology after the Genome*. Duke University Press.

Roberts, Dorothy. 2010. "Race and the New Biocitizen." In *What the Use of Race?: Modern Governance and the Biology of Difference*, edited by Ian Whitmarsh and David S. Jones, 259–76. Cambridge, MA: MIT Press.

Rohlfs, Rori V., Erin Murphy, Yun S. Song, and Montgomery Slatkin. 2013. "The Influence of Relatives on the Efficiency and Error Rate of Familial Searching." *PLOS ONE* 8 (8): e70495. doi:10.1371/journal.pone.0070495.

Rollins, Oliver E. 2014. "Unlocking the Violent Brain: A Sociological Analysis of Neuroscience Research on Violent and Aggressive Behaviors." Dissertation, San Francisco, CA: University of California, San Francisco.

Rose, Nikolas. 2000. "The Biology of Culpability:: Pathological Identity and Crime Control in a Biological Culture." *Theoretical Criminology* 4 (1): 5–34.

———. 2007. *The Politics of Life Itself: Biomedicine, Power, and Subjectivity in the Twenty-First Century*. Princeton: Princeton University Press.

———. 2010. "'Screen and Intervene': Governing Risky Brains." *History of the Human Sciences* 23 (1): 79–105. doi:10.1177/0952695109352415.

Rosenfeld, Richard, and Robert Fornango. 2017. "The Relationship Between Crime and Stop, Question, and Frisk Rates in New York City Neighborhoods." *Justice Quarterly*, January, 1–21. doi:10.1080/07418825.2016.1275748.

Roth, Andrea. 2013. "Maryland v. King and the Wonderful, Horrible DNA Revolution in Law Enforcement." *Ohio State Journal of Criminal Law* 11: 295–309.

Rowe, David C. 1986. "Genetic and Environmental Components of Antisocial Behavior: A Study of 265 Twin Pairs*." *Criminology* 24 (3): 513–32. doi:10.1111/j.1745-9125.1986.tb00388.x.

Rushton, J. Philippe. 1995. *Race, Evolution, and Behavior: A Life History Perspective*. Transaction Publishers.

Sankar, Pamela. 2010. "Forensic DNA Phenotyping: Reinforcing Race in Law Enforcement." In *What the Use of Race?: Modern Governance and the Biology of Difference*, edited by Ian Whitmarsh and David S. Jones, 49–61. Cambridge, MA: MIT Press.

Shim, Janet K, Katherine Weatherford Darling, Martine D Lappe, L Katherine Thomson, Sandra Soo-Jin Lee, Robert A Hiatt, and Sara L Ackerman. 2014. "Homogeneity and Heterogeneity as Situational Properties: Producing—and Moving beyond?—Race in Post-Genomic Science." *Social Studies of Science* 44 (4): 579–99.

Silverstein, Jason. 2012. "Stop and Frisk—and DNA Test?" *Huffington Post*. June 22. http://www.huffingtonpost.com/jason-silverstein/stop-and-frisk-and-dna-te_b_1608350.html.

Simon, Jonathan. 2006. "Positively Punitive: How the Inventor of Scientific Criminology Who Died at the Beginning of the Twentieth Century Continues to Haunt American Crime Control at the Beginning of the Twenty-First." *Texas Law Review* 84: 2135–72.

Singh, Ilina, and Nikolas Rose. 2009. "Biomarkers in Psychiatry." *Nature* 460 (7252): 202–7. doi:10.1038/460202a.

Spallone, Pat. 1998. "The New Biology of Violence: New Geneticisms for Old?" *Body & Society* 4 (4): 47–65. doi:10.1177/1357034X98004004003.

Strimbu, Kyle, and Jorge A. Tavel. 2010. "What Are Biomarkers?" *Current Opinion in HIV and AIDS* 5 (6): 463–66. doi:10.1097/COH.0b013e32833ed177.

Wacquant, Loïc. 2009. *Punishing the Poor: The Neoliberal Government of Social Insecurity*. First edition, Paperback issue edition. Durham NC: Duke University Press Books.

Walsh, Anthony. 2004. *Race and Crime: A Biosocial Analysis*. Hauppauge, NY: Nova Publishers.

Walsh, Anthony, and Kevin M. Beaver, eds. 2008. *Biosocial Criminology: New Directions in Theory and Research*. 1 edition. New York: Routledge.

White, Michael D., and Henry F. Fradella. 2016. *Stop and Frisk: The Use and Abuse of a Controversial Policing Tactic*. NYU Press.

Whitford, Emma. 2017. "New York Is Considering 'Genetic Stop and Frisk' DNA Testing Policy." *Gothamist*. April 13. http://gothamist.com/2017/04/13/dna_testing_genetics.php.

Wright, John P. 2009. "Inconvenient Truths: Race and Crime." In *Biosocial Criminology: New Directions in Theory and Research*, edited by Anthony Walsh and Kevin M. Beaver, 137–57. New York: Routledge.

Wright, John. P., & Cullen, Francis. T. (2012). "The Future of Biosocial Criminology: Beyond Scholars' Professional Ideology." *Journal of Contemporary Criminal Justice* 28, 237–253.

Wright, John P., and Mark A. Morgan. 2014. "Human Biodiversity and the Egalitarian Fiction." In *The Nurture Versus Biosocial Debate in Criminology: On the Origins of Criminal Behavior and Criminality*, edited by Kevin M. Beaver, J. C. Barnes, and Brian B. Boutwell. Thousand Oaks, California: SAGE Publications, Inc.

Yudell, Michael, Dorothy Roberts, Rob DeSalle, and Sarah Tishkoff. 2016. "Taking Race out of Human Genetics." *Science* 351 (6273): 564–65. doi:10.1126/science.aac4951.

Chapter Six

Racialized School Discipline and the School-to-Prison Pipeline

Thomas J. Mowen

Over the past few decades, scholars, teachers, policymakers, and members of the general public have become concerned with issues related to school safety and security (Addington 2009). Although all indicators demonstrate that schools have never been safer for teachers, students, and parents than they are today (Robers et al. 2016; see also Kupchik 2010, 2016), this same body of scholarship also demonstrates that schools have taken a very punitive turn toward the management of student misbehavior and student safety. As Hirschfield (2008) finds, school discipline has become "criminalized." Security measures including armed police, metal detectors, and drug sniffing dogs are becoming increasingly present within the hallways of schools in the United States (Robers et al. 2016). Not coincidentally, the use of punitive discipline—namely, in- and out-of-school suspensions and expulsions—has also been on the rise. Combined with research demonstrating that youth who are punished in school are far more likely to come into contact with the criminal justice system (Fabelo et al. 2011; Mowen and Brent 2016) there has been increased attention given to understanding, and preventing, the so-called school-to-prison pipeline (STPP). The school-to-prison pipeline refers to the phenomenon in which youth who are excluded from school find themselves at an increased risk of being arrested, adjudicated, and placed in prison than youth who are not excluded from school regardless of criminal involvement or delinquent offending.

While these trends are troubling for a variety of reasons, the impact of this punitive turn in school discipline is felt disproportionately by the more marginalized members of society: primarily poor and working-class, male, racial/ethnic minority students and their families (Irwin et al. 2013; Kupchik

2010; Losen and Martinez 2013; Morris, 2013; Skiba et al. 2002; Townsend 2000). At nearly every turn in this process, Black students in particular are likely to receive more punitive punishment, be punished more frequently, and—consequently—be more likely to experience collateral consequences such as dropping out of school or becoming enmeshed within the formal criminal justice system compared to their white counterparts (Ferguson 2001; Rios 2011; Welch and Payne 2010). Beyond affecting the student, these significant patterns of inequity also differentially affect Black and working-class families and communities.

This chapter reviews many of the theoretical explanations for the existing inequality in school discipline, and thus the school-to-prison pipeline, including racial threat and understanding school discipline as a reflection of broader trends in criminal justice and punishment in the United States. In conceptualizing the school-to-prison pipeline this way, understanding why the STPP impacts poor, Black males more than other demographics of society is—unfortunately—far from surprising. As a result of these trends, there are a host of individual- and structural-level outcomes reviewed in this chapter. Finally, this chapter concludes by positing some ways in which the inequality in school may be reduced, and the school-to-prison pipeline diverted.

TRENDS IN SCHOOL DISCIPLINE

Prior to exploring the inequality in school discipline and the school-to-prison pipeline, it is useful to explore both the historical and contemporary landscape of school discipline in the United States. School discipline and school security measures are two distinct components that, together, represent a school's approach to maintaining student safety. School security measures include specific apparatus and personnel used within the school such as police officers and metal detectors (Kupchik 2010). School discipline, on the other hand, refers to measures taken within the school to discipline and punish student misbehavior; primarily, the use of school exclusions such as in- and out-of-school suspensions and expulsions.

How Did We Get Here?

Prior to the 1950s, most middle-class white citizens viewed the public school system as an inclusive system of education (Phaneuf 2009), and concern for safety issues was minor. However, moving into the late 1950s and early 1960s, highly publicized social events such as the Vietnam War and the Civil Rights movement brought issues of violence and perceived disrespect for the existing social order into the center of public discourse. These events ushered in concern over problematic behavior in the public schooling system (Phaneuf 2009). The 1970s and 1980s saw the emergence of the "War On" initiatives and brought about increasing concern about gangs and drugs in the hallways of American schools (Casella 2006). As a result of these trends, schools began to adopt harsh disciplinary measures and policing mechanisms to maintain a "safe" school (Casella 2006).

Although there is not one specific event that led to the criminalization of school discipline, the Gun-Free Schools Act of 1994 led to mandatory punishment for certain infractions. For example, this act required that any student found with a weapon in school was subjected to a one year out-of-school suspension. While well intentioned, this policy—along with others—led to the criminalization of much more benign behavior (Skiba and Noam 2002) being targeted, discussed at greater length later on. What is clear, however, is that the contemporary landscape of school discipline is highly punitive.

Contemporary Landscape

Since the 1990s, the use of school security measures in public schools across the United States has increased exponentially. For example, in the 1999–2000 school year, approximately 19 percent of all public schools in the United States reported using security cameras to monitor student behavior. By the 2013–2014 school year, about 75 percent of all public schools reported using security cameras to monitor student behavior. Likewise, about 75 percent of all public schools controlled access to the school building during school hours in 1999–2000, but by 2013–2014 this number had increased to about 94 percent. Similar trends hold for the use of drug-sniffing dogs, armed security, and metal detectors (Robers et al. 2016) whereby public schools have seen significant increases in the use of these measures over time. In addition, schools are increasingly using police officers, often called School Resource Officers (SROs) in the hallways of K-12 schools to respond to, and manage, student behavior (Robers et al. 2016).

Like the use of school security measures, the use of school disciplinary measures has also increased. The current approach taken by many schools is often referred to as "zero tolerance," a term which refers to the orientation that discipline is "intended primarily as a method of sending a message that certain behaviors will not be tolerated, by punishing all offenses severely, no matter how minor" (Skiba and Noam 2002, 20). Unfortunately, zero tolerance policies have resulted in student's receiving punishment for normal childhood behavior such as play fighting, arriving late to class, or failing to wear a belt or tuck in a shirt (Fuentes 2011; Morris 2012). To this end, Kupchik (2010) finds, "When a punishment seems unfair, an administrator can hide behind the cloak of zero tolerance, as if he or she has no choice but to suspend or expel a student when really the administrator chose to prescribe such harsh punishments" (200). In other words, zero tolerance policies call for excessively harsh punishment to be used under the guise of "equality" (Skiba and Noam 2002). Like broader social trends, there is nothing "equal" concerning the distribution of school punishment across racial, ethnic, and social class boundaries.

In terms of trends in school discipline, Losen et al. (2015) find that about 3.5 million students in public schools across the United States are suspended each year. To place this into perspective, more students between grades K-12 are suspended each year than the entire number of high school seniors in the United States. Additionally, Schollenberger (2015) estimates that about one in three students will be suspended at some point between kindergarten and graduation from high school. To place within the historical context, suspension rates—mirroring broader punitive trends in crime control within the criminal justice system—increased sharply following the 1970s and remain near a record high (Losen et al. 2015).

Discipline and Security: Not Applied Equally

The use of school security measures and discipline, though increasing broadly, varies across important social contexts. For example, schools with higher percentages of low-income students report much more use of strict dress codes, school uniforms, and student picture IDs (Robers et al. 2016). Likewise, research has also demonstrated that schools with greater proportions of Black, and to a lesser degree Hispanic, students are significantly more likely to use more invasive types of school security, and greater numbers of school security measures (Mowen and Parker 2017). As Welch and Payne (2010) demonstrate, schools with greater proportions of Black—and to a lesser extent Hispanic—students are far less likely to respond to student misbehavior restoratively.

In a similar manner to the relationship between the racial/ethnic composition of the student body and the use of school security measures, the use of school discipline varies by race and ethnicity, too. For example, according to the 2014 civil rights data collection report by the U.S. Department of Education Office of Civil Rights, rates of suspension for Black youth are three times higher than rates for white youth; about 5 percent of white youth are suspended each year across the United States, while 16 percent of Black youth are suspended each year across all grades. This pattern holds for both males and females, though males are much more likely to be suspended in the first place (U.S. Department of Education Office for Civil Rights 2014). Removing elementary schools from this, in examining just middle- and high-schools, the racial gap in discipline is considerably larger and has gotten worse over time. For example, a report by the UCLA Civil Rights Project (Losen and Martinez 2013) indicates that inequality in suspension between Black and white students has nearly tripled in the few decades.

Mirroring trends in suspension, Black students are also disproportionately referred to law enforcement and arrested within the school at rates much higher than white students (U.S. Department of Education Office for Civil Rights 2014).

This body of research taken together provides for a number of firm conclusions about the relationship between school punishment and race. Although all students are affected by increases in punitive school disciplinary policy, like other aspects of the criminal justice system, the criminalization of school discipline has resulted in unequal outcomes. First, Black students are disproportionately targeted by school disciplinary policies (e.g., Kupchik 2010; Rios 2011). Black students are more likely to be suspended, expelled, and arrested compared to white students (Losen and Martinez 2013; Schollenberger 2015). Second, security measures are far more likely to be used in schools with greater proportions of Black students (e.g., Mowen and Parker 2017). Finally, although youth who experience punitive discipline all have the potential to experience negative outcomes, because Black students are more likely to receive punitive discipline, they are also more likely than students of any other race/ethnicity to experience negative outcomes as a result.

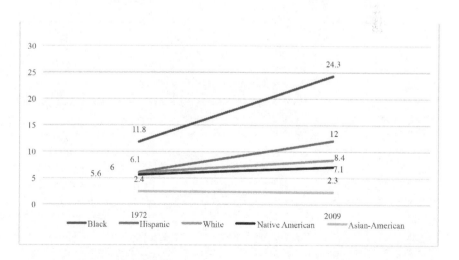

Figure 6.1.   Percent of students suspended by race/ethnicity between 1972 and 2009 (public middle and high schools). Graphic courtesy of the author. Data used to create the graph was taken from Losen and Martinez (2013, 1).

THEORETICAL EXPLANATIONS

Scholars have turned to a number of theoretical orientations to understand these trends. The simplest explanation for understanding why such disparate rates in punishment, discipline, and arrest within schools between racial/ethnic categories exist is that Black youth are much more criminal and delinquent than youth of other races and ethnicities. As with any simple explanation for a complex social phenomenon, this is, of course, simply wrong. In fact, rates of offending and delinquency are approximately equal across all racial/ethnic categories (Huizinga and Elliott 1986; Rocque and Paternoster 2011). As a result, differences in offending across racial categories cannot be the answer because no observable difference exists. Instead, scholars point to understanding trends in school punishment within the broader criminal justice system, and often apply the racial threat perspective.

The racial threat hypothesis asserts that members of the dominant class in society will wield their social and political power to control members of minority groups (Blalock 1967). More specifically, the threat presented by racial and ethnic minorities to whites must be met with economic and political sanctions and increased mechanisms of social control. From this perspective, the criminal justice system becomes a function of this threat and is then wielded as a tool to maintain and perpetuate existing inequalities along racial and ethnic boundaries. Although typically applied to understand police use of force or discretion (e.g., Stewart et al. 2009) or political/economic resources within police departments (e.g., Holmes et al. 2008), the racial threat hypothesis can be used to explain the disparate rates of school discipline and punishment across racial and ethnic lines. Recall, the "criminalization" of school discipline (Hirschfield 2008) has reoriented school discipline to the domain of the criminal justice system and school responses to student misbehavior are now much more in-line with the punitive nature of the criminal justice system than with traditional methods of school discipline.

Welch and Payne (2010) applied the racial threat hypothesis to explore racial inequality in school discipline. The authors found that schools with higher proportions of Black students were "more likely to use punitive and extremely punitive discipline, more likely to implement zero tolerance policies, and less likely to use mild and restitutive approaches" (40). Further, these findings remain even when school delinquency, drug use, perceptions of safety, and victimization are controlled. In other words, findings point to the fact that schools serving Black children are far more punitive in their approach to discipline *irrespective of actual issues of crime and safety.* Other research mirrors this finding as schools with more racial and ethnic minority youth are also likely to have security-based practices and more punitive forms of school discipline (see Irwin et al. 2013; Kupchik and Ward 2013; Mowen and Parker 2017; Payne and Welch 2010).

Another fruitful perspective in understanding the racial/ethnic differences in the application of school discipline concerns broader trends within the criminal justice system. Highlighting this connection, Ferguson (2001) finds in her book *Bad Boys: Public Schools in the Making of Black Masculinity*:

> Schools mirror and reinforce the practices and ideological systems of other institutions in the society. The racial bias in the punishing systems of the school reflects the practices of the criminal justice system. . . . Images of black male criminality and the demonization of black children play a significant role in the framing actions and events in the justice system (231).

From this perspective, school discipline has become "criminalized" (Hirschfield 2008) and responses to the control of citizens mirrors broader trends and "get tough" policies (Garland 2001). For example, Simon's (2007) *Governing through Crime* asserts that politicians draw from fears and insecurities in modern society and, as Ferguson (2001) highlights above, paint vivid pictures of the Black male as a looming and threatening figure. Like the massive inequalities in incarceration (Glaze and Kaeble 2016), Black male youth are subjected to the outcomes of these practices and policies. As a result, even the *potential* of violence to occur in schools has overwhelmed fearful teachers and members of the public to allow school discipline to— essentially—operate as a branch of the criminal justice system (Hirschfield 2008; Kupchik 2010). All youth, but particularly Black and working-class males, are viewed less as students and more as potential criminals. As Rios (2011) asserts, schools "systematically treat disadvantaged youth's everyday behaviors as criminal activity" (xiv). This finding mirrors the work of Ferguson (2001) as she finds that "bad boys" are constructed through school practices and reading of Black male bodies. Moreover, when Black males "act out" this behavior is seen as threatening while similar behavior by white males is seen as "boys being boys" (Ferguson 2001). Overall, this argument asserts that instead of developing pro-social solutions to modern day issues faced by schools, schools have instead enlisted criminal justice tactics to manage behavioral issues of students, particularly disadvantaged and marginalized youth (Ferguson 2001; Rios 2011).

Minority threat and broader trend perspectives on inequalities in school discipline are not incommensurate; in fact, they are two sides of the same coin. The portrait of the Black male as threatening occurs in both, and both perspectives understand schools as mechanisms of social control; essentially outgrowths of the criminal justice system. Unfortunately, the reality is, of course, that many racial and ethnic minority students' experiences are far different than their white counterparts and these differences mirror broader trends in inequality within the formal criminal justice system. The "criminal-

ization" of school discipline necessitates racial inequality in disciplinary outcomes.

OUTCOMES

As a result of the ascendancy of punitive school punishment and crime control, there are a number of important outcomes that affect all youth. For
example, punitive school discipline places the student at risk of dropping out
of school (Losen and Martinez 2013), and negatively impacts academic performance (Gottfredson et al. 2005). Increased levels of school security have
been shown to relate to lower levels of extracurricular participation among
students (Mowen and Manierre 2017), and high security environments can
contribute to less positive school environments (Lyons and Drew 2006).
Punitive school discipline can lead to feelings of frustration and anger; especially when individuals view the discipline as being motivated by racial bias
(see Kupchik 2016). Although rates of suspension disproportionately impact
Black males, emerging research has also explored the effects of discipline on
Black females. For example, Black females are often perceived as "loud" and
"assertive" (Morris 2012), and likely to be punished for failing to conform to
traditional gender roles expected of female youth (see also Blake et al. 2011).

In addition to the negative outcomes for students, there are also implications at the school level. For example, schools with higher levels of punishment actually report higher levels of disorder and delinquency (Way 2011).
This suggests that a punitive atmosphere within the school may actually
encourage students to act out. More punitively oriented schools also tend to
have lower test scores and higher dropout rates than schools with lower
levels of punitive discipline (Gottfredson et al. 2005). And yet, these policies
and practices have not resulted in schools that are any more or less safe than
they would be without these policies (Skiba and Peterson 2000). But what is
often lost in this growing conversation is that these effects are not equal; they
disproportionately impact working-class, racial, and ethnic minorities.

In addition to negative outcomes for the school and the individual student,
an emerging body of scholarship has demonstrated that school discipline
moves beyond impacting the student. For example, research has shown that
schools with armed security have parents who are less involved than schools
without armed security (Mowen 2015). Additionally, Kupchik (2016) documents the collateral consequences of school discipline on parents and families. In interviewing mostly single, poor, Black mothers in Mobile, Alabama,
Kupchik (2016) explores significant issues caused by school discipline.
These "collateral consequences" resulted in some parents losing their jobs,
experiencing an inability to care for their child and other ripple-effects within
the family. Single, working-class Black mothers felt angry, persecuted, and

victimized by punitive-school discipline and most of them believed their children (primarily Black males, but also Black females) were targeted because of their race. One parent likened her experiences in trying to advocate for her child to post-traumatic stress disorder. She finds:

> It's traumatizing . . . It's . . . You know when they were on the *Today Show* . . . they were talking about the soldiers and post-traumatic stress. When you go through it from year to year just dealing with the [school system] it's almost like you feel almost like a post-traumatic stress type of thing. I have been so stressed out . . . I cut my hair off because my hair would just come out. Your nerves, you know . . . When I went back into school, I just, you couldn't see it but I was just a nervous wreck. I never thought in a hundred years I'd have to endure this just to have her [the child] educated (Kupchik 2016, 66).

Overall, what this research demonstrates is that the impact of school discipline moves beyond the child and can impact the family. Although white parents, particularly working-class white parents, may experience similar frustrations and outcomes, Kupchik's (2016) work further demonstrates that families who are most likely to be victimized by school policies and the criminalization of school discipline are the very families who lack the resources to combat these issues: poor, racial/ethnic minorities. This experience is in stark contrast to the middle-class white experience within schools (see Lareau 2003). Not coincidentally, Noguera (2003) highlights, "as a 'captured market' they [poor individuals] are a group of consumers who are compelled to accept the quality of educational services provided to them, whether they like it or not" (94).

SCHOOL-TO-PRISON PIPELINE

Perhaps more so than any other issue related to school discipline, the school-to-prison pipeline (STPP) has received significant attention in recent years. The school-to-prison pipeline refers to a process in which youth who are punished in schools are increasingly likely to find themselves in contact with the formal criminal justice system (Skiba et al. 2014). This can occur through multiple avenues. For example, students who are punished in school are far more likely to drop out of school than those who are not punished (Fabelo et al. 2011). School dropouts are, in turn, far more likely to be arrested and/or incarcerated. As a result, we can trace the arrest/incarceration of the youth—at least in part—back to school punishment and thus, we see a school-to-prison pipeline emerge. Although this example is simplistic, situations like this have led many researchers and policymakers to wonder what would happen if students who misbehave in school were kept in school and given resources in order to correct the misbehavior as opposed to simply being met with punishment. That is, criminalized school discipline diverts students from school-based forms of rehabilitative justice into the more punitively oriented criminal justice system. There are two other non-mutually exclusive examples of the school-to-prison pipeline that contemporary research has observed: research on labeling theory, and research on the role of police in schools.

Labeling theory suggests that individuals often behave the way they are treated. For example, from a labeling perspective, youth who are punished in schools may be treated differently by school staff and even classmates, family, and members of law enforcement. In turn, the youth is presented with an undesirable label as a troublemaker or delinquent and may come to both *act* as the label and/or be *treated* like the label. For example, in analyzing four waves of the National Longitudinal Survey of Youth (1997), my own research has shown that youth who are suspended in school are placed at a significantly higher odds of arrest over time (Mowen and Brent 2016). In fact, each year a student experiences an arrest contributes to a significant increase in the probability that they will eventually be arrested regardless of levels of offending. Thus, there is a direct link between school suspension and involvement with the criminal justice system not explained by rates of offending alone. Other research has shown that students who are disciplined in school are more likely to drop out of school (Fabelo et al. 2011). These experiences can create a series of cumulative experiences that can drastically alter the life experiences of the youth (Laub and Sampson 2003).

From the labeling perspective, these research projects demonstrate that school discipline can serve as a "turning point" in the life of the youth (see Laub and Sampson 2003) whereby school discipline changes the path that the youth was on. In this case, school discipline acts as a turning point by directing the youth out of school and into the criminal justice system because of harsh school discipline. Thus, school discipline—a form of punishment— leads to more punishment in the form of arrest (Mowen and Brent 2016) and thus, the school-to-prison pipeline. But it is important to remember that at every step of this process, Black youth are far more likely to find themselves experiencing more punishment than white youth. As a result, the STPP is inherently tied to racialized school discipline.

In addition to labeling perspectives on school discipline, research also finds a much more direct school-to-prison pipeline link: school resource officers. SROs are becoming increasingly used in schools across the United States. SROs are formal police officers with the full authority of their agency (generally the local police department). Initially designed to operate as teachers, counselors, and law enforcement officers, research has found that SROs function far more as law enforcement officials than anything else (Schlosser 2014). As with other aspects of school discipline, SROs are far more likely to arrest Black and racial/ethnic minority students than white students (Nelson and Lind 2015; see also Wolf 2013). For example, in examining rates of arrest in New York City public schools, research shows that Black students are fourteen times more likely (and Hispanic students five times more likely) to be arrested for school-based issues than white students (New York City School-Justice Partnership Task Force 2013) despite no evidence that Black students offend more than students of any other race or ethnic background. Looking more broadly, Black students make up about 31 percent of all arrests in public schools across the United States, making them subject to significant disparities in arrest (United States Department of Education Office for Civil Rights 2015).

As a result of these trends, scholars have turned their attention to understand why placing police in schools exacerbates the school-to-prison pipeline. One study found that SROs use their power of arrest to arrest students for minor misbehavior, and will even arrest a student in order to "calm them down" (see Wolf 2013, 143–144). Other research has shown that schools with SROs report arresting students for "disorderly conduct" at rates five times higher than schools without SROs despite no evidence to suggest that these schools have any difference in rates of crime or disorder (Theriot 2009). This clearly creates a school-to-prison pipeline because when SROs arrest students, the students become subjected to the juvenile justice system. SROs funnel students out of school-based discipline into the hands of the criminal justice system.

More research on the school-to-prison pipeline is needed. But what remains clear is that the criminalization of school discipline has created this phenomenon in which youth are increasingly viewed and managed as criminals. As a result, the use of punitive disciplinary measures pushes students into the formal criminal justice system and, because school discipline is inherently unequal, punishes Black and Hispanic students much more than white students.

Can the "Pipeline" be Diverted?

Fortunately, concerned citizens and individuals impacted by the school-to-prison pipeline are making strong efforts to change these outcomes. For example, spurred on by the community-based advocacy organization *Padres y Jovenes*, the Denver Public School District and the Denver Police Department signed an Intergovernmental agreement in 2013 (Intergovernmental Agreement 2013). This effort grew out of citizens' concerns about the increasing use of arrest within the hallways of schools in Denver, and the disproportionate number of Hispanic males who found themselves funneled out of the school and into the police station. This agreement restricts the abilities of SROs to make arrests in schools, reserving arrest only for very serious offenses. It also provides parents with certain rights within this process. Further, this IGA requires community meetings between the SROs and community stakeholders. Instead of arresting and charging students for normal childhood behavior—like truancy or dress code violations—SROs are, instead, required to de-escalate the situation.

More broadly, the Department of Education has recently outlined a number of training objectives that SROs should adhere to in order to reduce the school-to-prison pipeline. SROs must be able to distinguish minor issues from major threats to the school, understand how to interact with both students and school personnel, learn and use conflict resolution and appropriate crisis management, understand civil rights and special education issues as they relate to students, and place an emphasis on restorative discipline. These recommendations are important—especially as the institutions of education and criminal justice continue to overlap more and more. More broadly, what is often left out of the conversation is that there is no evidence at all the SROs increase school safety. There is, however, ample evidence outlining the negative consequences of having SROs in schools, including racial inequality in arrest rates. Perhaps we would benefit from stepping back and asking if SROs should be used at all.

In addition to the steps outlined above, there has also been an increased awareness of the racial inequality in school discipline broadly, and the STPP specifically. For example, in 2014, the Department of Education released a "Dear Colleague" letter, published jointly with the Department of Justice, concerned with issues of racial inequity in school discipline (Department of Education 2014). In reference to a study performed by the Office of Civil Rights under the Department of Education, the letter finds, "For example, in our investigations we have found cases where African-American students were disciplined more harshly and more frequently because of their race than similarly situated white students. In short, *racial discrimination in school discipline is a real problem*" (no page, emphasis added). This "Dear Colleague" letter calls for an end to this racial issues within school and encourages individuals to openly recognize that these issues exist. Despite—seemingly—increased attention, racial inequalities in school discipline and the school-to-prison pipeline persist.

CONCLUSION

The goal of this chapter was to examine the racialized aspects of criminalized school discipline and the school-to-prison pipeline. Although issues of school safety concern families, teachers, school officials, and policy makers of all backgrounds, the current approach taken to safety in school is highly punitive and racialized. For example, there is no evidence that placing an SRO in a school makes the school any safer (see Kupchik 2016). Yet, there is ample evidence that placing an SRO in a school intensifies the school-to-prison pipeline (Nelson and Lind 2015) and increases racial inequity in discipline and arrest (United States Department of Education Office for Civil Rights 2014). We all want safe schools (Addington 2009), but without significant changes to the current approach taken across the United States, the "criminalization" of school discipline has resulted in severe and punitive punishment of youth (Hirschfield 2008) far more than it has increased school safety. This runs in stark contrast to broader trends in youth arrest. For example, the Office of Juvenile Justice and Delinquency Prevention (2015) has shown that arrests of youth across the United States decreased by about 50 percent between 2005 and 2014. Yet, during this same time, suspension and arrest of youth in schools increased.

Moreover, like all aspects of the criminal justice system, schools in the United States apply punishment along racial and ethnic boundaries. At every "step" of the school disciplinary process, Black youth are far more likely than white youth to receive punishment (Department of Education 2014). Black youth are far more likely to be suspended, expelled, and arrested than their white counterparts. When Black males engage in deviance, it is far more likely to be viewed as dangerous or threatening compared to white male delinquency, which is far more likely to be viewed as normal childhood (Ferguson 2001). Although always problematic, as a result of swift changes in disciplinary policies over the past two decades, this trend comes with increasingly severe implications. That is, because schools are using SROs more and more every day to implement discipline, school discipline now falls under the purview of the criminal justice system (Nelson and Lind 2015). Although Black youth have always been subjected to disproportionate punishment, there is a stark difference between a teacher giving a student detention or even an in-school suspension than an SRO arresting a student. Due—in part—to the expansion of SROs into schools, Black youth are significantly more likely to become enmeshed within the criminal justice system due simply to attending school (Kupchik 2016).

Although there are signs that these inequalities are becoming more openly acknowledged and challenged (e.g., Intergovernmental Agreement 2013; Department of Education 2014), the reality is there is no evidence these trends are changing. While some grass-roots efforts have been successful in combatting the school-to-prison pipeline and, particularly, the racial and ethnic disparities in punishment (see Intergovernmental Agreement 2013), these efforts appear largely localized and have not led to widespread change. That does not mean, however, that we must resign ourselves to accepting racial inequality in school discipline. Instead, we must find some way to overcome—and challenge—the prevailing myths of race and crime within the hallways of our public schools in the United States.

REFERENCES

Addington, Lynn A. 2009. "Cops and Cameras in Public School Security as a Policy Response to Columbine." *American Behavioral Scientist* 52: 1426–1446.

Blake, Jamilia, Bettie Ray Butler, Chance W. Lewis, and Alicia Darensbourg. 2011. "Unmasking the inequitable discipline experiences of urban Black girls: Implications for urban educational stakeholders." *The Urban Review* 43: 90–106.

Blalock, Hubert. 1967. *Toward a Theory of Minority-Group Relations.* Wiley and Sons.

Casella, R. (2006). Selling Us the Fortress: The Promotion of Techno-security Equipment for Schools. New York: Taylor and Francis Department of Education.

Dear Colleague Letter. U.S. Department Of Education. 2015. Available at: https://www2.ed.gov/about/offices/list/ocr/letters/colleague-201401-title-vi.html

Fabelo, Tony, Michael D. Thompson, Martha Plotkin, Dottie Carmichael, Miner P. Marchbanks III, and Eric A. Booth. 2011. *Breaking Schools' Rules: A Statewide Study Of How School Discipline Relates To Students' Success And Juvenile Justice Involvement.* New York: Council of State Governments Justice Center and Public Policy Research Institute.

Ferguson, Ann A. 2001. *Bad Boys: Public Schools and the Making of Black Masculinity.* Ann Arbor: University Of Michigan Press.

Fuentes, Annette. 2011. *Lockdown High: When The Schoolhouse Becomes A Jailhouse.* NY, New York: Verso Publishers.

Garland, Dave. 2001. *The Culture of Control: Crime and Social Order in Contemporary Society.* Chicago: University Of Chicago Press.

Glaze, Lauren E and Danielle Kaeble. 2016. "Correctional Populations in the United States, 2015." Bureau of Justice Statistics. Available at: Http://Www.Bjs.Gov/Index.Cfm?Ty=Pbdetail&Iid=5177

Gottfredson, Gary, Denise Gottfredson, Allison Payne, and Nisha Gottfredson. 2005. "School Climate Predictors of School Disorder: Results from a National Study of Delinquency Prevention in Schools." *Journal of Research in Crime and Delinquency* 42: 412–444.

Hirschfield, Paul J. "Preparing For Prison? The Criminalization of School Discipline in the USA. 2008." *Theoretical Criminology* 12: 79–101.

Holmes, Malcolm, Bruce Smith, Adrienne Freng, and Eduardo Munoz . 2008. " Minority threat, crime control, and police resource allocation in the Southwestern United States ." *Crime & Delinquency* 54: 128 –152 .

Huizinga, David and Delbert S. Elliott. 1986. "Reassessing the reliability and validity of self-report delinquent measures." *Journal of Quantitative Criminology* 2: 293–327.

Intergovernmental Agreement. Summary of 2013 Intergovernmental Agreement between Denver Public Schools and Denver Police Department. 2013. Available at: http://b.3cdn.net/advancement/e746ea2668c2ed19b3_urm6iv28k.pdf

Irwin, Katherine, Janet Davidson, and Amanda Hall-Sanchez. 2013. "The Race to Punish In American Schools: Class and Race Predictors of Punitive School-Crime Control." *Critical Criminology* 21: 47–71.

Kupchik, Aaron. 2010. *Homeroom Security: School Discipline in the Age of Fear.* New York: New York University Press.

———. 2016. *The Real School Safety Problem.* Oakland, California: University of California Press.

Kupchik, Aaron and Geoff Ward. 2013. "Race, Poverty, and Exclusionary School Security: An Empirical Analysis of US Elementary, Middle, and High Schools." *Youth Violence and Juvenile Justice* 12: 1–23.

Laub, John H. And Robert J. Sampson. 2003. *Shared Beginnings, Divergent Lives: Delinquent Boys to Age 70.* Cambridge, MA: Harvard University Press.

Lareau, Annette. 2003. *Unequal Childhoods: Class, Race, and Family Life.* University of California Press.

Losen, Daniel and Tina Martinez. 2013. *Out Of School and Off Track: The Overuse of Suspensions in American Middle and High Schools.* Los Angeles, CA: The UCLA Center for Civil Rights Remedies at the Civil Rights Project.

Losen, Daniel, Cheri Hodson, Michael A. Keith, Katrina Morrison, and Shkti Belway 2015. Are we closing the school discipline gap? The Civil Rights Project (2015). Available at: https://civilrightsproject.ucla.edu/resources/projects/center-for-civil-rights/remedies/school-to-prison-folder/federal-reports/are-we-closing-the-school-discipline-gap

Lyons, William and Julie Drew. 2006. *Punishing Schools: Fear and Citizenship in American Public Education.* Ann Arbor, MI: University Of Michigan Press.

Morris Edward W. 2013. "Tuck In That Shirt! Race, Class, Gender, and Discipline in an Urban School." *Sociological Perspectives* 48: 25–48.

Morris, Monique W. 2012. "Race, Gender, and the 'School to Prison Pipeline:' Expanding Our Discussion to Include Black Girls." African American Policy Forum (2012).

Mowen, Thomas J. 2015. "Parental Involvement in Schools and the Role of School Security Measures." *Education and Urban Society* 47: 830–848.

Mowen, Thomas J., and John J. Brent. 2016. "School Discipline as a Turning Point: The Cumulative Effect of Suspension on Arrest." *Journal of Research in Crime and Delinquency* 52:628–653.

Mowen, Thomas J., and Karen F. Parker. 2017. Minority Threat and School Security: Assessing the Impact of Black And Hispanic Student Representation on School Security Measures. *Security Journal* 30 (2): 504-522.

Mowen, Thomas J., and Matthew J. Manierre. 2017. School Security Measures and Extracurricular Participation: An Exploratory Multi-Level Analysis. *British Journal of Sociology of Education* 38 (3): 343-363.

Office of Juvenile Justice and Delinquency Prevention Statistical Briefing Book. 2015. Available: http://www.ojjdp.gov/ojstatbb/crime/qa05101.asp?qaDate=2014. Released on December 13, 2015.

Nelson, Libby. and Dara Lind. 2015. *The School to Prison Pipeline, Explained.* (Justice Policy Institute. Available at. http://www.justicepolicy.org/news/8775.

New York City School-Justice Partnership Task Force. 2013. *Keeping Kids in School and Out of Court.* New York State Permanent Judicial Commission on Justice for Children.

Noguera, Pedro. *2003. City Schools and the American Dream: Reclaiming the Promise of Public Education.* New York: Teachers College Press.

Payne, Allison A, and Kelly Welch. 2010. "Modeling the Effect of Racial Threat on Punitive and Restorative School Discipline Practices." *Criminology* 48: 1019–1062.

Phaneuf, S. W. (2009). Security in Schools: It's Effect on Students. El Paso, TX: LFB Scholarly Publishing.

Rios, Victor. 2011. *Punished: Policing The Lives Of Black And Latino Boys.* New York: New York University Press.

Robers, Simone, Jana Kemp, Amy Rathbun, Thomas D. Snyder. 2016. *Indicators of School Crime and Safety: 2015.* Washington, DC: US Department Of Justice, Bureau Of Justice Statistics And US Department Of Education, National Center For Education Statistics.

Rocque, Michael and Raymond Paternoster. 2011. Understanding the Antecedents of the "School to-Jail" Link: The Relationship between Race and School Discipline." *Journal of Crime, Law, and Criminology* 101:633–666.

Schlosser, Michael D. 2014. "Multiple Roles and Potential Role Conflict of a School Resource Officer: A Case Study of the Midwest Police Department's School Resource Officer Program in the United States." *International Journal of Criminal Justice Sciences* 9: 131–142.

Shollenberger, Tracey L. 2015. "Racial Disparities in School Suspension and Subsequent Outcomes: Evidence from the National Longitudinal Survey of Youth." In *Closing the School Discipline Gap: Equitable Remedies for Excessive Exclusion*, edited by DJ Losen, 31–43. New York: Teachers College Press.

Simon, Jonathan. 2007. *Governing Through Crime: How The War On Crime Transformed American Democracy And Created A Culture Of Fear.* New York: Oxford University Press.

Skiba, Russell J., and Reece L. Peterson. 2000. "School Discipline at a Crossroads: From Zero Tolerance to Early Response." *Exceptional Children* 66: 335–346.

Skiba, Russell, Robert Michael, Abra Nardo, and Reece Peterson. 2002. "The Color of Discipline: Sources of Racial and Gender Disproportionality in School Punishment." *Urban Review* 34: 317–342.

Skiba, Russell, Choong-Guen Chung, Megan Trachok, Timberly Baker, Adam Sheya, and Robin Hughes. 2014. "Where Should We Intervene? Contributions of Behavior, Student, and School Characteristics to Out-Of-School Suspension." In Daniel Losen (Ed) *Closing the School Discipline Gap: Equitable Remedies For Excessive Exclusion.* New York: Teachers College Press.

Stewart, Eric, Eric P. Baumer, Rod K. Brunson and Ronald R. Simons . 2009. " Neighborhood racial context and perceptions of police-based racial discrimination among black youth ." *Criminology* 47: 847 –887.

Theriot, Matthew T. 2009. "School Resource Officers and the Criminalization of Student Behavior. *Journal of Criminal Justice,* 280–287.

Townsend, Brenda L. 2000. "The Disproportionate Discipline of African American Learners: Reducing School Suspensions and Expulsions." *Exceptional Children* 66: 381–391.

United States Department of Education Office for Civil Rights. 2014. "Civil Rights Data Collection, Data Snapshot: School Discipline." Issue Brief No. 1. (2014). Available at: http://ocrdata.ed.gov/Downloads/CRDC-School-Discipline-Snapshot.pdf

Way, Sandra. 2011. "School Discipline and Disruptive Classroom Behavior: The Moderating Effects of Student Perceptions." *Sociological Quarterly* 52: 346–375

Welch, Kelly And Allison A. Payne. 2010. "Racial Threat and Punitive School Discipline." *Social Problems* 57:25–48.

Wolf, Kerrin. 2013. "Arrest Decision Making by School Resource Officers." *Youth Violence and Juvenile Justice* 12: 137–151.

Chapter Seven

Black and Blue: Analyzing and Queering Black Masculinities in *Moonlight*

Eric A. Jordan and Derrick R. Brooms

A number of studies have examined how Black males have been represented and portrayed in the media (Jackson 2006; Neal 2013). Much of this research has found that Black males often are framed in deficient rhetoric and projected in negative ways. In particular, scholars note that Black males are aggressive and involved in criminal behavior (Collins 2004; hooks 2004). Additionally, representations of Blackness seem fixated on tropes of pathology and deficiency within U.S. popular culture (see Gray 1995; Guerrero 1993; hooks 2004; Jackson 2006). Given the prominence of media as a social institution, socializing agent, and window of and to society, investigating how Black males are represented is of critical importance, especially with regard to media. As critical cultural scholar Stuart Hall (1992) argues, identities are linked to and shaped by both contemporary social positioning and self-constructed narratives. Thus, self-definitions and self-presentations always are situated within the social and, as a result, remain in constant negotiation.

In this chapter, we examine how the film *Moonlight* "queers" Black masculinities and how that queering of Black males shows more nuanced representations of black masculinities. We borrow from cultural critic Mark Anthony Neal's (2013) conception of "queering" Black masculinities. In particular, Neal conceptualizes a full range of Black maleness to unpack the simultaneous readings of the Black male body and Black masculine performance. The primary intention of our work is a reading, decoding, and analyzing presentations of Black masculine identities in the film. Thus, like Neal, we aim to "disturb the comfort of prevailing logics about Black male bodies"

(Neal 2013, 8). In making our case, we primarily focus on Chiron, the main character in the film for which the audience is engaged in viewing the challenges and triumphs of his coming of age and Black masculine identity development and awareness. In our analysis, we examine how Chiron's Black maleness is marked and queered throughout the film and how it informs his relationships, associations, and interactions with others.

In examining masculinities, we first are concerned with the broad definition of masculinity as a set of images, values, interests, and activities deemed important to a successful achievement of male adulthood (see hooks 2004; Lemelle 2010). Second, we intentionally focus on "masculinities" in the plural form to reaffirm the understanding that there is no one set form of masculine identity and, even more importantly, to reveal that ideals of manhood vary across space and time and through its intersection with other social identities. By examining how Black maleness is queered in the film, we necessarily move away from either/or dichotomies and simplistic reductions of Black men to a space that allows for a much broader understanding of the complexities and ambiguities of Black masculinities.

MEDIA PORTRAYALS OF BLACK MEN

Historically, Black men have been portrayed in media as sub-human, super-human, violent, criminal, or as buffoons (Guerrero 1993; hooks 2004). Throughout the twentieth century, representations of Black men in the media relied on overly negative and exaggerated framing that ultimately belied their humanity. In addition, up until the Blaxploitation period of the 1970s, Black men in the media were perversely represented as the constant "other." Images of their hypersexuality informed and, in many ways, were intended to justify why they faced physical violence, especially in the form of lynching. Depictions of Black men as aggressive and criminally prone helped to rationalize hypersurveillance and policing of them. And, projections of them as woefully foolish and dim-witted meant that they did not have to be taken seriously. Thus, as Collins' (2004) work informs, many of these portrayals are fashioned into "controlling images" that not only serve as a form to diminish Blacks, and Blackness, but also as a way to support racial oppression. Importantly, as we put forth in this chapter, representations of Black males are simultaneously raced and gendered. Images projected about them and their masculine identity take on a particular focus that is intended to be readable and deciphered by audiences.

Representations of Black men in film continue to be a contested terrain, dating back to the 1915 film *The Birth of a Nation*. Over a century later, moviegoers, scholars, and critics still find representations of Black men in need of restoration. At the center of debate and discussion are the troublesome representations that are continuously mass-produced throughout film and other mediums, including television, news, and music. Stuart Hall's (1997) Encoding/Decoding Theory is useful in analyzing media as text and, in our study, representations of Black maleness in *Moonlight*. He posits that encoding is the process by which a text is constructed by its producers (knowledge) while decoding is the process by which the audience reads, understands, and interprets a text (exposure).

The extant literature informs our reading of how media and their representations matter in the lives of Black males (Collins 2004; Drake 2016; hooks 2004; Jackson 2006; Neal 2013). Expanding on this scholarship, we examine how Black masculine identity is represented, expressed, and performed in the movie *Moonlight*. Building on Jackson's view that "Black bodies continue being commodified in a number of ways throughout everyday American life, and this practice is mirrored in popular culture" (Jackson 2006, 73), we argue that the Black male body as a commodity is not just permitted but required to define and detail the possibilities, expressions, and performances of Black masculine identities. Black manhood and masculinities (Drake 2016; Ikard 2007; McCune 2014; Neal 2013) are complex terrain often requiring Black males to view and perceive themselves through the eyes of others—or the broader society's purview.

CRITICAL RACE THEORY AND SCRIPTING THE BLACK MASCULINE

In an effort to better understand representations of Black maleness in *Moonlight*, we use scripts and critical race theory as the primary frameworks for our investigation. According to Jackson (2006), there are five "sensitizing constructs" represented throughout the literature on Black masculinity and are "indicative of Black masculine positionality: struggle, community, achievement, independence, and recognition" (134). While these factors can offer some explanation for how masculinities are selected and enacted, we assert that they also can help reveal how masculinities are performed and expressed. Even further, Jackson (2006, 135) offers seven assumptions that ground Black masculine identity theory:

1. Struggle is a human activity that solidifies one's sense of community.
2. Struggle is defined by group experiences.
3. Struggle is the centerpiece of the Black masculine identity model because of the complexity of defining and negotiating Black masculine identity.

4. All identity theories in some way call for dialectics. In this case, Black masculine identities are enwrapped in an I-Other dialectic involving politics of recognition.
5. Black masculine persons are usually preoccupied with a sense of self-efficacy, which, when achieved, offers a sense of life satisfaction, autonomy, and stability.
6. Black masculine persons' motivation to achieve is culturally, historically, and socially founded.
7. Without struggle, recognition, independence, and achievement, commitment to community is virtually impossible.

These assumptions, or scripts, provide a suitable framework for analysis because they help reveal the grounds for which Black masculine identities may be projected or expected. Thus, we follow Jackson's guide in understanding that in film, bodies are presented in ways that always are intended to be read—and consumed (also see Neal 2013). Understanding these scripts, then, also can inform us about the possibilities and limitations of behaviors and performances that Black males can engage in.

Our viewing of *Moonlight* uses a Critical Race Theory (CRT) lens to analyze representations of Black masculinity. Emerging from critical legal studies in the 1970s, CRT places race at the center of critical analysis and challenges colorblind approaches to social justice (see Bell 1992; Crenshaw 1995; Delgado and Stefancic 2000). We situate our study within multiple CRT tenets. First, we acknowledge the centrality of race and racism in society. Our study examines the intersections of race and gender provided within the film, as we take into account how race plays a prominent role in one's identity development. Second, CRT challenges the dominant ideology. Our focus on how Black masculinity is queered resists the mainstream framing of Black males as having or espousing a one-dimensional Black masculine identity. Third, CRT asserts the centrality of experiential knowledge. In this study, we examine how Chiron's, the movie's main character, life provides a window to perceive and analyze masculine identity development. And, finally, CRT uses a multidisciplinary perspective. We depend on multiple methods (such as performance and expression) and lean on multiple disciplines (e.g., sociology, Black studies, cultural studies) in order to inform our analyses.

WHY *MOONLIGHT*?

Our analysis was focused on analyzing one film, *Moonlight*, as a case study, for which we employed content analysis to gather and interpret the data. By using the case study method, this study was not intended to suggest that the data are rigid and generalizable to all films with Black male characters. Rather, this study aims to be transferable instead of generalizable. We want our analyses to be detailed enough so that the reader can determine whether the analyses resemble scenarios the reader may be familiar with in other films, literature, or interpersonal experiences, and whether our findings can be applied to other concepts in the aforementioned domains. Ultimately, this study aimed to be systematic and structured, and we aimed to be nuanced in our analysis of the selected film in order to make sense of the cultural significance and import that we present in our findings.

To structure our methodology, we developed a study population from the total population of Hollywood produced, mainstream, and feature films produced over the past ten years. First, we looked at the Internet Movie Database's (IMDb) lists that archive the most popular or highest rated Black films, specifically, films that prominently feature Black male protagonists. We analyzed the most popular films because we believed these films would be the most recognizable since the film we analyzed was released in the previous year, has been met with critical acclaim, and has larger social reach compared to lesser-known films. We looked at IMDb and created a list of eight movies we thought we wanted to analyze based on these criteria.

Film Criteria and Selection

Inclusion criteria primarily rested on selecting films that focused specifically on the experiences of Black male protagonists, as we were interested in investigating representations of Black males in contemporary film. Next, the film had to have been released in the past ten years. We did not want to use movies from the early 2000s or any time prior to the year 2000 as we felt like movies made in those time periods were outdated representations of Black males in films from another era. We only wanted to look at the most recent representations of Black males in film. Finally, we also wanted to consider films that delve into Black masculinity, its performance, and its representation. Based on our criteria, we deciphered a list of eight films that we considered for analysis (listed in order of release): *The Great Debaters* (2007), *The Dark Knight* (2008), *Hancock* (2008), *Django Unchained* (2012), *Dope* (2015), *Fences* (2016), *Moonlight* (2016), and *Get Out* (2017).

From this list of eight, we deliberated on a focus for the study and determined that we would analyze *Moonlight* and *Dope*. We specifically wanted to analyze these two movies because they were released around the same time, *Moonlight* came out in 2016 and *Dope* in 2015, and also because they are in the same coming-of-age genre and deal with characters of similar backgrounds. After careful consideration, we decided to focus exclusively on one movie, *Moonlight*, as we did not want to default to an uneven comparison between the movies. Even further, we believed that comparing or juxtaposing the two movies necessarily would take away from what each had to offer. Stated differently, we did not see these movies in completion and, in an effort to ensure that readers understood this desire, we focused exclusively on *Moonlight*. Additionally, *Moonlight* was appealing particularly given its overarching messages and narratives about Black masculinities. And, also, we desired to produce an in-depth analysis of the film, specifically, analysis of Black masculinity, and such an in-depth analysis would allow us to have a more robust discussion of Black masculinities and their representation in modern film.

Procedure

Moonlight was analyzed as a case study of Black male representation in film. As we watched the film, we analyzed it for recurrent themes such as: what are the major motifs of the film as they pertain to Black masculinity? What problems are the Black characters dealing with? What ways does the film address Blackness and Black masculinity? What is the status of the characters and their families? What roles, assigned and/or performed, do the Black characters play in the film? And, how is Black masculinity performed? We compared these findings both within and between narratives in order to detect salient patterns, themes, and observations.

MOONLIGHT, MASCULINITY, AND BLACK MEN

Moonlight, directed by Barry Jenkins, is an adapted screenplay of a play by Tarell Alvin McCraney titled, *In Moonlight Black Boys Look Blue*. *Moonlight* is a coming-of-age story about a Black boy named Chiron, and the exploration of his sexual orientation and the struggles that come with Chiron's journey of self-discovery. The movie chronicles Chiron's life across three key periods: his naive, innocent, childhood (played by Alex Hibbert); his angry, anxious high school teenage life (played by Ashton Sanders); and his life as an adult who has adopted the hardened elements of what we have come to define as the "thug" (played by Trevante Rhodes). We provide an analysis of each period individually through the following themes: (1) The Naivety of Black Masculinity; (2) Discovering and Unmasking Masculinities; and (3) Blackening Masculinities, and follow with analysis of representations of Black women in the film as well.

The Naivety of Black Masculinity

The first act, "Little," begins with Chiron (who goes by the nickname "Little") playing with, and being bullied by, other kids for being "soft"—a derogatory term used to describe a (Black) male perceived to be meek and effeminate. This "softness" is what first begins to alienate Little from other Black children. We see the use of this concept of being a "soft" Black male toward the beginning of the film where Little, and his friend Kevin (played by Jaden Piner), play kickball with other Black kids. While Kevin plays kickball with the other kids and manages to keep up with them, Chiron does not seem to be able to; he struggles kicking the ball and keeping up with other kids and the other kids tease him for it. Chiron eventually walks away from the game and Kevin follows him to ask him why he left. Upon making some small talk with Chiron, and Chiron staring at blood on Kevin's face, that he got from playing the game, the two boys have a conversation:

> Kevin: "Why you always lettin' people pick on you, man?"
> Chiron: "What you mean?"
> Kevin: "You always lettin' 'em pick on you."
> Chiron: "So? What I gotta do?"
> Kevin: "All you gotta do is show these n****s you ain't soft."
> Chiron: "But I ain't soft."
> Kevin: "I know, I know. But it don't mean nothin' if they don't know it."

Kevin openly encourages Chiron to be tough and put up a stereotypical masculine persona, a persona that is aggressive. We watch Chiron and Kevin wrestle and fight on the field for a short period of time, after which Kevin gets up, and feels reassured about Chiron's ability to adhere to a "code of the streets" (see Anderson 1999). He looks down at Chiron and says, "See Little, I knew you wasn't soft." The two boys get up and return to the game only after Chiron allowed himself to be assimilated into the generic schema of Black maleness, a schema that suggests that Black boys are to be hardened and calloused all the time, at least for a moment around *others*. As per the "code," the tough guy persona was only to be used around others as if the tough brand of Black masculinity was only a performance, survival mechanism, and an inclusive force for Black boys in the presence of other Black boys who more easily fit the expectations of a Black male. The fact that Kevin, a child, expressed this complex idea to Chiron showed that this idea of what it means to be a Black male—the idea that a Black boy cannot be "soft" around other Black boys—shows that the tenets of hypermasculinity are programmed into Black boys at an early age.

In essence, Black hypermasculinity becomes a defense mechanism, an equal but opposite force against the societal forces that push down and pressure Black males who might be "soft." Around other Black boys, Chiron could not be himself, he had to be what others expected him to be, what Kevin wanted him to be. In many ways, throughout this film, Black masculinity is a mask to be worn, so much so that it should be called Black *mask-ulinity* in the context of this film. The dichotomous struggle between toughness and "softness" plays a key role in the presentation of Black males in this film as these two concepts remain in tension with each other and manifest in various ways that ultimately create an image of Chiron as a complex Black male character. While Chiron is encouraged by Kevin to be a stereotype to fit in and survive among others, Chiron's relationship with Juan (played by Mahershala Ali) encourages him to embrace his "softness"—his authentic self.

"Little" continues in Liberty City, Miami, where Juan, a Cuban drug dealer, finds Chiron hiding in an abandoned crack house from the children who are chasing and bullying him. Juan allows Chiron to stay the night at his own apartment with him and his girlfriend, Teresa (played by Janelle Monáe). Juan returns Chiron to his home the next morning where they are greeted by Paula, Chiron's mother (played by Naomie Harris). Throughout the first act, Chiron and Juan increasingly spend more time with each other. Juan takes Chiron to the beach and teaches him lessons and imparts his wisdom to him. Juan and Chiron go swimming at the beach together in a moment of non-sexual intimacy. Juan holds Chiron and teaches the boy how to swim. Juan gently places Chiron's head in the water and tells him to relax and that he will not let him go. As he goes to place Chiron's head in the water, Juan says, "See right there, you in the middle of the world, man" and lets Chiron gently lay in his arms.

This scene allows Chiron to explore his male identity even further via the guidance of another Black male who is more open to Black male choice in his own identity; Chiron can fully be, and explore, himself around Juan where he could not be around other Black boys. The swimming lesson liberates Chiron's humanity in a moment that frees him, in an inclusive space that is non-judgmental, free from the external male gaze, and open to exploration of his identity. Where Chiron was dirtied on the kickball field literally wrestling with Kevin, another image of masculinity in Chiron's life, Chiron's time with Juan washes all of the dirt and pretense of masculinity away. All of this happens in an intimate moment between two Black male characters, and this intimacy near a body of water is a common motif throughout the film. Each moment where Chiron develops a stronger sense of self takes place in or near water and will begin to take place at night.

After they swim, they sit on the beach and discuss history, Black identity, and Black agency. Juan tells Chiron, "There are Black people everywhere in the world. Remember that, okay? Ain't no place in the world ain't no Black people. We were the first on the planet," and even tells him to be himself and to decide who he is going to be, the opposite message Kevin gave him. Juan tells Chiron the story of a Cuban woman who refers to Juan as "blue." He quotes the woman, "Runnin' around catching the morning light. In moonlight, Black boys look blue. You blue. That's what I gon' call you. Blue." After a beat, Juan tells Chiron, "At some point you gotta decide for yourself who you wanna be—can't let nobody make that decision for you." Juan becomes Chiron's first male role model, a symbol of hopeful Black agency, and one of the only people in the film to embrace Chiron for who he is and openly encourages Chiron to choose who he is in a world that constantly seeks to label him and tell him who he should be. This scene highlights the fact that Chiron's and Juan's experiences can be linked to the experiences of many Black males all around the world: the experiences of having the world label you and try to define you based on preconceived notions, expectations, and limitations. Juan is giving Chiron permission to be himself and never to allow others to define him. Juan rejects arbitrary definitions of masculinity and seems to believe that no one makes the rules on Black male identity or masculinity.

Toward the end of the first act, Juan sells Chiron's mother, Paula, crack cocaine and notices her smoking it with one of his customers in the same spot where Juan sells his drugs. Juan confronts Paula and lambasts her for her addiction. Paula chastises him for selling her the drugs in the first place and proceeds to mock his relationship with her son and questions if he, given his position as a drug dealer, would serve as some ideal of a surrogate parent or caretaker for Chiron:

> Paula: "So you gon' raise my son now? Huh? You gon' raise my son?" Juan is silent. "Yeah, that's what I thought."
> Juan: "You gon' raise him?"
> Paula: "You gon' keep sellin' me rocks? Huh?" Juan watches silently as Paula smokes more crack and blows the smoke in his face. "Motherf*****. Don't gimme that 'you gotta get it from somewhere' shit, n****. I'm gettin' it from *you*. But, you gon' raise my son though, right? Hm? You ever see the way he walks?" Paula imitates Chiron's supposed "walk."
> Juan: "You better watch your mouth."
> Paula: "You gon' tell him why the other boys kick his ass all the time? Huh? You gon' tell him?" Juan continues to stare at her silently. "You ain't shit." Paula gets in the car with her smoking partner and drives away.

In this scene, we can see that Juan and Paula fight over Chiron. The tug of war for Chiron, even if just ideologically, is situated on a veiled morality that leaves one questioning if a bad mother (e.g., as a drug addict) can raise a son better than a bad man (e.g., a drug dealer). Implied in Juan's positioning is his own stature as a Black man, thus supplanting the notion that he has more to offer for Chiron—financially, materially, and relationally. In a number of ways, this is displayed in the suggestion of Juan's care for Chiron, and his development, which seems to be at a more distinct level than his mother. Additionally, as a way to diffuse her accusations and reveal the limits of her understanding, Juan silently rejects Paula's assertion that boys pick on Chiron because he is gay—or at least seems to acknowledge that fact but refuses to accept it.

Juan seems to want to deny labels since they can be seen as mechanisms through which people try to define, and debase, others. Paula indirectly defines who her son is during her conversation with Juan. She then goes home and yells at her son, calling him a "faggot" and it is clear that she connects her son's gay identity to his tendency to be bullied—she connects her son's gay identity to his "softness." Interestingly, both Paula and Juan attempt, in their own ways, to shield Chiron from the harsh realities of his marginalized masculine identity. Juan tells him to define himself and never let anyone define him, while Paula doesn't tell him about who he is at all, almost as if she resents who and what Chiron is, until she decides to belittle him with a slur.

We can see in these scenes that Black male identity is constantly being pushed and pulled by those who encourage openness like Juan and his girlfriend Teresa, and those who don't like Paula and Kevin. Black masculinity is depicted as a fortress under siege. Black males have to walk the tightrope of their identities in order to avoid appearing "soft," but the cost of that is that they live according to someone else's definitions of who they are and are not being true to themselves. Black males are expected to be stoic and aggressive to survive, but hiding their emotions under a cool-pose (see Majors and Billson 1992) patina deprives them of who they really are. Chiron, for the first time in his life, has to come to grips with who he really is when he asks Juan what "faggot" means. In this moment, Juan also has to come to terms with who Chiron really is in another moment of intimacy between the two characters. Chiron goes to Juan's house and begins to deduce his identity. In responding to Chiron's inquiry about the meaning of "faggot," Juan informs him that (1) it is a word used "to make gay people feel bad" and (2) he is not a "faggot." In particular, seemingly in a way to encourage Chiron to protect his masculine self, Juan encourages Chiron by asserting, "You could be gay but don't let nobody call you no faggot." Additionally, Juan affirms Chiron's questions about being a drug dealer and his mother using drugs.

The end of Act I helps Chiron come to an understanding of who he is as a Black male, and his identity is further represented as something he should suppress, since people continue to try and hurt him for his identity—both verbally and physically. In this sense, Chiron's Black gay identity is shown to be hidden, but under construction, something to be explored silently and privately under the guise of stereotypical Black masculinity. In Acts II and III, we see that Chiron's efforts to hide who he is in favor of more conventional representations and performances of his Black masculine identity catch up with him and begin to affect his social life and his emotions.

Discovering and Unmasking Masculinities

Act II, titled "Chiron," takes place during Chiron's high school teenage life. Like his childhood self, he is bullied by other Black males. His new bully is classmate Terrel (played by Patrick Decile), who bullies Chiron for being gay and presumably for being too "soft." Chiron spends time with Teresa, who lives alone after Juan dies. Paula has become a prostitute to make the money to fund her addiction and forces Chiron to give her the money that Teresa gives him, berating him for being unwilling to support his own mother in favor of supporting Teresa.

In school, Chiron is ostracized while his friend Kevin (played by Jharrel Jerome), the same friend from his childhood, is not. Kevin is part of social groups that Chiron is not a part of and cannot gain access to. Kevin is portrayed as a heterosexual male who openly discusses with Chiron the sex he has with girls and tells Chiron to keep his sex stories between the two of them because he knows Chiron can "keep a secret." It is clear Kevin uses cool-pose around Chiron and other Black males, probably to avoid being seen as soft since this movie establishes that being cool and tough is how a Black male survives. Kevin's sexuality, and his expression of it, lies in contrast to Chiron's, who is a closeted, troubled, gay teen. Act II really analyzes the performance of Black masculinity, and picks up on the discussion of Black masculinity where Act I left off. What do Black men need to do to be considered Black men? Who comes up with the arbitrary rules of Black masculinity? These questions are answered within the context of Act II's demonstration of how a Black man exploring his sexuality in ways that do not directly conform to the heteronormative standards society has set up, can be, and often is, conceived as a negation of a Black man's masculinity.

It appears that Black masculinity is something that is, first and foremost, strictly and conventionally heterosexual. Next it appears that Black masculinity, and its representation, is something strong, muscular, aggressive, hypersexual, dominant, and in some ways violent and/or criminal—all of which are byproducts of the colonial white gaze, propaganda, and rhetoric concerning Black males. Anyone who explores and performs his sexuality outside of the pre-packaged norms of masculinity are excluded, teased, and met with violence; Chiron is met with all three.

Chiron is awkward, thin, and discovering his sexuality by himself. He is teased by Terrel and others for not performing or expressing his Black masculinity in the same ways as other Black boys, like Kevin. While Chiron does not feel safe to freely explore his sexuality in high school, Kevin is able to explore his sexuality and is not teased, bullied, or excluded from any groups because he operates within the parameters of Black masculine heteronormativity, and has managed to keep his own sexual fluidity hidden from others. We find out later that Kevin is bisexual in private but is publicly heterosexual—thereby engaging in "passing" in his public performance. Kevin's passing is based on his practicing discreet sexual acts "while privileging spaces that are more heteronormative" (McCune 2014, 4). Act II shows us that Chiron and Kevin are foils of one another and take different paths to reach the same destination at the end of the movie. One of the most poignant scenes in Act II is the scene where Chiron and Kevin meet by the beach at night and talk. While smoking a blunt, the two teens discuss their goals, emotions, and Chiron's nickname "Black." In this interaction, they gain greater insight into each other's and their own interiorities. In response to Chiron admitting that he cries quite frequently, Kevin discourages him from masking his pain or drowning in sorrow. This is a critical scene in the film as it centers on their needs and vulnerabilities. After completing a great majority of the dialogue, the two of them share an intimate moment.

It is in this moment, under the moonlight, the two Black boys were "blue." It can be interpreted that Juan's story about the Cuban lady meant that, under the cover of night, Black boys could drop their guard, shed masculine pretenses and personas that they use to survive, and become vulnerable, beautiful, and free to be themselves by the water, a romantic symbol in this movie about Black male liberation from societal pressure and complexes of what Black men should be. Kevin and Chiron were not hardened men putting up a tough guise to avoid being seen as "soft." They were authentically themselves with each other. Two Black men, exploring their sexualities and themselves in just a single moment of truth and reconciliation of who these men are: Chiron is gay, Kevin is bisexual. Chiron apologizes for the sexual encounter, but Kevin reassures him that he had nothing to be sorry for, echoing, indirectly, Juan's message about being oneself and being okay with that choice.

It is here where the movie's title begins to make sense. In moonlight, Black boys look blue. In moonlight Black boys are shown for who they truly are; they are vulnerable at night. In the day they are "Black," hardened, cloistered, performative, and in many ways repressed. At night they are softer, more genuine and open, they are "Blue." For this reason, Chiron is "Black" because he hides his vulnerabilities as best he can. While he was alive, Juan was "Blue" because he more readily showed his vulnerabilities. The Cuban lady's phrase could also be a warning that Black boys should never let their environment define who they really are, much like Juan's message to Chiron that he needs to choose his own identity. Other kids bully Chiron and thus his environment dictates his demeanor and who he is, but with Kevin, he chooses to be his true authentic self, regardless of his previous bullying.

The kissing scene with Kevin highlights the film's message that true Black masculinity is sincere, emotional, connected, intimate, and is nothing to be ashamed of. In a world where a Black gay man is demonized for being

Black and gay (because the intersection of those two identities do not mix according to the conventions of heteronormative society and hegemonic masculinity scripts), Black men are expected to be "hard" and the only real way to survive in such a world is to be "soft" and vulnerable with others. This scene shifts the movie's original meaning of the word "soft" from weak to sincere, genuine, and loving with other Black men. Thus, in essence, this scene obliterates other films' colonial interpretation of Black men as harsh thugs who seek to harm others with a detached attitude. "Moonlight" represents Black males as people under construction and languishing under the oppressive forces of the colonial white male gaze. It is only when Black males escape from that colonialism that they can truly be free as Black men. This moment between these two Black males comes to an end afterward as Kevin reverts back into cool-pose as he drops Chiron off at home, their intimate moment kept between them.

The next day, Terrel decides to haze Kevin and forces him to fight Chiron; Kevin spent a lot of his time trying to fit into Terrel's group, and trying to maintain an air of heterosexuality as a result. Kevin, seeking to show that he isn't "soft," and possibly to avoid being bullied and ridiculed himself, punches Chiron in the face. In this moment, Kevin seems trapped between sincerity and performance of his Black masculinity. We know Kevin has romantic feelings for Chiron, but he pretends not to in order to fit in; in effect, he is performing masculinity for people in order to keep from being mistreated. Kevin is a victim of toxic masculinity. As Kevin keeps punching Chiron, he tells Chiron to stay down as a way of saving Chiron from the world around him; Chiron refuses to stay down and Terrel and his group beat Chiron until security breaks up the fight with Kevin looking on, disturbed. Kevin was "Black" by day, allowing his environment to make him ruthless and hard.

Chiron makes his way toward Terrel after the assault and hits him with a chair during class. Chiron unleashed his pent up rage and frustration about being bullied and that is when Chiron, much like Kevin, became "Black" as he is being led away by police officers. Toxic masculinity makes Black males unfeeling and angry in these situations, and these Black boys are represented as victims of said masculinity that compels them to fight each other, hate each other, and guard themselves from each other to survive.

Being Black and Blackening Masculinities

The final act of the film, Act III, titled "Black," shows Chiron as an adult. He has transformed his body from that of a scrawny teen to one seemingly hardened by jail time, weightlifting, and he goes by the nickname "Black" on the street. In addition, he deals drugs in Atlanta, becoming what Juan was before his death. Chiron did not heed the warning about allowing the environment to shape and define you and he had become what Juan tried to steer him away from. He became the face of the toxicity that tormented him and informed his performance of Black masculinity in stereotypical ways. He performs Black maleness by day to survive ("Black"), and he is implied to lack intimacy at night, so he doesn't have an outlet to be his true self: a queer Black man.

Chiron gets a call from Kevin one day and he wants to meet Chiron again after several years of not communicating. Kevin also apologizes for everything that happened between them in high school. The two of them eventually meet at a diner and reconnect. Kevin, who is now a cook, makes Chiron the diner's "chef special" and they talk at a table. Chiron begins telling Kevin that he is selling drugs, how he got involved, and his ultimate goal to "get my shit straight." Kevin examines Chiron's presentation of self, which includes fake gold teeth, and questions him about what he sees as a masculine performance that does not resemble the Chiron he once knew.

Importantly, Kevin sees that Chiron is still performing an idea of Black masculinity and putting up a front to seem tough and untouchable. Kevin knows that Chiron is more than a Black male construct; he knows Chiron intimately underneath the mask. As they continue in their dialogue, Kevin sees Chiron opening and letting him in; he is slowly taking down his guard and being vulnerable—or "Blue." The two spend an intimate moment listening to a song from the jukebox that Kevin selected. They leave the diner in Chiron's car, with the music blasting and drowning out any communication between them—another defense mechanism and performance of masculinity.

The men reflect back to the last time they saw each other. Chiron admits his attempts to "forget all of those times. The good, the bad; all of it" while Kevin acknowledges that he "never did anything I actually wanted to do." For Chiron, forgetting was an important attempt of self-healing and coping; for Kevin, his awareness opened him to see that he "wasn't never myself." As they continue to talk, Chiron finally opens up to Kevin after all these years as he admits, "You're the only man who's ever touched me. The only one. I haven't really touched anyone, since." The two of them share one final intimate moment of silence as the waves of the ocean hit the shore, under the moonlight. The film fades to Black.

Black Masculinities and Representations of Black Women

In exploring the representations of Black men and their masculine selves, it also is necessary to understand how Black women are positioned and projected within the film project as well (Collins 2000, 2004; Crenshaw 1995; hooks 2014). Paula, Chiron's mother, and Teresa, girlfriend to Juan, the two prominent women in the film, offer the audience dichotomous views of Black women. Paula is relegated as a "bad Black mother" because of her drug addiction, poverty, and lack of parenting of Chiron (see Collins 2004). Throughout the film, Paula's character suffers from a lack of capital, agency, and know-how. The family's lack of financial capital is set as a backdrop for the first half of the film, primarily viewed in how Paula attempts to raise Chiron. There are very few representations of Chiron's home life in the film, which, in a sense, can suggest that his home was not a space that played a prominent role in his development. Thus, by implication then, Paula is repositioned as unsupportive and incapable of helping Chiron develop a positive self-identity. In many ways, Paula's continuous chiding and denigrating of her son marks her as an unfit mother. At the least, she expresses a lack of empathy and understanding of Chiron's development and, at the worst, uses his sexuality and masculine identity as cause and reason for the physical violence that he experiences. Even further, Paula's verbal chiding of her son at various moments throughout the film creates a toxic home environment that also suffocates his emotional and holistic development.

In addition, as cited earlier in the chapter (in "The Naivety of Black Masculinity" section), Paula and Juan's interaction on the street is a critical moment in the film. In that scene, while Juan's position as a drug dealer is highlighted and problematized for the negative impact it has on the community, his identity as a male presents itself as an ontological positioning of "knowing" what Chiron needs. At the same time, Paula's drug use and addiction, and thus dependency, are spotlighted as well. In fact, one might argue Paula's use of drugs places her sense of mothering and care for Chiron on trial. The scene occurs late in the evening and shows Paula in search of buying drugs. Self-removed from the home in search of illegal drugs, this scene seems representative of how Paula's personal choices place her self-interests over and above her role as caregiver and caretaker of her son. Later in the film, in efforts to support her drug use and lack of financial capital, we see Paula willing to sell her body for money and demanding that Chiron give her money. Not only is she, then, unfit for motherhood, but she also is inept to support Chiron, his needs, and his masculine identity development.

Teresa's role is much more complex. In one sense, she is the girlfriend to a known drug dealer. This positionality allows her to benefit financially from Juan's endeavors without problematizing drug dealing. In another sense, she is portrayed as genuinely caring and supportive of Chiron. Throughout the first half of the film, Teresa appears but is mostly silent (or silenced) as she plays a background role and is a supporter of Juan's developing relationship with Chiron. In the second half of the film, her position is elevated to a caretaker/parent for Chiron. In many ways, the second half of the film reveals her repositioning and her replacing of Juan in caring for Chiron, in a sense. However, as was the case with Juan, this is a contested positioning. In Paula's view, Teresa is still an outsider and has no familial relation with Chiron; thus, she is to be distrusted. After Juan's death, Teresa allows Chiron to stay at her house whenever it is needed or convenient for him. As a result, her home becomes a refuge for Chiron from the spaces and people that continuously denigrate, ridicule, and violate his being and masculinity. At Teresa's, he is nourished, supported, and loved. Teresa's place, and role, then, can be seen as a "home" with a number of supportive elements to allow Chiron his own space for healing, shelter, and security.

In sum, also revealed in this dichotomous view is the absent presence of Black women. Both Paula and Teresa are positioned as sideline viewers of Chiron's development. Whereas Paula openly ridicules his sexuality, ultimately blaming him for his own physical and emotional suffering, Teresa gives him space, literally and figuratively, to just be—and keep his humanity intact. As a result of the constant barrage of external pressures that Chiron faces and experiences in his home life, within the neighborhood, and at school, these spaces remain unrelenting and unforgiving of and to his masculine identity. He has neither the sociocultural capital nor the disposition to present himself in traditional masculine ways—e.g., as one who can physically stand up for himself and, even more mundane, as one who might dare speak up on his own behalf. Thus, his masculine identity is viewed as deficient and neither of the women contributes specifically to his positive identity development. Even in Act III, when Paula apologizes for her ineptitude, Chiron ("Black" as he is called as an adult) is hesitant to accept her love. In the end, neither Paula nor Teresa actually helps Chiron learn more about himself or explicitly assists him in developing his masculinity. As a result, one insinuation in the film is that Black males' masculine identity development primarily rests on their own self-learning and exploration and is dependent upon other males, both those in their peer group and older males as well.

QUEERING THE BLACK MASCULINE IDENTITY

Moonlight shows that there exists a number of Black men who long for intimacy but have no one to turn to. Where do some men go to be touched and held if they are, as Black men, socialized into and toward the myths of masculinity: told that they should be tough and strong all the time? Furthermore, where do they go when they do not receive the intimacy they long for? How does the lack of intimacy affect Black men? The film also subtly discusses the effects of socio-economic factors, unemployment, lack of an education, and the school to prison pipeline that Black men (and families) have to deal with that also can harden them. As opposed to focusing solely on the symptoms, we also must examine the roots. A good deal of the hardening of Black men—stoicism, distrust, moved toward aggression—can come from systemic oppression and disenfranchisement. Both Chiron and Kevin follow the same pathway through life. They both go through prison but come out of it and live their lives in different ways: Kevin becomes a cook, Chiron becomes a drug dealer. Their paths represent the either/or dilemma that plagues healthy Black male development; they are forced to endure a reality that is racialized, gendered, and scripted onto Black male bodies. Additionally, they are forced into a "Black male reality" that comes as a result of systemic oppression and repression of their emotions, ambitions, hopes, and dreams. In order to survive this system, Black men must find ways to adapt and survive either through legitimate or illegal means.

Ultimately, *Moonlight* provides a diverse representation of Black men primarily as complex human beings instead of constructs sculpted by the white gaze or white domination (though we do acknowledge the prison industrial complex as a manifestation of white domination). The Black maleness represented in *Moonlight* is thoughtful, reflective, and, most of all, soft, genuine, and sincere. Black masculinity and sexuality are byproducts of colonial oppression that continues to disenfranchise Black men. Cultural critic bell hooks asserts, "At the center of the way Black male selfhood is constructed in white-supremacist capitalist patriarchy is the image of the brute— untamed, uncivilized, unthinking, and unfeeling" (hooks 2004, xii). Chiron's and Kevin's minds had been colonized and warped to fit a typical hypermasculine guise that turned them into the stereotypical images of Black men we often see in film today. However, *Moonlight* pushes back by queering Black masculinities. In effect, the film shatters the "same old stories" and stereotypes by allowing Black men to express themselves and be vulnerable in ways not often expected of or allowed for Black men. This is especially true for Chiron, who adopted a "thug" persona that we typically associate with violence, anger, aggression, and criminality. However, and most importantly, underneath that thuggish veneer (as displayed in Act III) we find a man who is hurting, while searching and in need of love and intimacy.

Each of the acts shows Chiron's growth into his own Black maleness along with his embracing of who he is and the vulnerability that comes with such an evolution. It is during Chiron's evolution that we see the utility of queering Black masculinity. In particular, we see the possibility of how modern cinema can humanize Black men and afford them nuance and emotional gradients, which is a stark contrast to the one-dimensional controlling images of Black men in the media of yesteryear (e.g., see hooks 2004; Collins 2004). Chiron's humanity and struggle to reconcile himself and how he interfaces with the world around him is the key story in this film, ultimately offering viewers insight into new ways of seeing Black men—especially with regard to how they are represented in film.

CONCLUSION

While, as depicted in the film, Black males may, in fact, venture into the middle of the world, a space where they can reclaim a semblance of freedom, rekindle hope in being their authentic selves, ultimately, this middle is but borrowed space. The water is the fixed space where those seeking wholeness can escape. However, they cannot bring elements of this middle back to their homes, families, and environments. Even further, while they may have a moment in the middle of the world, Black men, and their masculine selves, cannot be the center of the world. As the film and our analysis shows, there is a critical need for a rewriting of Black bodies in popular media, especially for Black bodies that are seemingly always commodities and commodified. We must create space both beyond and within the dialectic that allows for healthy masculine selves to develop and thrive. By queering Black masculinity, *Moonlight* both invites and pushes the audience into new(er) considerations of Black maleness. These selves, and bodies, must be freed from the wrangle holds of hegemonic and heteronormative masculine scripts—and the white gaze. Invariably, both of these scripts reposition Black male bodies into a schizophrenic dialectic of dominator-dominated, strong-weak, hard-soft, tough-meek. These dialectics cannot liberate the Black masculine self and can be corrosive to relational, familial, and communal dynamics.

As opposed to the typical struggles of men to come to terms with their own masculinities, Chiron's character allows us to see how others struggle to come to terms with masculine identities that are neither traditional nor hegemonic. Chiron's quietude, even as an adult, is an invitation to better see, and better appreciate, Black men's interiorities. The projections of and socializations toward traditional masculinity are problematic and unhealthy for Black males and unhealthy for families and communities. Additionally, these forms of masculinity can stunt Black males' holistic growth and development. However, these discursive frameworks are part of a larger system that organizes our lives. In queering Black masculinity, *Moonlight* allows space for Black males' youthful innocence, problematizes the contested terrain that hegemonic masculinity demands and envelops, and reveals the complexities of the Black masculine self. Importantly, as evinced throughout the film, we need more spaces that allow young Black males the opportunity to decide who they can and will be.

REFERENCES

Anderson, Elijah. 1999. *Code of the Street: Decency, Violence, and the Moral Life of the Inner City*. New York: Norton.
Bell, Derrick A. 1992. *Faces at the Bottom of the Well: The Permanence of Racism*. New York: Basic Books.

Collins, Patricia Hill. 2000. *Black Feminist Thought: Knowledge, Consciousness, and the Politics of Empowerment* (Second edition). New York: Routledge.

———. 2004. *Black Sexual Politics: African Americans, Gender, and the New Racism.* New York: Routledge.

Crenshaw, Kimberlé W. 1995. "Mapping the Margins: Intersectionality, Identity Politics, and Violence against Women of Color." In *Critical Race Theory: The Key Writings that Formed the Movement*, edited by Kimberlé Crenshaw, Neil. Gotanda, Gary Peller and Kendall Thomas, 357–83. New York: New Press.

Delgado, Richard and Jean Stefancic. 2011. *Critical Race Theory: An Introduction* (Second edition). New York: New York University Press.

Drake, Simone. 2016. *When We Imagine Grace: Black Men and Subject Making.* Chicago: University of Chicago Press.

Gray, Herman. 1995. *Watching Race: Television and the Struggle for "Blackness."* Minneapolis: University of Minnesota Press.

Guerrero, Ed. 1993. *Framing Blackness: The African American Image in Film.* Philadelphia, PA: Temple University Press.

Hall, Stuart. 1992. "What is this Black in Black Popular Culture?" In *Black Popular Culture*, edited by Gina Dent, 21–33. Seattle, WA: Bay Press.

———. 1997. *Representation: Cultural Representations and Signifying Practices.* London: Sage Publications.

hooks, bell. 2004. *We Real Cool: Black Men and Masculinity.* New York: Routledge.

———. 2014. *Ain't I a Woman: Black Women and Feminism* (2nd edition). New York: Routledge.

Jackson, Ronald L., II. 2006. *Scripting the Black Masculine Body: Identity, Discourse, and Racial Politics in Popular Media.* Albany, NY: SUNY Press.

Ikard, David. 2007. *Breaking The Silence: Toward a Black Male Feminist Criticism.* Baton Rouge, LA: Louisiana State University Press.

Lemelle, Anthony J. 2010. *Black Masculinity and Sexual Politics.* New York: Routledge.

Majors, Richard and Janet Mancini Billson. 1992. *Cool Pose: The Dilemmas of Black Manhood in America.* New York: Lexington Press.

McCune, Jeffrey Q. 2014. *Sexual Discretion: Black Masculinity and the Politics of Passing.* Chicago: University of Chicago Press.

Neal, Mark Anthony. 2013. *Looking for Leroy: Illegible Black Masculinities.* New York: New York University Press.

Chapter Eight

New Rules to the Game

Neoliberal Governance and Housing in Atlanta, Georgia

Cameron Khalfani Herman and
Theresa Rajack-Talley

Since the 1970s, neoliberal restructuring has reshaped economic and governance strategies at the global, national, and sub-national levels of society (Brenner and Theodore 2002b; Harvey 2005). At the sub-national level, many cities have taken on entrepreneurial strategies to maintain local development initiatives in the face of declining federal fiscal support. As a result, cities have become more attuned to the needs of businesses and industrial institutions and increasingly less responsive to the needs of economically marginalized citizens living within the city limits. Moreover, marginalized city residents are rendered powerless in the city's decision-making process.

The electoral system is the traditional vehicle for citizens to influence decision-making regarding their needs and those of their communities. Citizens elect public officials with the well-intentioned belief that the elected representatives will honor their promises and responsibility to meet the needs of all their constituents. However, elected officials face the increasing reality of balancing the fiscal health of their cities with the needs of the electorate, particularly those that are economically and socially disadvantaged. Noted sociologist Manuel Castells (2005, 9) describes this growing gulf between citizens and political representatives and institutions as "the crisis of political legitimacy." While Castells spoke of the "crisis" in a global context, this "crisis" is also applicable and observable at a local level in major cities of the United States.

There are, however, a number of questionable issues linked to the crisis of political legitimacy and local and national governance. First, it appears that there is an increasing accountability gap between the citizenry and the politicians who are elected to represent them. Secondly, the question is raised as to whether there are mechanisms in place that allow politicians to avoid their representative responsibility, especially to those most marginalized. Further, are there options that exist to allow citizens to regain a foothold in the governance process so that their needs can be addressed? Equally important, can such options exist within the neo-liberal structures adopted by cities?

In an attempt to respond to some of these questionable issues, this chapter employs a case study of Atlanta's governance strategy related to citizens' housing rights between 1992 and 2012. The relationship between marginalized groups in the city of Atlanta and urban governance structures, particularly the Black Urban Regime, is examined. Moreover, the extent to which different groups influence the political decision making processes within a neoliberal framework is explored.

NEOLIBERALISM AND THE RESTRUCTURING OF POLITICAL GOVERNANCE

Neoliberalism, an ideological commitment to free market capitalism as a panacea for socioeconomic development and human well-being, emerged in the 1970s. It quickly became the predominant political-economic perspective informing the global economy (Curtis 2016; Harvey 2005; Theodore, Peck, and Brenner 2011). The widespread turn towards neoliberalism is characterized by deregulation, privatization, and state withdrawal from the provision of social services (Harvey 2005). These practices are in direct contradiction to the social democratic tradition initiated after the Second World War in which the state was heavily concerned with, and involved in, maintaining the welfare of its citizens. This was commonly achieved by the redistribution of capital and resources across society. In the process of implementing the free-market ideology of neoliberalism, the state is reengineered to deregulate critical areas of society and facilitate the spread and implementation of market rule (Peck and Tickell 2007; Theodore et al. 2011; Wacquant 2012). Rather than shrink the state, neoliberals have worked to reconfigure it in ways that serve the ends of market rationale (Soss, Fording, and Schram 2011).

Neoliberalism is a process that rejects the egalitarian liberal tradition of the Keynesian economy[1] that shaped the state's relationship with American citizens between 1930 and 1970. In response to the crisis of the Great Depression, the U.S. government instituted a number of social welfare policies and programs to address basic needs and provide economic opportunities for its citizens. Neoliberalism emerged in the 1970s following the global oil crisis and redefined the relationship between the state and the citizen. The federal government absolved its social welfare position touting individuality, followed an unfettered free market, and adopted a non-intervening state protocol. These measures were considered essential components needed to ensure freedom for the individual (Hackworth 2007; Harvey 2005).

Where adopted, the process of neoliberalism has significantly altered each scale's relationship with governance. Contrary to the theoretical idea that the state's power is waning or its level of importance is diminishing, the state's role in society is actually changing to advance the neoliberal agenda (Castells 2000; Castells 2005; Hackworth 2007; Harvey 2005). The state no longer prioritizes the social well-being of its citizens as was the case during the Keynesian era of governance. With this shift, the state rolled back many of its resources and opportunities to its citizens to engender competition among all social actors (Harvey 2005; Nicholls 2008). In its current iteration, the state's primary task is to enact policies that allow capital to flow unabatedly to the most competitive market participants. Effectively, the state that once facilitated redistribution of wealth and resources among its citizens began promoting a form of upward redistribution (Harvey 1989).

From an ideological and theoretical perspective, neoliberalism is a clean and straightforward process. However, its processes and effects are articulated differently according to the particular geographical location, a reality Brenner and Theodore (2002, 3) deemed "actually existing neoliberalism." In the United States, multi-scalar neoliberal restructuring of society focused primarily on its growing cities. However, the shift in the political and economic frameworks of cities produced certain dubious outcomes. For example, Atlanta's adoption of neoliberal governance practices between 1992 and 2012, along with the collapse of the housing market in 2008, led to the complete demolition of its public housing stock and the dramatic rise of foreclosed homes. Interestingly, political scientist Clarence Stone (1989), in his book *Regime Politics: Governing Atlanta, 1946–1988*, delineates the rise of a coalition between the city's white political and business leaders and Black leaders as the core governing body, as occurring around the same time—the latter half of the twentieth century. This coalition steered the city towards its rise as a globally recognized metropolis, an ascension that has often occurred at the expense of the city's poor and working-class citizens.

ATLANTA: NEOLIBERALISM AND PUBLIC HOUSING

Atlanta, Georgia, is often referred to as the crown jewel of the United States' southern region. Georgia Pacific, Coca-Cola, Home Depot, Delta Airlines, and United Parcel Service (UPS) are among the Fortune 500 companies that call the metro-Atlanta area home. Music artists, actors and actresses, and other entertainers have added to the city's fame. Home to the late Reverend

Dr. Martin Luther King, Jr., the most prominent leader of America's Civil Rights Movement, it was dubbed the "City too Busy to Hate" by elected officials in the 1960s, in an attempt to distance Atlanta from the legacy of racism associated with the region. To many, Atlanta has everything a person could ask for in a city.

Despite these many accolades, Atlanta does have its share of problems. According to a 2011 report from the U.S. Department of Commerce, Atlanta had the largest measure of income inequality between 2005 and 2009 among places in the United States with more than 100,000 residents (Weinberg 2011). Moreover, the income inequality gap keeps increasing. For example, the *Brookings Institute Community Survey* (2015) reported that once again Atlanta ranked as the city with the highest gap between rich and poor. Researchers compared the incomes of the highest-earning 5 percent of a city's residents with those in the lowest fifth. The findings showed that the richest Atlanta households earned almost 20 times more than the city's poorest residents: $288,159 compared to $14,988. Residents were concerned about the growing inequality also linked to low job creation and high unemployment. They saw these problems as a blemish on Atlanta's public image and were looking towards the elected officials in the 14-karat gold-plated capitol building for solutions. Overall, there was an urgent need to counteract the local effects of a slowly recovering national economy and a restructuring of the global economy.

Urban Regimes and the Atlanta Way

Since the post–World War II economic expansion, a long-term business cycle, following the end of World War II in 1945 and lasting through the mid-1970s, Atlanta's governance structure has operated on a coalition built on informal arrangements between the city's business elite and its public officials, a governance structure known as the urban regime (Arena 2003; Reed Jr. 1999; Stone 1989). The coalition is typically comprised of any combination of elected officials, business owners, supporters of the electorate, major property owners, and governmental administrators (Banks 2000). Members of the coalition are tied together by common interests that guide their policy development. Atlanta's urban regime developed in the post-war era when its business elite recognized that the city was more likely to engage in a service-based economy rather than the large industrial type economic model adopted by other cities at that time. The business elite sought out informal partnerships with elected officials so as to create conditions that could protect and maintain their capital in a changing economy (Stone 1989).

Atlanta's urban regime has, however, evolved since its inception in the 1940s. Protests from Atlanta's Black residents over housing, education, and work opportunities in subsequent decades forced several compromises from

Atlanta's historically White governing coalition (Bayor 1996; Bayor 2000). Blacks used their vote to influence the decisions of the governing coalition and to build their influence in the regime. By 1973, the size of Atlanta's Black electorate had grown large enough to elect Maynard Jackson as the city's first African American mayor. Jackson's election marked an important step in establishing Atlanta's Black urban regime (BUR), a regime led by Black mayoral leadership with a majority or near-majority Black electorate (Arena 2011; Banks 2000; Reed Jr. 1999). While the desire for community representation in the governance structure drove the election of Maynard Jackson, the tenure of Black mayors in the following four decades resulted more in a commitment to a pro-growth agenda, rather than addressing the inequities faced by a significant portion of their Black and economically disadvantaged urban communities.

The Black electorate responsible for Jackson's election waned in the following decades. Manley Banks' (2000) analysis of Atlanta's changing electorate provides some insight into the influence of electoral politics on urban governance. For example, during the 1970s, middle class Blacks moved out of the city to Atlanta's nearby suburbs while affluent Whites returned to the city. Since voting registration is often concentrated among Atlanta's middle class residents, White voters gained significant voting powers in the city's electoral process. The concerns of White middle-class urban dwellers were not the same as the economically disadvantaged African American residents who remained in the city. Consequently, to remain electable, Black mayors had to balance the needs of the less politically active and economically dispossessed African American citizens with the needs of the more politically active and economically powerful, predominantly white citizens and business elites. The needs of the two groups rarely overlapped. Consequently, political leaders often overlooked the needs of the Black poor in favor of the latter group, whose goals were more aligned with the municipal administration's vision. This is highly observable in governance decisions around public housing where the urban regime catered to a pro-growth agenda much to the detriment of the city's impoverished communities and citizens.

Political Marginalization and Public Housing

Similar to other major U.S. cities, public housing has been a significant issue facing Atlanta's poor since the postwar era. Public housing is one of the last vestiges of the Keynesian era of national governance. Atlanta's construction of Techwood Homes in 1936 was the first public housing unit in the nation, commissioned under President Franklin Roosevelt's New Deal (Atlanta Housing Authority 2010; Ferguson 2002; Ruechel 1997). Techwood Homes initially housed white residents only. University Homes, John Eagan Homes, and John Hope Homes were built in Atlanta's westside communities to house some of the city's poor Black residents. Several public housing units were subsequently created over the next three decades to provide basic amenities to Atlanta's underprivileged citizens of all races. In contrast, in the 1980s, Mayor Andrew Young pursued the construction of middle and upper class homes advancing the pro-growth agenda despite the continued need for more public housing (Banks 2000). In 1993, Mayor Bill Campbell appointed Renee Glover, a former corporate finance attorney, CEO of the Atlanta Housing Authorit. Moving away from any commitment to rehabilitate or renovate the city's public housing, Campbell's administration initiated the destruction of Atlanta's public housing on the eve of the 1996 Olympics. Techwood Homes was demolished and the subsequent building served as the dormitory for visiting world-class athletes.

By 2010, the Atlanta Housing Authority, a non-governmental institution, oversaw the demolition of a majority of Atlanta's public housing stock and the construction of several mixed-income housing developments funded by the federal HOPE-VI program (Oakley, Ruel, and Reid 2013). The destruction of public housing and subsequent construction of mixed-income housing was promoted as a salve to the concentration of high poverty rates, crime, drug use, and low educational attainment because it dispersed low-income and indigent residents. This line of thought and policy implementation reflected neoliberalism's reliance on market-based solutions to social issues. That is, the city government absolved its responsibility of social welfare and placed it on the individual, irrespective of disparity in resources and opportunities based on race/ethnicity, gender, and social class. Within this neoliberal framework, there was also a shift from public investment to the involvement of private entities. Support for the neoliberal model was espoused by Atlanta Housing Authority's former CEO Renee Glover (2010), who credited the federal government's deregulation of public housing as the key to Atlanta's successful transition beyond the public housing model. According to Glover:

> In part, [the improved living conditions of tenants receiving assistance] is made possible because private investment now leverages the federal funds allocated to the authority. Thus, instead of being barely able to keep up with critical repairs to the decrepit projects, the infusion of private investment has made possible the creation of livable, affordable and quality neighborhoods.[2]

Not all of Atlanta's public housing has been removed. Atlanta's private investment also supports the maintenance of the remaining public housing units left in the city—11 high rises and one apartment community (Torpy 2010). However, these are more likely to house elderly European immigrants rather than the residents of the razed homes (Husock 2010). Mixed income developments replaced the demolished public housing but very few of the original residents were able to return to these sites. Between 1994 and 2011, nearly 50,000 residents were relocated from demolished public housing communities (Oakley, Ruel, and Reid 2013). Most residents were awarded Section 8 Vouchers to relocate to other areas. However, displaced citizens' ability to relocate to areas of their choice was often undermined by prospective rental agency staff who used criminal background and credit checks to select new tenants, nullifying the voucher's intended purpose. Oftentimes, it is difficult to find affordable housing outside that of public housing, and it is difficult to find public housing outside city limits.

In Atlanta, public housing concerns were specific to its poorer residents who were (and still are) disproportionally African Americans. Governance decisions headed by Mayors Young and Campbell and carried out by private corporations resulted in dispossession and hardship for this group of citizens. The need for affordable housing was outweighed by the interests of improving capital gains via more expensive housing stock, and the global prestige generated by hosting the Olympic Games. Thus, in the 1990s, economically disadvantaged African Americans were politically marginalized, abandoned by their Black electoral representatives, their homes demolished and their families displaced.

The analysis of Atlanta's governing structure during this twenty-year period found that the city displayed a strong commitment to business-first governance reflecting the entrepreneurial thrust of neoliberalism. Additionally, the dwindling relationship between Atlanta's public housing residents, largely African American, and the city's political leadership affirms Adolph Reed, Jr.'s (1999) assessment of the Black Urban Regime's (BUR) commitment to its business and middle-class constituency. Lastly, Atlanta's citizens' collective action to protect residents from foreclosed home seizures provides a glimpse into extra-political resistance to neoliberalism. The analysis of Atlanta's BUR demonstrates how this "new" state's relationship with citizens cuts across race and ethnicity and is intersected by social class. The housing outcomes are a direct result of Atlanta's neoliberal governance structure and its public-private partnerships. Businesses and corporations collaborate with state actors to influence legislation, determine public policies, and establish regulatory frameworks (Hackworth 2007; Harvey 1989). The public-private partnerships operate as the managing vessel for neoliberalism and to safeguard the neoliberal schema. Resisting neoliberal policies at the local level is difficult but not impossible.

RESISTANCE TO NEOLIBERAL POLICYMAKING ON HOUSING

American cities have always been prominent sites for social movements against unpopular state policies and mandates since the 1960s (Castells 1983). Urban social movements, in Castells' seminal work *The Grassroots and the City* were contextualized by a climate of social unrest. Several groups wanted to change aspects of their society and created opportunities to do so. For a while, it seemed as if the contemporary social climate was not the same. In Mayer's (2006) estimate, the state, and cities in particular, were no longer the antagonists they were in the previous era. As cities' federal support waned during the neoliberal shift in the state, many groups who were on the frontlines of social movements were invited to participate as stake-holders in the governance process. Civic organizations and interest groups engaged in partnerships with the municipal governments to address issues such as poverty, unemployment, and welfare dependency, among others, ran the risk of being neutralized because of a dependency on state resources (Nicholls 2008).

To say, however, that American cities are any less antagonistic today is not accurate. For example, the recent political climate in the United States with the propagandistic polemics, attempted policies, and structuring of Donald Trump's presidency has spurred the rebooting and rebirth of social movements around a wide range of social issues. Similarly, anti-globalization movements constitute another trend in contemporary social movements (Arena 2003; Mayer 2006). Local chapters of the anti-globalization networks work with older social movement organizations and groups to address the local effects of neoliberal restructuring. Again, while the identification of these groups is beyond the purview of this research, a brief glimpse into Occupy Wall Street's Atlanta cohort offers an insightful example of this latter trend.

Like other Occupy groups around the country and the globe, Occupy Atlanta (OA) is comprised of a variety of people from various backgrounds vocalizing their angst against the institutions sustaining the debt crisis, and the growing gap between the classes. Atlanta protestors have fought bank foreclosures in a related movement called "Occupy Our Homes." OA members went to the homes of Atlanta and metro-Atlanta neighborhoods and provided moral support, financial, and legal resources to citizens facing foreclosure. They were successful in their advocacy on behalf of Brigitte Walker—a former army personnel who was critically wounded during a tour in the Iraq War, and who ended her career with medical retirement. With her wages cut in half and medical bills piling up, Occupy Atlanta protestors worked with Walker to stave off the banks and acquire a loan modification allowing her to keep her home (Occupy Atlanta 2011). This local response is a small victory in a larger movement. However, it is evidence that there is potential for resource mobilization across networks as was actualized in this instance, and perhaps many more like it in other cities.

As the parameters for who is considered "marginal" under the current economic crisis are diverse, the realization of common interests may engender collective action between groups who would not have thought to work together before. It is important, however, to be mindful that cities are extensions of the state and will attempt to neutralize and/or retaliate against change agents so as to sustain the dominant power structure (Graham 2010). For example, citizens utilizing non-violent protest tactics are arrested and jailed with high bail. In other parts of the nation, police have utilized brute force to subdue movement activists. The lengths to which the state would go to neutralize and repress citizens' actions can have a direct impact upon the success and setbacks of social movements.

CONCLUSION

Urban governments have the arduous task of attempting to preserve their cities in the wake of severely diminished fiscal support from the federal government. Such is the case in Atlanta. In this chapter, we illustrate how Atlanta's governance structure operates with uneven input from its citizens, particularly its economically disadvantaged citizens. In an ideal democracy, elected public officials would address the needs and issues of the entire electorate responsible for their tenure in office. However, the case study of Atlanta's city housing shows that urban regimes operating in the era of neoliberal restructuring do not wholly abide by this democratic sentiment. The governance coalition between Atlanta's business elite and its public officials marginalized its electorate along class lines. As a result of structural racism those most likely to be negatively affected by neoliberal policies are poor and working class Blacks and other minority groups.

Additionally, the desire to remain integrated into the global network of capital flow is a clear motivator in Atlanta's governance strategy. Reshaping the city's landscape is done with the focus on making it a viable place to do business and a destination for upper class residents. Atlanta is a city for those who can contribute to its capital accumulation, for people and businesses with money in hand. Those who cannot contribute are ignored, made invisible, or removed from sight altogether. If this is the Atlanta Way, where and how do marginalized groups enter and influence the decision-making process in a city governed by regime politics? This situation places urban governance actors in precarious positions where they must choose whether they will implement policies to improve the conditions of the citizens or follow policies that will keep the city afloat in a global economy. As Beall (2000, 84) emphasized in her analysis of urban policy for the marginalized poor, "the power of local governments to shape outcomes in favor of the poor is easily undermined by the influence of forces beyond their control." Yet agency exists in the decision-making process. The urban regime is not completely beholden to the will of the macro-level processes.

Thus, the fundamental concern underlying this brief analysis of Atlanta's urban regime is how cities are restructured and for whose benefit it is being done. It is unclear that when decisions are made based on capital pro-growth interests that marginalized citizens can still influence the governance process. Furthermore, if marginalized citizens and groups can no longer influence the decision-making process through their votes, then what mechanisms for involvement in the governance process is there beyond the electoral process? Social movements can play an important role in advocacy and peer pressure for state officials and elected representatives to hear the voices of the marginalized and the views of democratic-thinking citizens.

Working within the established governance system to influence the decision-making process is also an option. There are alternatives to the regime structure of Atlanta; urban regimes can be comprised of diverse partners. Electing public officials who come from marginalized groups may be a way to develop a progressive regime that is committed to addressing the needs of the economically deprived populations. Needless to say, this can be difficult to accomplish if the person elected is in the minority within the governance structure. A concerted effort to elect multiple public officials with commitments to social investment will be necessary to begin shifting the direction of the regime. Moreover, the understanding that there cannot be pro-growth without socio-economic development of all groups is important.

NOTES

1. According to the Oxford Reference online, Keynesian economic theory is based on the ideas of John Maynard Keynes (1883–1946), developed in the 1930s, which assigned an important role to the state as well as to the private sector. Central elements of this theory are the failure of prices, especially wages, to adjust to clear markets; and the effect of changes in aggregate demand on real output and employment. Keynesian economics asserts that aggregate demand is the driving force in the economy; in particular, during a recession, the government can boost economic activity by increasing its spending, thereby inducing private consumption and investment. Post-Keynesian economics, which prevailed in the 1960s and 1970s, emphasized the role of uncertainty, path dependence, and the effects of money on the real economy. From the early 1990s, the ideas of Keynes have been further developed in New Keynesian economics which endeavors to derive them from micro foundations, in particular, assuming rational expectations for the economic agents. http://www.oxfordreference.com/view/10.1093/oi/authority.20110803100035353.

2. Glover, Renee Lewis, "AHA Lessons Learned: Looking Back After 15 Years." *Lessons Learned* (blog), Atlanta Housing Authority, June 13, 2010, http://ahalessonslearned.blogspot.it/2010/06/looking-back-after-15-years.html.

REFERENCES

Arena, John. 2003. "Race and Hegemony: The Neoliberal Transformation of the Black Urban Regime and Working-Class Resistance." *American Behavioral Scientist* 47 (3): 352–80. doi:10.1177/0002764203256191.

————. 2011. "Bringing in the Black Working Class: The Black Urban Regime Strategy." *Science & Society* 75 (2): 153–79.

Atlanta Housing Authority. 2010. "Techwood Homes." Atlanta: Atlanta Housing Authority. http://www.atlantahousingauth.org/pressroom/index.cfm?Fuseaction=quickfacts.

Banks, Manley Elliot. 2000. "A Changing Electorate in a Majority Black City: The Emergence of a Neo-Conservative Black Urban Regime." *Journal of Urban Affairs* 22 (3): 265–278

Bayor, Ronald H. 1996. *Race and the Shaping of Twentieth-Century Atlanta.* Chapel Hill, NC: University of North Carolina Press.

————. 2000. "Atlanta: The Historical Paradox." In *The Atlanta Paradox*, edited by David L Sjoquist, 42–58. New York: Russell Sage Foundation.

Beall, Jo. 2000. "From the Culture of Poverty to Inclusive Cities: Re-Framing Urban Policy and Politics." *Journal of International Development* 12 (6): 843–56.

Brenner, Neil, and Nik Theodore. 2002a. "Cities and the Geographies of 'Actually Existing Neoliberalism.'" In *Spaces of Neoliberalism: Urban Restructuring in North America and Western Europe*, edited by Neil Brenner and Nik Theodore, 2–31. Malden, MA: Blackwell Publishing.

————. 2002b. "Spaces of Neoliberalism: Urban Restructuring in North America and Western Europe." Malden, MA: Blackwell Publishing.

Castells, Manuel. 1983. *The City and the Grassroots: A Cross-Cultural Theory of Urban Social Movements.* Berkeley and Los Angeles, CA: University of California Press.

————. 2000. "Towards a Sociology of the Network Society." *Contemporary Sociology* 29 (5): 693–99.

————. 2005. "Global Governance and Global Politics." *Political Science and Politics* 38 (1): 9–16.

Ferguson, Karen. 2002. *Black Politics in New Deal Atlanta.* Chapel Hill, NC: University of North Carolina Press.

Glover, Renee Lewis. 2010. "AHA Lessons Learned: Looking Back After 15 Years." *Lessons Learned.* http://ahalessonslearned.blogspot.com/2010/06/looking-back-after-15-years.html.

Graham, Stephen. 2010. *Cities Under Siege: The New Military Urbanism.* New York: Verso.

Hackworth, Jason. 2007. *The Neoliberal City: Governance, Ideology, and Development in American Urbanism.* Ithaca, NY: Cornell University Press.

Harvey, David. 1989. "From Managerialism to Entrepreneurialism: The Transformation in Urban Governance in Late Capitalism." *Geografiska Annaler. Series B, Human Geography* 71 (1): 3–17. doi:10.2307/490503.

————. 2005. *A Brief History of Neoliberalism.* New York: Oxford University Press.

Husock, Howard. 2010. "HUSOCK: Reinventing Public Housing." *The Washington Times.* http://www.washingtontimes.com/news/2010/nov/8/reinventing-public-housing/.

Mayer, Margit. 2006. "Manuel Castells' The City and the Grassroots." *International Journal of Urban and Regional Research* 30 (1): 202–6. doi:10.1111/j.1468–2427.2006.00652.x.

Nicholls, Walter J. 2008. "The Urban Question Revisited: The Importance of Cities for Social Movements." *International Journal of Urban and Regional Research* 32 (4).

Oakley, Deirdre, Erin Ruel, and Lesley Reid. 2013. "Atlanta's Last Demolitions and Relocations: The Relationship Between Neighborhood Characteristics and Resident Satisfaction." *Housing Studies* 28 (2): 205–34. doi:10.1080/02673037.2013.767887.

Occupy Atlanta. 2011. "Ocupy Atlanta Helps Save Iraq War Veteran's Home." Atlanta, GA. http://occupyatlanta.org/2011/12/20/occupy-atlanta-helps-save-iraq-war-veteran's-home/#.TwyzXkoVwy4.

Peck, Jamie and Adam Tickell. 2007. "Conceptualizing Neoliberalism, Thinking Thatcherism." In *Contesting Neoliberalism: Urban Frontiers*, edited by Helga Leitner, Jamie Peck, and Eric S. Sheppard, 26–50. New York, NY: Guilford Press.

Reed Jr., Adolph. 1999. "The Black Urban Regime: Structural Origins and Constraints." In *Stirrings in the Jug: Black Politics in the Post-Segregation Era*, 79–116. Minneapolis, MN: University of Minnesota Press.

Ruechel, Frank. 1997. "New Deal Public Housing , Urban Poverty , and Jim Crow : Techwood and University Homes in Atlanta." *The Georgia Historical Quarterly* 81 (4): 915–37.

Soss, Joe, Richard C. Fording, and Sanford F. Schram. *Disciplining the Poor: Neoliberal Paternalism and the Persistent Power of Race*. Chicago: University of Chicago Press.

Stone, Clarence N. 1989. *Regime Politics: Governing Atlanta, 1946—1988*. Lawrence, KS: University Press of Kansas.

Theodore, Nik, Jamie Peck, and Neil Brenner. 2011. "Neoliberal Urbanism: Cities and the Rule of Markets," in *A New Companion to the City*, edited by Gary Bridge and Sophie Watson, 15–25. London: Blackwell.

Wacquant, Loïc. 2012. "Three Steps to a Historical Anthropology of Actually Existing Neoliberalism." *Social Anthropology* 20 (1): 66–79.

Weinberg, Daniel H. 2011. "U.S. Neighborhood Income Inequality in the 2005–2009 Period." *American Community Survey Reports*. Washington D.C.

Chapter Nine

Black Farmers' General and Gendered Strikes against the USDA

Willie Jamaal Wright

On December 9, 2010, President Barack Obama signed into law House Resolution 4783 (H.R. 4783), also known as the Claims Resolution Act of 2010. This piece of legislation authorized the United States (U.S.) Department of the Treasury to allot payment to claimants who could prove that officials within the United States Department of Agriculture (USDA) used racial bias in order to preclude Black farmers, landowners, and would-be farmers from acquiring various forms of assistance and loans (United States House of Representatives 2010). Agricultural agencies such as the Farmers Home Association (now Farm Service Agency) and the Cooperative Extension Service (CES) provide financial, technical, and agricultural assistance to landowners, farmers, and future farmers. The landmark class-action lawsuit, *Pigford et al. v. Glickman*, by Black agrarians, argued that employees of the USDA's county-level agencies[1] denied applications from, and assistance to, Black applicants or would-be farmers.[2] According to Pigford claimants, once he was made aware of these issues, then Secretary of Agriculture Dan Glickman, failed to move with all deliberate speed to redress these problems (*Pigford et al. v. Glickman* 1996). Due to issues such as the forced removal from land, access to capital, loss of their property), Black farmers have experienced higher rates of foreclosure and land loss than their white counterparts (Gilbert, Sharp, and Felin 2001; Gilbert, Sharp, and Fezlin 2002; Wood and Gilbert 2000; USCCR 1982). Once the suit was filed, Secretary Glickman instituted a moratorium on all farm foreclosures and formed the Civil Rights Action Team (CRAT) to investigate the claims of discrimination made by over 400 Pigford claimants (Civil Rights Action Team 1997).

The CRAT conducted twelve listening sessions in eleven states through-out the southern United States. These town hall meetings culminated in a report, on the "Civil Rights and the USDA." The scathing dossier was defini-tive proof that county-level agencies under the auspices of the USDA were ensconced with racism. Racial discrimination was said to have resulted in differential treatment and unequal access to resources for Black farmers and landowners (Civil Rights Action Team 1997). Carmen Harris (2008) believes Black applicants were treated in this manner due to an all too pervasive belief of Black inferiority (i.e., white supremacy):

> The popular belief in African American inferiority and pragmatic political compromises aimed at creating a bureaucracy serving the nation's agricultural constituency and ensuring its longevity, led to a conscious marginalization of African American interests within the program. Federal extension officials not only tolerated, but actively supported, discrimination within the southern branches of the service (193).

Applicants knew all too well the power of county-level officers. During one CRAT listening session, an attendee stated local farm committees held the power to send a farmer "up the road to fortune or down the road to foreclo-sure" (Civil Rights Action Team 1997, 7). This is but a snapshot of Black farmers' and would-be farmers' history with structural racism in the South. Their histories are connected to the eras of sharecropping, debt peonage, and enslavement times when scores of Black agrarians were kept tied to the lands of white planters (Daniel 1990; Daniel 2013; Du Bois 1935; Du Bois 1994).

Though a step forward, Pigford I did not take into account the generations of exploitation that occurred prior to 1981.[3] Nor does it account for the ongoing acts of aggression against Black farmers and landowners. In what some argue was too narrow a window, in order to be eligible to join the Pigford lawsuit, one must have met the following criteria:

> All African American farmers who (1) farmed, or attempted to farm, between January 1, 1981, and December 31, 1996; (2) applied to the United States Department of Agriculture (USDA) during that time period for participation in a federal farm credit or benefit program and who believed that they were discriminated against on the basis of race in USDA's response to that applica-tion; and (3) filed a discrimination complaint on or before July 1, 1997, regard-ing USDA's treatment of such farm credit or benefit application (*Pigford et al. v. Glickman* 1996, 36).

The following section presents research on the significance of landowning to Black rural families and communities. For decades scholars have studied the effects of landownership on Black men and women as well as the attitudes held by Black people regarding the significance of owning farmland.[4] Under-standing the varied importance of land to Black families and communities may help explain why Black landowners went to such lengths to challenge the USDA.

SIGNIFICANCE OF BLACK LANDOWNERSHIP

Since Emancipation, the ownership of property has provided a litany of social, economic, and political benefits for African American families. In the foreword to the landmark study, "The Black Rural Landowner—Endangered Species: Social, Political and Economic Implications," Frederick S. Humphries, former president of Tennessee State University wrote, "Since the turn of the century, it is estimated that blacks have loss in excess of 9,000,000 acres of rural land. The economic impact of this great lost is incomprehensible to many Americans" (Humphries 1976, 3). Considering that at the time of its publication, land constituted, "possibly the largest equity base under black control," the decline of Black-owned land was an all the more disconcerting phenomenon (Humphries 1976, 3). More than a mere landmass, landownership contributed to a number of positive effects among individual Black landowners and landowning families.

In a study of four Black families in Promise Land, Tennessee, Charles Nesbitt argues that throughout the postbellum history of this small, all Black town, landownership was a prerequisite for political power: "As one might suspect, where the zeal to acquire property existed to such a strong extent other attributes of citizenship could be likely found" (Nesbitt 1979, 40). Free, landholding Black men were more likely to challenge the racial hierarchy of the Jim Crow South with bold declarations of Black humanity and self-determination. Landownership was a key asset during the Civil Rights Movement. Landowning Black Southerners were known to house Freedom Riders and organizers with the Student Nonviolent Coordinating Committee (SNCC). And when sharecroppers were evicted for attempting to vote, some Black farmers offered up their land for the purpose of creating tent communities (Jeffries 2010). Furthermore, many of the Black men and women willing to engage in armed self-defense of their lives and livelihoods were landowners, or people making explicit claims to land and territory in the Deep South (Kelley 1991; Obadele 1970, 1974; Umoja 2013).

In a study of 147 Black landowners across three majority Black counties in rural Tennessee, Leo McGee and Robert Boone demonstrated that across generations, rural African Americans held land in high regard. Participants 55 and older believed owning land was more fulfilling than renting. Participants ages 23–28 believed owning land was important to one's self image and esteem (McGee and Boone 1979). Writing thirty plus years later, Pennick, Gray, and Thomas (2007) inquired further about the attitudes regarding landownership, and emphasized the perspectives of multiple generations and genders. Using a focus group method, the authors found that many women associate success and wealth with owning land. Ultimately, all of their participants, regardless of age and gender, associated owning land with economic success and political enfranchisement. Older generations, in particular, those who experienced the exigencies and excesses of the Civil Rights Movement viewed land as a source of political power (Pennick, Gray, and Thomas 2007). Moreover, Manning Marable (1979), William Nelson Jr. (1979), and Edward Pennick (1990) have all highlighted the political empowerment garnered through the effect of Black landowners.

In a review of 100 interviews conducted with Black residents of New Deal resettlement camps, Lester Salamon found that Black landowning farmers felt a sense of independence and had a more positive outlook about their lives than Black tenant farmers. They also fared better economically (Salamon 1979). To this day, Black descendants of the New Deal resettlement communities value and fight to retain land bestowed upon them by their farmer ancestors (Minkler 2000). Conducting a query of the affective aspects of landownership, Brown, Jr., Christy, and Gebremedhin (1994) found that owning land contributes to positive feelings of self-worth and self-identity, not to mention, the health and well-being of elderly Black landowners (Groger 1987). In a study of kinship affiliations in a rural community in North Carolina, Yvonne Jones (1980) posits ownership of land adds to the stability of kinship patterns and supports annual homecomings. Janice Dyer supports this position in her work on partition sales by Black heirs, stating that land is a "source of pride" for the rural Black residents (Dyer 2007, 95). In short, land provides Black rural families "a place to call home," one they are willing to defend (Dyer and Bailey 2008, 322).

THE ENSLAVED STRIKE BACK

W. E. B. Du Bois's magnum opus, *Black Reconstruction*, articulates the agency of enslaved Black men and women in the waning days of the Civil War.[5] In addition to providing an extensive history of the Civil War and the role of enslaved Black men in its development and conclusion, *Black Reconstruction* represented a shift in Du Bois's politics and writings toward the articulation of a deep-seated Black radical tradition in the United States. According to Cedric Robinson, Du Bois's ability to produce this tome— particularly following his elitist conceptualization of the talented tenth[6]— was the result of Du Bois's self-extrication from the Black petit bourgeoisie, their habits and norms, from "the notion that only a Black elite could realize the task of Negro resurrection" (Robinson 1983, 191). Rather than see liberation among Black elites, who, following Emancipation, had become power brokers in the space that separated white and Black life and who were known for "ruthlessly repressing mass Black mobilization," Du Bois turned to the self-determined political praxis of the Black masses (Robinson 1983, 191).[7] This transformation in Du Bois's politics, one inspired by Marxist analyzes and socialist revolutions (Horne 1686), came when he embarked on a quest to write a history of the radical Reconstruction that articulated the intersection of slavery, capitalism, and the agency of the enslaved.

Du Bois argues that the enslaved were workers. He indicates that though unpaid and unfree, their labor facilitated the development of the United States and the territorial expansion of Britain. As the focal motor of the American economy and Britain's cotton-based industrial economy, enslaved Black women became laborers who were the catalyst for the Civil War. He writes:

> Black labor became the foundation stone not only of the Southern social structure, but of Northern manufacture and commerce, of the English factory system, of the European commerce, of buying and selling on a world-wide scale (Du Bois 1935, 5) . . . It was thus the Black worker, as founding some of a new economic system in the nineteenth century and for the modern world, who brought civil war in America. He (and she) was its underlying cause, in spite of every effort to base the strife upon union and national power (Du Bois 1935, 15).

Du Bois makes clear that it was not the desire of the Union army to free the millions of slaves across the South. On the contrary, communities of enslaved men and women liberated themselves through an act of cunning. "What the Negro did was to wait, look and listen and try to see where his interest lay," says Du Bois (1935, 57). The strategic decision to leave plantations upon the advance of Union soldiers into Confederate territory and to transplant their self and service among Union encampments crippled the South's plantocracy beyond repair. This massive, leaderless movement, what Du Bois coined a "general strike," challenged his earlier belief that it would be educated Black men who would lead Black communities from exploitation and into enfranchisement (Du Bois 1994).

It also called into question notions held by Northern and Southern whites regarding the intelligence, inferiority, and docility of enslaved Black men and women. Their collective flight toppled a political economy reliant upon the exploitation of their labor and challenged a civil society incumbent upon their social death[8] (Wilderson III 2003; Hartman and Wilderson III 2003) and the exploitation of their labor. Over a century later, descendants of this roving mass of men and women would strike, this time in response to the USDA and its agents of authority.

PIGFORD CLAIMANTS' GENERAL STRIKE

Evidence of a general strike was not among the acts of the initial claimant within the Pigford case. Indeed, the conferencing of these men and women was due to many months of organizing by legal teams, Black farmer organizations, and other advocacy groups. Following the closing of the suit, it became known that there had been a discrepancy in the due date for claims. Officials with the USDA failed to make clear whether applications were to be submitted or postmarked by the due date. Thus, many applicants whose forms were postmarked on and not received by the due date were excluded from the original class of claimants (Pigford I). To make good on their error, the USDA created another class of claimants, known as Pigford II.

Following the reopening of the suit an unprecedented number of applicants. Given ample time and opportunity to express their grievances and to demand justice and recompense, Black farmers enacted a modern-day general strike, one that took advantage of the law and a clerical oversight. The response of Black farmers after the reopening of the case stupefied legal representatives and threatened to jeopardize the lawsuit in its entirety. The impact of the massive and unexpected enrollment of applicants in Pigford II was expressed in a court memorandum by District judge Paul Friedman:

> The size of the class, which the parties originally estimated would reach 2,000 farmers, quickly ballooned to more than 21,000 farmers. In light of this enormous and unforeseen expansion of the class . . . [and] faced with the need to assist a class more than 10 times larger than expected, Class Counsel made a wise decision: rather than tell potential class members that they could not participate in this case because there were not enough lawyers to assist each and every one of them with every aspect of the filing of their claims, Class Counsel chose to allow non-lawyers to assist some class members to assemble their claim packages, so long as an attorney ultimately reviewed and signed each claim before it was filed (as required by the Consent Decree) (*Pigford et al. v. Glickman* 2001).

The unexpected number of applicants required lawyers for both parties and the court to allow "non-lawyers" to support claimants in completing, filing, and managing their claims. Some of these supporters included nationally recognized organizations such as the Federation of Southern Cooperatives (FSC), the Black Farmers & Agriculturalists Association (BFAA), and the Land Loss Prevention Project (LLPP). These groups provided applicants with information and technical assistance needed to complete and submit applications. They also challenged the USDA to make structural changes at the federal and county levels, in order to eliminate its racist, classist, and patriarchal culture of discrimination (USCCR 1982; USCCR 1967).

There were other unforeseen results of the Black farmers' general strike. The original consent decree agreed upon by both legal teams included a financial reward in the amount of $500,000,000. However, the expanded number of applicants within the class-action suit *and* those who filed claims independently would require legal teams and the court to consider a larger sum—$1.5 billion to be parceled out in payments of $50,000 per applicant. Moreover, there was a fear that additional claims would stall or "obliterate" the suit. The following quote illustrates the trepidation induced by applicants' increasing claims:

> As Class Counsel, government counsel and movants' counsel all note in their briefs, the Consent Decree approved by the Court on April 14, 1999, is a grand, historical first step toward righting the wrongs visited upon thousands of African American farmers for decades by the United States Department of Agriculture. In the 20 months since the settlement was approved, more than 11,000 African American farmers have filed successful claims for relief and have received monetary compensation and/or debt relief totaling more than $500,000,000. This motion, brought on behalf of seven farmers out of the class of more than 21,000, seeks to obliterate this achievement and the possibility that thousands of additional farmers will receive additional millions of dollars by having the Court vacate the Consent Decree. Such an action would not only mean that the thousands of hours and hundreds of millions of dollars spent to this point administering the Decree would all be for naught, but also would mean that the thousands of farmers who have already prevailed on their claims would be forced to return their monetary awards to the government and would have to reassume the debt of which they just recently were relieved (*Pigford et al. v. Glickman* 2001).

The 2,000 applicants that were speculated to join the Pigford I claimants grew to an unanticipated 11,000 successful claimants in a matter of 20 months. Though the USDA had conducted a series of listening sessions with farmers throughout the South, the agency, Judge Friedman, and attorneys for the plaintiffs and defendants had not anticipated such a response from a leaderless mass of agrarians. Contemporary Black farmers, like their enslaved forebear Black farmers, had taken advantage of an opportunity to assert their agency in the aftermath of the Pigford case. Black farmers and their advocates continue to mobilize to ensure that all just claimants receive settlements and to oppose attacks against their character (Daniel 2013).

Attack Against Applicants

In 2013, a *New York Times* (NYT) reporter, Sharon LaFraniere, published a lengthy polemic about the Pigford lawsuit insinuating widespread fraud. In the article, "U.S. Opens Spigot after Farmers Claim Discrimination," LaFraniere (2013) made it appear that because many applicants did not have evidence (other than testimony) of racism and that some disingenuous claims were filed, the entire suit was fraught. In response, Black farmer organizations rallied to expose inaccuracies within LaFraniere's article. The Network of the Black Farm Groups and Advocates, a collective of nine Black farmer groups/advocates, immediately published a press release adding context, truth, and clarity to a longstanding issue of discrimination within the USDA (The Network of the Black Farm Groups and Advocates 2013).

Rachel Slocum, who at the time was an Assistant Professor of Geography at the University of Wisconsin–La Crosse, a scholar who is concerned with race and food access, challenged the biased article in a letter to the editor of the NYT. Slocum (2013) insisted:

> "Federal Spigot Flows as Farmers Claim Bias" underplays the history of racial dispossession, uses cherry-picked examples, and creates needless antipathy to the lawsuit and the settlement with Black farmers. Focusing on fraud and invoking familiar, racially freighted stereotypes of undeserving opportunists serves to throw into question all payouts rather than explaining why they were ordered in the first place. The Agriculture Department acknowledges racial and gender discrimination against farmers. The loss of farms we have witnessed over the past 90 years has disproportionately affected African-American farmers. Had the Agriculture Department provided loans and other assistance to everyone equitably, the landscape of the United States would look quite different.

In addition to clearing the names of countless applicants, Black farmers and their advocates called for structural changes within the USDA.[9] It is commonly believed the USDA has not cleaned house and that many of the perpetrators who instigated the injustices that led to this legal process are still employed by the agency and have, perhaps, risen to supervisory positions. As of yet, the only USDA employee who has been publicly reprimanded and terminated for racial discrimination is Shirley Sherrod,[10] a Black woman.

In the next section, Angela Davis's reflections on the role of Black women within enslaved communities serves as a guide to understanding Shirley Sherrod's work as an advocate for Black farming families. Her untimely and unwarranted termination by the USDA, and her necessary and ongoing role in what has been presented as a male-dominated struggle for land and justice are both discussed.

THE ROLE OF THE BLACK AGRARIAN WOMAN

Confined in a prison cell and empowered with information distilled from the pages of a limited prison library, Angela Davis reflected upon on the role of the Black woman in the slave community. Her purpose for doing so was to refute the "matriarchal Black woman . . . as one of the fatal by-products of slavery" (Davis 1972, 82). The stereotype of the emasculating Black woman, that gained traction in politics and America's popular imagination, suggested Black women capitulated to the dehumanizing pressures of enslavement by becoming caricatures of Black men. The Moynihan report, which was taken up by various segments of white and Black society, perpetuated these presumptions (Office of Policy Planning and Research 1965). As a challenge, Davis advanced a community-centered approach to understanding Black women's emancipatory roles within enslaved communities, not unlike Du Bois's (1935) work on radical Reconstruction.

Davis (1972) argues that during chattel slavery, a system in which the majority of the daily movements of the enslaved were surveilled, the slave cabin was a place where one could move beyond the watchful eye of an overseer. As a result, the domestic sphere of the slave cabin became a place where an ethics of redemption was made possible and from whence insurrection could be fomented:

> But the community gravitating around the domestic quarters might possibly permit a retrieval of the man and the woman in their fundamental humanity. We can assume that in a very material sense it was only in domestic life—away from the eyes and whip of the overseer—that slaves could attempt to assert the modicum of freedom they still retained (Davis 1972, 86).

Considered to be the abject opposite of white women (i.e., docility, beauty, purity, etc.), Black women were forced to perform the same back-breaking fieldwork, suffered the same punishments (and then some), and shared in subversive tactics alongside Black men. And because their subjection was both raced and gendered, Davis suggests[11] that it is from the subject position of Black womanhood where a liberatory praxis would derive.

One of the many roles Black women held was agent provocateur of resistance as women "would prepare to ascend to the same levels of resistance which were accessible to her man" (Davis 1972, 89). Forms of resistance varied; simple harassment through slowed work, the destruction of tools, attempts to poison food, and outright attacks were ways that Black women fought to curtail the ubiquitously dehumanizing social structure of slavery. The efforts of Black women did not go unnoticed and unchecked by white enslavers. Black women's bodies were subject to the same tortures as their male counterparts (i.e., lashing, hangings, rape, and beatings). According to Davis (1972), these acts of counterinsurgency were meant not only to demean Black women but also to wound and make impotent any pang of resistance within the Black man (Davis 1972, 89). Nevertheless, challenges to enslavement persisted:

> the few uprisings—too spectacular to be relegated to oblivion by racism of ruling class historians—were not isolated occurrences. . . . The reality, we

know now, was that these open rebellions erupted with such a frequency that they were as much a part of the texture of slavery as the conditions of servitude themselves. And these revolts were only the tip of an iceberg: resistance expressed itself in other grand modes and also in the seemingly trivial forms of feigned illness and studied indolence (Davis, 1972, 86).

It is within this legacy, of Black women's resistance to domination and oppression that the case of Shirley Sherrod is examined. Through her role in establishing a Black land cooperative, along with her support for Black farmers, Shirley Sherrod—the once unduly disgraced USDA employee—embodied an agrarian tradition of resistance in the face of a right wing counterinsurgency.

Shirley Sherrod and the Counterinsurgency of the Right

Shirley Sherrod's activism on behalf of Black farmers extends back decades. In the mid-1970s, Sherrod, along with her husband and other Black farmers/landowners created New Communities, Inc., a Black-owned collective designed to acquire rural land and produce Black homesteads. By 1985 New Communities, Inc. had amassed approximately 6,000 acres of land. However, due to spurious schemes including the denial of much-needed loans from their local Farmers Home Administration (FmHA), the collective lost much of its acreage. Sherrod, her husband, and their partners enrolled and received financial settlements in the Pigford case (Pickert 2010).

In keeping with the tradition of resistance put forward by Angela Davis, Sherrod's stance, along with those of other Black women, past and present, illustrate the central importance of a collective stance to improvement of Black life in rural America. Furthermore, it suggests that the survival mechanisms engendered by Black women were meant to push the Black community ahead, not to supplant a patriarchal position born of Western ideals of manhood and family structures. On the contrary:

> alongside her man, accepting or providing guidance according to her talents and the nature of their tasks. She was in no sense an authoritarian figure; neither her domestic role nor her acts of resistance could relegate the man to the shadows. On the contrary, she herself had just been forced to leave behind the shadowy realm of female passivity (Davis 1972, 98).

Such acts, whether in the past or the present, do not go unchallenged. In 2012, Shirley Sherrod became the face of a national debacle that concluded in her being relieved of her position as the director of the USDA's Georgia Rural Development office. Sherrod was terminated by Secretary of Agriculture Tom Vilsack after a video surfaced that appeared to show Sherrod discussing how she had discriminated against a white farmer. The video created a firestorm of media attention and thrust Sherrod into the limelight as a bigot who allowed a bias to override her moral compass and civic duty. Andrew Breitbart, the conservative blogger who leaked the strategically edited tape, called for her immediate resignation. In short order, Sherrod was admonished by Secretary Vilsack, President Barack Obama, and Ben Jealous, then president of the National Association for the Advancement of Colored People (NAACP). Breitbart's attack defamed and demoralized Sherrod's character in the eyes of the public.[12] What is worse is that he was successful in enlisting those who should have been her fiercest supporters into her public castigation. Hence, so-called seekers of racial justice were mere pawns within a web of deceit. In the midst of the firestorm, Sherrod would submit a hurried resignation to Secretary Vilsack via Blackberry, while parked on the side of a country road (Condon 2010).

Following a careful investigation of the entire video and Sherrod's strong defense of her character and her record as a civil rights advocate—not to mention a CNN interview with the alleged aggrieved white farmer and his wife—Secretary Vilsack apologized and offered her another position with the agency, which she declined. For his part in the matter, President Obama called Sherrod to offer an apology (Montopoli 2010), while Ben Jealous issued his *mea culpa* via a press release on the NAACP website. In part he wrote:

> Having reviewed the full tape, spoken to Ms. Sherrod, and most importantly heard the testimony of the white farmers mentioned in this story, we now believe the organization that edited the documents did so with the intention of deceiving millions of Americans. I apologized to Ms. Sherrod, clearly a committed and selfless public servant, who had been unfairly maligned (Jealous 2010).

Secretary Vilsak, President Obama, and Ben Jealous had not watched the video in its entirety. The portion shown to television audiences had been edited to portray Sherrod as a bigot who had abused her power to hinder Roger and Eloise Spooner from retaining their farmland. The unedited recording shows Sherrod discussing how the demands of her job, combined with her experience with white terrorism in the Jim Crow South, tested her sense of justice and equality:

> When I made that commitment [to accept the position], I was making that commitment to Black people, and to Black people only. But you know God will show you things, and he'll put things in your path so that, that you realize that the struggle is really about poor people. You know, the first time that I was faced with having to help a white farmer save his farm, he took a long time talking. But he was trying to show me that he was superior to me. I knew what he was doing. But he had to come to me for help. What he didn't know, while he was taking all that time trying to show he was superior to me, is I was

> trying to decide just how much help I was gone give him. I was struggling with
> the fact that so many Black people had lost their farmland, and here I was
> faced with having to help a white person save their land. So, I didn't give him
> the full force of what I could do. I did enough. (NAACP 2010).

Sherrod goes on to say that she introduced the farmer to a white lawyer with
the belief that he would feel more comfortable with a member of his own
race and gender and that he would get the help he needed. The results of her
decision would give her a crash course in intra-class bias:

> Chapter 12 bankruptcy had just been enacted for the family farmer. So, I
> figured if I take him [the white farmer] to them [a white lawyer], that his own
> kind would take care of him. That's when it was revealed to me, that y'all, it's
> about poor versus those who have. . . . But, during that time we would have
> these injunctions against the Department of Agriculture. So, they couldn't
> foreclose on him. . . . So, everything's going fine [and] I'm thinking he being
> taken care of by the white lawyer. And then they lifted the injunction against
> [the] USDA in May of '87 for two weeks. And he was one of 13 farmers in the
> state of Georgia who received [a] foreclosure notice. . . . But, working with
> him made me see that it's really about those who have versus those who don't.
> And they can be Black. They could be white. They could be Hispanic. And it
> made me realize that I needed to work to help poor people, those who don't
> have access the way others have (NAACP 2010).

Sherrod's speech was an allegory, an oral depiction of how she overcame her
client's racism, his patriarchy, and the animus she had for white Southerners—feelings tied to saddening memories formed while coming of age in Jim
Crow Georgia. Sherrod was also impacted by the memory of her father who
was killed in 1965 by a white man who went unpunished (Pickert 2010). In
spite of these tragic encounters with the manifestations of white supremacy,
Sherrod helped Roger and Eloise Spooner save their land, knowing full well,
that if the roles were reversed a white USDA agent may not have been as
supportive.

Sherrod is but one example of a Black woman challenging white supremacy, patriarchy, and classism in service of farmers in need. Monica White's
research has highlighted the role of Black women in promoting self-determination through food security. In her study of the Freedom Farms Cooperative
(FFC), formed by Sunflower County, Mississippi, sharecroppers, White discusses how Fannie Lou Hamer and her counterparts used the FFC to feed and
organize Black sharecroppers. Its initiatives included a community garden
and a pig bank, both of which helped supplement sharecroppers' meager
food rations. More than figureheads, "community women built fences and
shelters for the pigs and the community men did the pig ringing," says White
(2017, 28). Again, Black women and men worked side-by-side for the good
of the community. Though the FCC only lasted a few years, White (2017)

asserts "Hamer made food and its production an act of resistance and a strategy to build a sustainable community. Freedom Farms represented her vision of the centrality of food and agriculture in building self-reliant communities as a base for political activism" (33).

Black women remain cornerstones of Black agrarian resistance,[13] and are taking a leading role in procuring provisions and securing communities in the cities. Detroit, Michigan, has surfaced as a site where residents have taken to agriculture as a means of challenging disinvestment, of producing a sense of place, and fostering food security in communities abandoned by grocers. There, Black women have assumed formative roles in the Detroit Black Community Food Security Network (DBCFSN), D-Town Farms, and Freedom Growers (Quiznar 2014, White 2011a, 2011b), three urban farm initiatives formed in communities on the city's east and west sides. Early in the formation of D-Town Farms, women represented 80 percent of its membership (White 2011a). As a result, these "sisters of the soil," became key decision makers whose labor has helped transform an abandoned city park into an agricultural oasis wherein a sense of safety and communal well-being is nourished (White 2011b, 13):

> Gardening in Detroit, for these women activists, demonstrates self-reliance and self-determination. When members of the community face harsh economic realities, gardening becomes an exercise of political agency and empowerment. Instead of petitioning the city government to increase access to fresh food, or lobbying for more grocery stores and markets to locate in the city, they transform vacant land into a community-based healthy food source that allows them to be able to feed themselves and their families and to provide an example to their community of the benefits of hard work (White, 2011a, 19).

In Washington, D.C., community gardening contributes to what Ashante Reese (2014, 2) calls "geographies of self reliance." Geographies of self-reliance call attention to how spatial, historical, and racial dynamics intersect. Reese suggests that Black folks navigate inequalities with a creativity that reflects a reliance on self and community. Through the practice of garden construction and upkeep, Black men and women not only build community but a communal ethic of survival. Rashad Shabazz (2015) suggests urban farms emerged as one way residents whose lives have been overdetermined by the prison industrial complex, HIV/AIDS, racist urban planning, and localized violence have begun to alter the feel of their physical geographies. He states, "gentrification . . . is not the entire story of Chicago's changing landscapes. Nor is it the most compelling" (Shabazz 2015, 115). Similar to Detroit, residents of the South Side are turning abandoned lots into active urban gardens, green spaces that are said to improve the overall health of community members. Though Shabazz does not state the gender of the proprietors of the South Side's green renaissance, given the focus of his text is on "the impact the prisonization of space has had on Black men," both on the South Side and in the Illinois Department of Corrections, one may presume that many of these initiatives are spearheaded by Black women who carry on an agricultural tradition of communal uplift that xtends from the Deep South to the Midwest and beyond (Shabazz 2015, 116).

CONCLUSION

This chapter places the Pigford I and Pigford II class action lawsuits and Black farmers' continued protests against the USDA in conversation with W. E. B. Du Bois's commentary on enslaved Black men and women's role in bringing an end to the Civil War. Using analyses of court documents, I posit that through sheer determination, litigants in Pigford II—the second round of the Pigford case, enacted their general strike through a mass enrollment in the class action lawsuit that overwhelmed the USDA, Judge Paul Friedman, and attorneys for the defendant. Building on Angela Davis's study of the role of Black women in enslaved communities, I posit that Black women today and throughout the Pigford case have been essential to thwarting threats against Black agrarians and their livelihoods. Shirly Sherrod, the Black farmer advocate is brought to the fore as an exemplar of the underacknowledged, yet vital role Black women have had in Black farmers' struggle to retain land and agricultural livelihoods. Despite ongoing assaults by the USDA, legislators, and critics who accuse Pigford claimants of fraud, Black farmers continue to assert (via multiple forms) their right to a livelihood based on the control of farmland. In doing so, they invoke a tradition of struggle initiated within enslaved communities, and one that continues, to date, throughout Black agricultural communities.

Presently in cities throughout the United States, Black women continue to sustain communities through urban agricultural efforts.

NOTES

1. The county level is where life altering decisions are made as to whether an applicant is fit for financial assistance. Hence, throughout countless rural counties, discrimination continued generations following the end of *de jure* racism in the Jim Crow South.

2. I use the phrase "would-be farmers" because a number of Pigford claimants were applicants who sought farm ownership (to purchase land) and farm operation loans (for seed, steer, and implements) in order to become farmers. An inability to acquire the necessary capability (due to racist practices) kept them from entering the farming industry.

3. In the 1980s the powers of the Office of Civil Rights was hampered by the Reagan administration, as President Ronald Reagan appointed a conservative Secretary of Education who facilitated the attrition of the Department of Education and the Office of Civil Rights.

4. Black scholars serving Historically Black Colleges & Universities (HBCU) conducted some of the earlier studies of this sort.

5. By, "enslaved," I, drawing from Afro-pessimism, speak of those caught within chattel slavery, and their descendants, those of us harangued into its present-day permutation, into slavery as a grammar of suffering.

6. Du Bois realized this concept that states only one tenth of educated Black men would rise to lead the masses of Black people.

7. This turn toward the freed and fugitive slaves, and away from Black elites, was a stark departure from the talented tenth presented in Du Bois's *The Souls of Black Folk*.

8. I speak of social death as it is described by Orlando Patterson: (1) general dishonor; (2) gratuitous violence; and (3) natal alienation.

9. S. Sherrod, personal communication, October 10, 2013.

10. Shirley Sherrod and her husband, Charles Sherrod, were successful litigants in the Pigford case.

11. See Hortense Spillers's "Mama's Baby, Papa's Maybe" for more detail on the revolutionary potential of Black womanhood.

12. By proxy, the video was also an attack on the NAACP, President Obama, and the Black farmers who were exposed and demanded compensation for the USDA's racist legacy.

13. Through her roles as a board member with the Detroit Black Community Food Security Network (DBCFSN) and an Assistant Professor of Environmental Justice at the University of Wisconsin–Madison, White demonstrates and documents Black women's food justice advocacy.

REFERENCES

Brown, Jr., Adell, Ralph Christy, and Tesfa Gebremedhin. 1994. "Structural Changes in US Agriculture: Implications for African American Farmers." *Review of Black Political Economy* 22 (4): 51–71.

Civil Rights Action Team. 1997. "Civil Rights at the United States Department of Agriculture: A Report by the Civil Rights Action Team." Washington, D.C.

Condon, Stephanie. 2010. "Shirley Sherrod: White House Forced My Resignation." *CBS News*. http://www.cbsnews.com/news/shirley-sherrod-white-house-forced-my-resignation/.

Daniel, Pete. 1990. *The Shadow of Slavery: Peonage in the South, 1901–1969*. Urbana: University of Illinois Press.

———. 2013. *Dispossesion: Discrimination against African American Farmers in the Age of Civil Rights*. Chapel Hill: University of North Carolina Press.

Davis, Angela. 1972. "Reflections on the Black Woman's Role in the Community of Slaves." *The Massachusetts Review*, 81–100.

Du Bois, W. E. B. 1935. *Black Reconstruction in America: An Essay toward a History of the Part Which Black Folk Played in the Attempt to Reconstruct Democracy in America, 1860–1880*. Temecula, CA: Reprint Services Corp.

———. 1994. *The Souls of Black Folk*. New York: Dover Publications, Inc.

Dyer, Janice. 2007. "Alabama Agricultural Experiment Station Heir Property: Legal and Cultural Dimensions of Collective Landownership." 667. Auburn, Alabama.

Dyer, Janice, and Conner Bailey. 2008. "A Place to Call Home: Cultural Understandings of Heir Property among Rural African Americans." *Rural Sociology* 73 (3): 317–38.

Gilbert, Jess, Gwen Sharp, and M Sindy Felin. 2001. "The Decline (and Revival?) Of Black Farmers and Rural Landowners: A Review of the Research Literature." 44. North America Series. Madison, Wisconsin.

Gilbert, Jess, Gwen Sharp, and M. Sindy Felin. 2002. "The Loss and Persistence of Black-Owned Farms and Farmland: A Review of the Research Literature and Its Implications *." *Southern Rural Sociology* 18 (2): 1–30.

Groger, Lisa. 1987. "The Meaning of Land in a Southern Rural Community: Differences Between Blacks and Whites." In *Farmwork and Fieldwork: American Agriculture in Anthropological Perspective*, edited by Michael Chibnick, 189–205. Ithaca, NY: Cornell University Press.

Harris, Carmen V. 2008. "The Extension Service Is Not an Integration Agency": The Idea of Race in the Cooperative Extension Service." *Agricultural History Society* 82 (2): 193–219.

Hartman, Saidiy and Frank Wilderson III. 2003. "The Position of the Unthought." *Qui Parle* 13(2). 183–201.

Horne, Gerald. 1986. "Black and Red: W. E. B. Du Bois and the Afro-American Response in the Cold War, 1944–1963." Albany, NY: State of New York Press.

Jealous, Ben. 2010. "Statement on the Resignation of Shirley Sherrod." *NAACP*. http://www.naacp.org/press/entry/naacp-statement-on-the-resignation-of-shirley-sherrod1/.

Jeffries, Hasan Kwame. 2010. *Bloody Lowndes: Civil Rights and Black Power in Alabama's Black Belt*. New York: NYU Press.

Jones, Yvonne. 1980. "Kinship Affiliation through Time: Black Homecomings and Family Reunions in a North Carolina County." *Ethnohistory* 27 (1): 49–66.

Kelley, Robin. 1991. *Hammer and Hoe: Alabama Communists during the Great Depression*. Chapel Hill: The University of North Carolina Press.

LaFraniere, Sharon. 2013. "U.S. Opens Spigot After Farmers Claim Discrimination." *The New York Times*, April 25. http://www.nytimes.com/2013/04/26/us/farm-loan-bias-claims-often-unsupported-cost-us-millions.*ht*ml.

Marable, Manning. 1979. "The Politics of Black Land Tenure: 1877–1915." *Agricultural History Society* 53 (1): 142–52.

McGee, Leo, and Robert Boone, eds. 1979. *The Black Rural Landowner—Endangered Species: Social, Political and Economic Implications*. Westport, Connecticut: Greenwood Press.

Minkler, Meredith. 2000. "Using Participatory Action Research to Build Healthy Communities." *Public Health Reports* 115 (2–3): 191–97.

Montopoli, Brian. 2010. "Vilsack: I Will Have to Live With Shirley Sherrod Mistake." *CBS News2*. http://www.cbsnews.com/news/vilsack-i-will-have-to-live-with-shirley-sherrod-mistake/.

NAACP. 2010. "Shirley Sherrod: The FULL Video." *YouTube*. https://www.youtube.com/watch?v=E9NcCa_KjXk.

Nelson Jr., William. 1979. "Black Rural Land Decline and Political Power." In *The Black Rural Landowner—Endangered Species: Social, Political, and Economic Implications*, edited by Leo McGee and Robert Boone, 83–96. Westport, Connecticut: Greenwood Press.

Nesbitt, Charles. 1979. "Rural Acreage in Promise Land Tennessee: A Case Study." In *The Black Rural Landowner-Endangered Species: Social, Political, and Economic Implications*, edited by Leo McGee and Robert Boone, 67–81. Westport, CT: Greenwood Press.

The Network of the Black Farm Groups and Advocates. 2013. "Sharon LaFraniere Got It Wrong! Response to the Coverage of the Pigford Settlement in the April 26, New York Times." Federation of Souther Cooperatives. http://www.federationsoutherncoop.com/pigford/Response to Pigford NYTimes Coverage[2].pdf.

Obadele, Imari. 1974. "The Struggle of the Republic of New Africa." *The Black Scholar*, 32–41.

Obadele, Imari Abubakari. 1970. *Revolution and Nation-Building: A Strategy for Building the Black Nation in America*. Detroit, MI: The House of Songhay, Publishers.

Office of Policy Planning and Research. 1965. "The Negro Family: The Case for National Action." Washington, D.C.

Patterson, Orlando. (1982). *Slavery and Social Death*. Cambridge, MA: Harvard University Press.

Pennick, Edward. 1990. "Land Ownership and Black Economic Development." *The Black Scholar* 21 (1): 43–46.

Pennick, Edward, Heather Gray, and Miessha Thomas. 2007. "Preserving African-American Rural Property: An Assessment of Intergenerational Values Toward Land." In *Land & Power: Sustainable Agriculture and African Americans*, edited by Jeffrey Jordan, Edward Pennick, Walter Hill, and Robert Zabawa, First, 153–73. Waldorf, Maryland: Sustainable Agriculture Publications.

Pickert, Kate. 2010. "When Shirley Sherrod Was First Wronged by the USDA." *TIME Magazine*. http://content.time.com/time/nation/article/0,8599,2006058,00.html.

Pigford et al. v. Glickman. 1996.

Pigford et al. v. Glickman. 2001.

Quizar, Jessi. 2014. "Who Cares for Detroit?: Urban Agriculture, Black Self-Determination on, and Struggles Over, Urban Space." University of Southern California.

Reese, Ashanté. 2014. "We Will Not Perish; We're Going to Keep Flourishing: Race, Food Access, and Geographies of Self-Reliance." *Antipode*, 1–18.

Robinson, Cedric J. 1983. *Black Marxism: The Making of the Black Radical Tradition*. Chapel Hill: University of North Carolina Press.

Salamon, Lester. 1979. "The Time Dimension in Policy Evaluation: The Case of the New Deal Land Reform Experiments." *Public Policy* 27 (2): 130–83.

Shabazz, Rashad. 2015. *Spatializing Blackness: Architectures of Confinement and Masculinity in Chicago*. Urbana: University of Illinois Press.

Slocum, Rachel. 2013. "Bias and a Settlement with Black Farmers." *The New York Times*, May 3.   http://www.nytimes.com/2013/05/04/opinion/bias-and-a-settlement-with-black-farmers.html.

Spillers, Hortense, J. (2003). "Mama's Baby, Papa's Maybe: An American Grammar Book," in *Black, White, and in Color: Essays on American Literature and Culture*, edited by Hortense J. Spillers, 203–229. Chicago: Chicago University Press.

Umoja, AO. 2013. *We Will Shoot Back: Armed Resistance in the Mississippi Freedom Movement*. New York: New York University Press.

United States House of Representatives. 2010. *Claims Resolution Act of 2010*. Vol. 156. Washington, D.C.: 111th Congress.

USCCR. 1967. "Equal Opportunity in Federally Assisted Agricultural Programs in Georgia." Washington, D.C.

———. 1982. "The Decline of Black Farming in America." Washington, D.C.

White, Monica. 2011a. "D-Town Farm: African American Resistance to Food Insecurity and the Transformation of Detroit The Detroit Context." *Environmental Practice* 13 (4): 406–17.

———. 2011b. "Sisters of the Soil: Urban Gardening as Resistance in Detroit." *Food Justice* 5 (1): 13–28.

———. 2017. "'A Pig and a Garden': Fannie Lou Hamer and the Freedom Farms Cooperative." *Food and Foodways* 25 (1): 20–39.

Wilderson III, Frank. 2003. "Gramschi's Black Marx: Whither the Slave in Civil Society?" *Social Identities* 9(2).

Wood, Spencer D, and Jess Gilbert. 2000. "Returning African American Farmers to the Land: Recent Trends and a Policy Rationale." *Review of Black Political Economy; Spring* 27 (4): 43–64.

Conclusions

Derrick R. Brooms and Theresa Rajack-Talley

This book is based on the premise that race and racism are well-entrenched elements of U.S. society. Throughout the pages of this book, we have argued that race and racism are more than mere concepts; instead, we see and treat these as part of the fabric that constitutes and organizes our lives. Consequently, race and racism are maintained through structures such as social institutions (e.g., schools and media) and are carried by individual actors through ideologies, beliefs, practices and etiquette that inform how we relate to and interact with one another (or not). As we have expressed throughout this book, the notion of *living racism* is twofold. On the one hand, *living racism* denotes the ways in which racism is embodied and active, much like a living organism. On the other hand, *living racism* connects with the ways that we must navigate racism in our individual and collective lives. As Reverend Dr. Martin Luther King, Jr. (1967, 83) quips, living with the "pretense that racism is a doctrine of a very few is to disarm us from fighting it frontally as scientifically unsound, morally repugnant and socially destructive. The prescription for the cure rests with the accurate diagnosis of the disease."

This chapter summarizes some of the more salient ideas presented in the preceding chapters of the book and offers a brief compilation of some of the suggestions and ideas offered by the volume's authors to better understand how we live racism and how racism impacts our lives. The book is organized around two heuristic sections. First, it provides a theoretical perspective of the nature of race as a concept separate from but intersected with social class, gender and other social variables. Throughout this book, we explain some of the contradictions in U.S. society along with the divergences in ideology and positions that historically and contemporaneously privilege whites above and beyond people of color. Second, we take a historical approach to explore the nature of race and racism through three key epochs: slavery and the plantation model, the Jim Crow era, and the post-Civil Rights periods.

PERSISTENT NOTIONS OF RACE AND RACISM

In efforts to make sense of racism, and to provide an accurate diagnosis of it, chapters 1 through 3 offer a focus on race and racism as structure and racial ideologies, specifically the nature of white privilege, white supremacy and Black subordination and perceived inferiority during these three periods. This perspective contributes to the body of literature on racial theories that focus on racial formation, internal colonization, social stratification and critical race theory, but is unique because it incorporates the idea of human agency. The incorporation of human agency allows for the nuances and diversity (populist, extremist, conservative and liberal) that exists in racial ideologies within the white group (seen today as well) and for the persistence of these varying racial ideologies across time. Incorporation of human agency also allowed us to look at racial etiquette—how race is played out across groups between whites and Blacks and within groups in private spheres (also seen today). Additionally, incorporating human agency helps explain racial thinking and racial stereotyping and how racial practices are rationalized. And, finally, human agency also furthered our understanding that with white domination there is Black resistance. In all of these ways, human agency allowed us to understand how racism lives and is lived.

In chapter two, the authors offer a nuanced framework for understanding the persistence of racism. Building on the previous chapter, which examines racial structures, this chapter pushes our racial understanding a bit further by exploring the role of racial ideology in maintaining beliefs of white supremacy and practices of racial ideologies. Importantly, the authors show that racial ideologies result from people's experiences, historical structures and experiences, and internalized racial thinking embedded in society. Racial ideologies emerge from and through these explanations; in addition, racial ideologies, then, are capable of diverse manifestations even in periods that are not leveled in overt forms of racism—such as slavery, Jim Crow, and Civil Rights eras. Indeed, racial ideologies are supported through and by racial beliefs, racial stereotypes, racial customs and traditions, and racial practices. Each of these, individually and collectively, pushes us beyond simplistic views of racism as hatred based on race. As the authors detail, while racial ideologies have been incorporated in a range of racial theories, in some degree, greater attention is needed on the intersecting nature of these ideologies. Racial ideologies reflect both change and continuity, which makes it incumbent to understand how divergent racial ideologies and competing ideologies develop *within* the same group. Thus, we must resist the temptation of offering, or attempting to apply, a single categorization of a particular group and instead seeks ways to understand the creation and re-creation of racial ideas of white superiority and Black inferiority—and, even more broadly, inferiority of all racially marginalized groups.

BLACK MALE NARRATIVES

Chapter four examined how a range of men, primarily contributing authors as well as two of Dr. Talley's former students, lived with racism and made meaning of Black male mentoring in their lives. The men's experiences amplify what is offered in the foundational chapters by giving voice to the realities of race and racism. The men shared their experiences through examples and stories that revealed the continuing significance of race. In the first half of the chapter, focusing specifically on racism, the men's narratives highlight microaggressions and anti-Black sentiments in schooling contexts and in interactions with police officers. From the men's experiences, we can identify and call even more attention to their experiences of learning while Black—a proposition that Black students in general, and Black males as described within the chapter, face a number of schooling challenges precisely because of their Black maleness.

In the second half of the chapter, the men offered narratives that focused on male mentoring. Here, we see how their efforts were supported and enhanced by mentors across a spectrum of adults, such as parents and families in general and institutional agents in particular. In effect, mentoring helped increase the men's own individual efforts geared toward academic achievement and self-learning. Additionally, mentoring played a key role in helping the men learn how to navigate educational contests, prepare themselves for their futures, and learn more about who they wanted to be. These findings reaffirm the benefit that mentors and caring adults can contribute in these and other men's holistic development. Also, as the men shared, the benefits that they accrued from their mentors have given them a charge to serve as a mentor and engage in mentoring practices in their own lives as well. Collectively, their experience with negotiating racism and being mentored by Black men channeled their education and scholarship to also focus on race and social inequality.

BLACK MALES IN SOCIAL INSTITUTIONS

Chapter five starts with the premise that there is a troublesome and unsettled racial history that foreground the use of genetics, or biological approaches, to crime and violence. In particular, the author argues that the fixation of linking race to crime has continued from centuries ago. As opposed to relying on physical characteristics, such as phenotype or skin color, both of which continue to face scrutiny, police departments can use scientific knowledge as a way to combine the desire to "know" with socio-political interests and cultural discourses of power. The author maintains that we are in a historical moment that may signal a return to a biopolitics of race by empowering biological knowledge and measures as "more" accurate or complete. These approaches manifest themselves in a "genetic stop-and-frisk" by relying on biomarkers of risk and masking racial ideologies and beliefs. As explored in the earlier chapters, the author highlights scientists' adoptions as their (underlying) thirst for "race-neutral" and "objective" practices that can, somehow then, remove racial (or racist) interpretations of criminal behavior. By appearing to be "colorblind," this approach also ignores the sociopolitical dynamics that disproportionally shape the interactions between the criminal justice system and different populations—namely, Black and brown folks. As opposed to doing away with race, or engaging in policies and practices through a colorblind prism, this biological approach reproduces racialization in society, reinforces its own biopolitics, and repurposes race as biologic fact.

Chapter six examines racialized school discipline and the school-to-prison pipeline. The author highlights the problematic trends in school discipline, which rely on overly harsh penalties and consequences for students' infractions in schools. By adopting harsher disciplinary measures in the 1970s and 1980s under the guise of making schools "safer," invariably, school policies and approaches turned into more punitive practices that ultimately criminalized students. As opposed to achieving "equality" and treating students within the same standards, schools now punish students for behavior that is consistent with adolescent maturation and development.

Additionally, these increased measures have resulted in a greater maldistribution of school punishment across racial, ethnic, and social class lines. Not only are discipline and security applied unequally, they also exacerbate challenges that students face in school as the racial gap in discipline has increased over time. Additionally, the author reviews a number of theoretical explanations, namely the racial threat hypothesis, broader trend perspective, and labeling theory, to explore the disproportionate school discipline practices. The author highlights that the criminalization of school discipline necessitates racial inequality in disciplinary outcomes, impacting not only students but families as well. The racial experience in schools is particularly important given that the narratives of many of the Black male authors and mentees reveal that they became intensely aware of racism in this public arena.

Chapter seven provides a critical race analysis of the film *Moonlight*. The authors start from the premise that, historically, mainstream representations maintain distorted images of Black males and their masculinities. The lessons about the representations of Black masculinities in film, and other forms of media, provide critical insight into Black maleness and Black males' interiorities. In the film, the authors argue that Chiron's life and development are reflected in a number of meaningful associations and decisions about protecting his Black masculine self. His physical presence and awkwardness during his adolescent years queered his masculinity. He could not present or project himself as "tough" because this image was belied by his physique. Thus, his development into and embodiment of "Black" was critical to a new presentation of self—a presentation that easily could be decoded as a tough front. Importantly, it was in the liminal space between Acts II and III that Chiron's physical transformation occurred. This particular discursive screenplay, a disappearance of one self and the reappearance of a new self, uses Chiron's removal from the school via the criminal justice system (not depicted within the film) as a way to mark his body and queer his Black masculine self. First, throughout the film, Chiron's body is marked as different from others and as deficient.

Second, his body is marked as a target for physical violations, both in attempting to play soccer in the neighborhood and being bullied at school. Third, his mother and a number of others mark his body for verbal assault and ridicule. And, finally, in his presentation of self as "Black" in the third act, his body is marked as one that physically can dominate others. The liminal space, the transition between acts II and III (where there is no action), is important in this regard as it was not necessary for the film writers and producers to show how Chiron transformed his body. Thus, for viewers, it was completely plausible that Chiron's physical maturation and transformation could occur in this liminal space—away from the audience's view. In the same vein, queering of Black masculine bodies also relies on developing oneself away from the view, or gaze, of others. Here, the authors argue for perceiving this development with an eye toward understanding the delicate balance between vulnerability and tenderness—spaces rarely ever saved or allowed for Black men.

As argued within these chapters, race and racism play critical, active roles in how students and youth engage in and across social institutions. Not only does racism exist in these spaces, but it also is used to inform how actors frame, think about, and (re)position Black males. At the same time, each of these institutions—criminal justice system, schools, and media—are highly interactive where behavior, interactions, or projections in one domain have consequences for youth in another. That is, with the increased presence of school resource officers and more punitive discipline practices and policies, youth are much more likely to come into contact with law enforcement personnel outside of school. Similarly, how Black males are represented in films can be used to inform (or reaffirm) perspectives, especially given the historical legacies of Black males as criminals and threats. As these tropes and characterizations continue to be prominent on screen, and other forms of media, they will continue to impact the racial beliefs, attitudes, and practices that people harbor about Black males—and other youth of color.

THE DISPOSSESSED: URBAN AND RURAL IMPACT OF RACISM

Chapter eight focuses on the impact of neoliberal governance and housing in Atlanta, particularly the Black Urban Regime. The authors argue that the electoral system, the traditional vehicle for citizens to influence decision-making regarding their needs and those of their communities, has been supplanted by neoliberalism. Importantly, neoliberal politics and processes have rejected egalitarian liberal traditions and significantly changed different locale's relationship with governance. By focusing in explicitly on Atlanta, the authors point out that the city has a range of problems, including increasing income inequality gaps as well as local effects of a national economy that has been slow in recovering along with a restructuring of the global economy. Of significant concern, the public housing market has failed to keep up with demand, housing units have been demolished to accommodate more wealthy residents and the construction of mixed-income housing have all occurred at the expense of living options for less affluent residents.

These processes reveal some of the latent functions of a continued pro-growth agenda and the political elite's lack of responsibility to social welfare. As opposed to leading the city in these areas, the city government reframed responsibility to the individual. The authors show how these shifts placed a disproportionate burden on African American families and communities and, at the same time, ignited collective action to protect housing availability for residents—particularly through Occupy Atlanta. Still, the contests remain, as these groups, and others, can wage resistance battles that can reach only so far. Most notably, as the authors detail, however, they still must contend with the state, which has shown great dexterity in neutralizing and repressing citizens' actions.

Chapter nine focuses on Black farmers' resistance to systemic racism within the United States Department of Agriculture (USDA). The author looks specifically at the *Pigford et al. v. Gilckman* court case, a class-action lawsuit levied by Black farmers against USDA. The author frames this action as a self-emancipatory praxis, akin to the efforts taken by formerly enslaved Blacks during the Civil War. Keys to these efforts were Black landowner-ship, which helped ground Black families and communities throughout the late nineteenth and early twentieth centuries, and labor, which helped facilitate the development of U.S. infrastructure, economy, and territorial expansion. Blacks' decisions to leave plantations following the war, not only displayed a massive, leaderless movement, they also resulted in a significant shift in labor power—and the economy.

This movement, in some ways, served as a precursor to the Pigford claimants' general strike. By joining the class-action lawsuit, Black farmers demonstrated and asserted their agency and legitimacy. The case's significance is tied to and cannot be separated from these actions. In this display, Black farmers not only resisted capitalistic ventures and practices but their resistance also refuted and undermined prevailing racial ideologies and beliefs that often denigrated and diminished Blacks—such as claims of inferiority, lack of intelligence, and submissiveness. The author also points to the role of Black women farmers in resisting white supremacy, patriarchy, and classism and asserting their agency. In one view, the author examines Angela Davis's analysis of the importance of Black women in enslaved communities. In another view, Black women's resistance, discussed through Shirley Sherrod's efforts, illustrates a level of collective consciousness, other-centeredness, and dedication to Black liberation much needed today.

As these two chapters show, Blacks have not quietly acquiesced to uneven power relations and systemic racism. Even in the face of great odds, many Blacks remain committed to liberation efforts that not only are intended to elevate their own individual plight but also are intended to alleviate the plight of the masses. Although the chapters are two case studies, they help to reveal the manifold efforts that Blacks take to resist various forms of oppression. Much like that discussed in their personal narratives (chapter four), it is incumbent upon individuals and groups to rise up against forces that threaten their lives and livelihoods. The example of a massive, leaderless movement connects well with the #BlackLivesMatter movement in our current time frame. #BlackLivesMatter is a "forum intended to build connections between Black people and our allies to fight anti-Black racism, to spark dialogue among Black people, and to facilitate the types of discussions necessary to encourage social action and disengagement" (BlackLivesMatter). What is revealed across each of these examples is the need to stand in solidarity. There is a great need for us to continue to show our massive dissatisfaction with the status quo.

In general, understanding the multiple and malleable components of racism that permeate our society requires that we see racism for what it is. Racial ideologies, beliefs, and practices help inform the policies and structures that organize and sustain our society. The events that transpired in Charlottesville, Virginia, are not an anomaly. We cannot allow ourselves to be disarmed by a lack of willingness to call out, name and oppose the forces and actors that threaten our health, well-being, and livelihood—individually and collectively. Recent water crises at Standing Rock and in Flint, Michigan, along with a host of other locales threaten us all. The killing of unarmed Black and brown men, women, and children reveals state-sanctioned and extrajudicial threats to our lives. Reservations exist because of particular racial ideologies, beliefs and practices that forced indigenous peoples to relocate—or else. Though concentration camps no longer exist in their previous forms, urban areas are filled with "iconic ghettos" that recreate a "new" color line (see Anderson 2012; Du Bois 1903/2005). The old and nascent forms of oppression, which accost us in various social institutions and social spaces, continue to be steeped in ideologies, beliefs, and practices that all point toward anti-Black racism. For, as psychiatrist/philosopher Frantz Fanon offers, "Each generation must discover its mission, fulfill it or betray it, in relative opacity" (1961, 145).

REFERENCES

Anderson, Elijah. 2012. "The Iconic Ghetto." *The ANNALS of the American Academy of Political and Social Science* 642 (1): 8–24.

BlackLivesMatter. 2017. "About the Black Lives Matter Network." http://blacklivesmatter.com/about/

Du Bois, William Edward Burghardt. 1903/2005. *The Souls of Black Folk*. (Original work published in 1903).

Fanon, Frantz. 1961/1963. *The Wretched of the Earth*. Translated by Richard Philcox. New York: Grove Press.

King, Martin Luther, Jr. 1967. *Where Do We Go from Here? Chaos or Community*. New York: Beacon Press.

Index

About the Contributors

Derrick R. Brooms is faculty in sociology and Africana Studies at the University of Cincinnati and serves as a youth worker as well. He specializes in the sociology of African Americans, particularly Black males, with research and activism that focuses on educational equity, race and racism, diversity and inequality, and identity. His education research primarily centers on Black male schooling experiences in both secondary and post-secondary institutions, with particular focus on school culture, engagement, resilience, identity, and sense of self. He is author of *Being Black, Being Male on Campus: Understanding and Confronting Black Male Collegiate Experiences* (2017).

Cameron Khalfani Herman is a PhD Candidate in the Department of Sociology at Michigan State University where he specializes in the department's Community and Urban program focus. As an urban studies scholar, Cameron is concerned with the ways marginalized social groups experience the shifting landscape of urban communities in the twenty-first century. His research broadly examines issues of urban inequality with specific interests in the areas of youth culture and community development. Cameron has published single-authored articles in several publications including *The Journal of Urban Youth Culture* and *Race, Gender and Crime Anthology* along with several other co-authored publications on local groups' collective responses to urban and rural development. Cameron Khalfani Herman received his MA in Pan-African Studies at the University of Louisville.

Eric A. Jordan is currently pursuing a PhD in Applied Sociology at the University of Louisville. He received his MA degree in Sociology from the University of Louisville where he studied and analyzed modern films as racial projects and their impact on our understanding of race and racism. Eric's work on racial tropes and representations in film can be found in *The Encyclopedia of Racism in American Cinema* where he analyzes the white savior trope and representations of white characters in film.

Thomas J. Mowen is an Assistant Professor in the Department of Sociology at Bowling Green State University. Tom's past research have examined the link between school punishment, policing, and security on youth and family outcomes as well as how family dynamics shape—and are shaped by incarceration. His current research focuses on the implications of punishment within the life-course of young people by examining how experiences such as arrest and incarceration affect criminal offending, delinquency, and family relationships. Mowen's work has appeared in a variety of publications including *Criminology, Justice Quarterly, Journal of Research in Crime and Delinquency,* and *Criminology & Public Policy.* Thomas Mowen received his PhD in sociology from the University of Delaware and his MA in Sociology from the University of Louisville

Theresa Rajack-Talley is a Professor in the Department of Pan-African Studies and the Associate Dean for International, Diversity and Engagement Programs in the College of Arts and Sciences, University of Louisville. Her research centers on social inequality and its intersection with race/ethnicity, gender, social class, and social location at the community, household and group levels. Specifically, she looks at social relations of power and its impact on marginalized groups across the Diaspora. Her numerous publications center on race and racism in the United States and poverty and gender inequality in the Caribbean. Her book *Poverty is a Person: Human Agency, Women and Caribbean Households* was published in 2016. Her commitment to linking teaching and research to community development has won her numerous awards and recognition for her social activism. Theresa Rajack-Talley is a Fulbright scholar and received her PhD in Sociology from the University of Kentucky.

Oliver Rollins is a postdoctoral fellow in the Pennsylvania Program on Race, Science & Society and Visiting Scholar in the Center for Neuroscience and Society at the University of Pennsylvania. His research focuses on the social and ethical implications of neuroscience research on social behaviors, and especially the conceptualization and use of race/ethnicity in the mind and brain sciences. His current project examines the social and policy impacts of neuropsychological research on implicit bias, including the way neuropsychologists conceptualize and measure bio-social factors related to behavior, and the potential promises, challenges, and consequences of operationalizing racism (and race) at the neurobiological level. Additionally, Rollins's pending book, *Unlocking the Violent Brain* traces the development of neuro-science research on anti-social behaviors, with particular attention to the way neuro-criminologists think about and address longstanding debates and controversies surrounding biological research on crime and violence. Oliver Rollins received his PhD in Sociology from the University of California, San Francisco and his MA from the Department of Pan-African Studies, University of Louisville.

Clarence R. Talley was employed as an Associate Professor in the Department of Sociology at the University of Louisville where he taught a variety of courses including his department's milestone "Race in the U.S." Talley supervised numerous MA theses and mentored many of his young students to pursue PhD programs. His primary research area focused on social stratification and inequality in the United States with a focus on race, ethnicity, gender and social class. He later expanded his research to include the African continent and the Caribbean and Latin American regions. Over his short career, Talley won numerous grant awards. Clarence Talley received his PhD in Sociology from the University of Maryland. Clarence passed away on January 28, 2011, before this book was published. As he rests in peace, his ideas and spirit refuse to rest but live in and through his students and their good work.

Willie Jamaal Wright is an Assistant Professor in the Department of and Geography at Florida State University. His research focuses broadly on revolutionary social movements, critical theory, and the relationships between Blackness and the social production of space. More specific, Wright investigates Racial Violence as Environmental Racism, the Black Farmer's Struggle and its Importance to the Local Food Movement. Using a combination of participatory, archival, and ethnographic methods. His research has been published in a wide range of journals. Over his career, Wright has received several awards and recognitions. Willie Wright received his PhD in Geography from the University of North Carolina at Chapel Hill, and his MA in Pan-African Studies at the University of Louisville.

Made in the USA
Columbia, SC
01 March 2022

57037248R00133